Cuban Cinema After the Cold War

Cuban Cinema After the Cold War

A Critical Analysis of Selected Films

ENRIQUE GARCÍA

McFarland & Company, Inc., Publishers
Jefferson, North Carolina

LIBRARY OF CONGRESS CATALOGUING-IN-PUBLICATION DATA

García, Enrique, 1975–
    Cuban cinema after the Cold War : a critical analysis of selected films / Enrique García.
        p.   cm.
    Includes bibliographical references and index.
    Includes filmography.

    ISBN 978-0-7864-9910-6 (softcover : acid free paper) ∞
    ISBN 978-1-4766-2060-2 (ebook)

    1. Motion pictures—Cuba—History—20th century.   I. Title.
PN1993.5.C8G28 2015
791.43097291—dc23   2015009751

BRITISH LIBRARY CATALOGUING DATA ARE AVAILABLE

© 2015 Enrique García. All rights reserved

No part of this book may be reproduced or transmitted in any form or by any means, electronic or mechanical, including photocopying or recording, or by any information storage and retrieval system, without permission in writing from the publisher.

Front cover: still from the 2003 *Havana Suite* (ICAIC/ Wanda Visión/Photofest)

Printed in the United States of America

McFarland & Company, Inc., Publishers
  Box 611, Jefferson, North Carolina 28640
    www.mcfarlandpub.com

Table of Contents

Preface   1

Introduction: The Legacy of Cuba's "Imperfect Cinema"   5

1. Daniel Díaz Torres' *Alicia en el pueblo de Maravillas* and the Controversial Use of Surrealist Techniques and Intertextual Subjects   25

2. Political Melodrama in the New Nationalist Vision of Tomás Gutíerrez Alea's *Strawberry and Chocolate* and Humberto Solás' *Honey for Oshún*   41

3. Entertainment and the Proletarian Avant-Garde in the Films of Juan Carlos Tabío and Fernando Pérez   71

4. *Paradise Under the Stars* and *Habana Blues*: The Revival of Cuban Musical Coproductions   99

5. Ideology, Realism and Fantasy in Juan Padrón's Animated Franchises *Elpidio Valdés* and *Vampires in Havana* Before and After the Special Period   123

6. *Juan of the Dead* and the Ideological Evolution of the Caribbean Zombie   151

Conclusion   177
Chapter Notes   185
Bibliography   203
Filmography   210
Index   215

Preface

In the late 1990s, when I was completing my Ph.D. in comparative literature with a film track at the University of Massachusetts Amherst, I decided to specialize in Cuban cinema because, as a comparatist, I was fascinated with how Cuba's revolutionary cinema had been influenced by different national cinematic traditions from countries such as the United States, Mexico, Argentina, the Soviet Union, France, Italy, and Japan. By reading the official Cuban journal *Cine Cubano* and other scholarly writing, I was able to understand how revolutionary Cuban filmmakers and critics studied and analyzed the works of important filmmakers such as Sergei Eisenstein, Luis Buñuel, Glauber Rocha, Vittorio De Sica and Alfred Hitchcock. I learned how these prominent artists' techniques became influential in modern filmmaking, and how the Cuban filmmakers were able to apply them to a revolutionary cinematic intertextuality in their ideological narratives.

As part of my research, I visited Cuba in the summer of 2000, and was able to experience two often conflicting aspects of the country's mythology: its status both as a legendary site of social revolution and as the evidence of socialism's obsolete qualities. To me, it was very interesting to observe the accomplishments of the Cuban revolution in terms of social justice, the arts, and health care, but also to experience the economic devastation of the island brought about by the American embargo, the disappearance of Soviet funds, and the outdated socialist economic models that needed to be rethought for a new post–Cold War reality.

After the collapse of the Soviet Union in 1991, and as a consequence of the economic crisis that ensued, Cuban filmmakers had to rethink the revolutionary values and aesthetics that were developed in Cuba after the revolution of 1959. A number of these precepts, originally encapsulated in the 1965 manifesto "For an Imperfect Cinema," had been influential not only in Cuban filmmaking but also in the rest of Latin America's socialist or leftist cinema. The film market had begun to change in the 1980s and ICAIC (Cuban Film Institute) funds for new movies had begun to be supplemented with investments from abroad (and particularly Spain). As a partial result of the influx of foreign capital, Cuban cinema began to broaden its scope, and package its ideological message with old-fashioned entertainment in its attempt to target wider international audiences. Thus many of the "imperfect cinema" cultural concepts had to be reinvented for a new, more skeptical era disinclined to romanticize their legacy.

This book examines the post–Cold War cinema of some internationally acclaimed Cuban filmmakers working within the framework of the ICAIC. I analyze their struggle to create a new film vocabulary that depicts more accurately the new Cuban reality and the evolving ideals of the Cuban revolution.

As Raúl Castro officially fully replaced his brother Fidel at the helm of the Cuban government in 2011, Cuba underwent some economic reforms that have begun to decentralize the control of the government on commerce. These reforms have also opened new venues for both the funding and exhibition of Cuban movies, and have relaxed the control of the ICAIC on Cuban filmmakers. These trends are particularly visible in *Juan of the Dead* (dir. A. Brugués, 2010), the first Cuban film made completely independent of ICAIC funding. I analyze this and other recent genre films (e.g. musicals and horror) that I believe might point to the direction that Cuban cinema is currently taking.

In the U.S., the study of Cuban cinema has been limited to occasional articles and other short publications, with a few notable exceptions. The most important English-language manuscript about Cuba's post-revolutionary cinematic production is undoubtedly Michael Chanan's *Cuban Cinema*. The book is very comprehensive, as it touches on a large number of Cuban films, and explores clearly and in depth a number of important aesthetic and political topics. More recently, researchers such as Ann Marie Stock, Hector Amaya, and Sujatha Fernandes have tackled more specifically the reception and production of

Preface

Cuban cinema. My book differs from all these projects in the primary texts that it addresses, as well as in its approach to these texts. My goal is not to provide a comprehensive history of Cuban cinema, its production or reception. Instead, I discuss specifically revolutionary cinematic techniques and their development in the Special Period, by examining in detail a few important films in each chapter. I focus on the transformation of filmmaking techniques inherited from the Surrealist movement, proletarian revolutionary cinema, and the European avant-garde, and the reasons why these changes took place.

It was very important to me to integrate American, Latin American, and Cuban criticism into my book. I wanted to avoid presenting a completely foreign interpretation of Cuban cinema, yet I did not want to limit my discussion to the revolutionary discourse. An example where foreign theories were essential to understanding the Cuban texts is the fourth chapter, where I explain how issues of race have developed in Cuba in different ways to the United States. Black minstrelsy, for instance, has long been considered racist in the U.S., but some aspects of it remain in Cuban cinema. The struggles to create a balance in the discussion from an American *and* a Cuban perspective created an interesting topic about perceptions of race in different national cultures. At the same time, integrating the Cuban criticism allowed me to explain certain debates from the Cubans' point of view and outside of the typical American media studies discourse.

In my interactions with undergraduate students, I have noticed that Cuban film criticism is often written for readers who have seen a lot of Cuban films that are not widely available. I decided to prioritize the analysis of films that can be acquired within the United States (and with English subtitles) with the goal of making the chapters accessible for discussion in a wide range of film classes. My goal was to write an accessible book, which can be used in college classes taught in English, as well as Spanish courses, and to students who do not necessarily have much background in Latin American and Caribbean film. My hope is that my book will create a broader interest in Cuban cinema among wider audiences and emerging scholars, including those interested in global genres such as horror and musicals. I hope this will be the first step towards eradicating the stigma that Cuban culture is isolated in an

Preface

ideological vacuum, and can only be studied for political or abstract aesthetic purposes. I strongly believe that Cuban cinema has a lot to offer to scholars of genre, film movements, animation, and other general topics in cinema, as well as to filmmakers who wish to explore new techniques.

Introduction

The Legacy of Cuba's "Imperfect Cinema"

Since the end of the Cold War, Cuba has been the site of multiple and contradictory perceptions. Some see the island and its now recovering economy as evidence of the futility of socialist governments, while others still like to promote the legendary revolution that was once one of the main inspirations for revolutionary activists in Latin America and other parts of the world. My first contact with Cuban revolutionary culture was during my high school years in Puerto Rico, when I acquired a bootleg VHS copy of the Cuban film *Se permuta* (*House Swapping*, 1983). Although the plot of the film was based on the communist, and hence foreign to me, concept of house swapping,[1] I was surprised to decode a variety of typically Caribbean locales, humor, language, food, and music on screen. Still more impressive, despite the fact that the film was a comedic melodrama made for a mass audience, it was charged with avant-garde references such as the documentary-style intrusive appearance, midway through the narrative, of a film critic pointing out the film's flaws. Although at the time I was unaware of the importance or meaning of this narrative transgression, I was fascinated by its departure from the typical corporate and straightforward Latin American narrative.

In addition, *House Swapping* promulgated a "progressive" social agenda by representing a daring interracial love story rarely found in comparable films, and even less so in commercial Puerto Rican productions that tend to adopt a condescending attitude toward race debates.

Introduction

Appreciating the cultural significance of this small, unknown film, I began to take more seriously such interesting samples of Caribbean cinema. I thus focused my research on cinema, and began to study in depth particularly Cuban cinema. This book is the product of my longstanding interest in the Cuban film industry, one of the most stable and consistent national cinema industries in the Caribbean, which has produced some of the most aesthetically and thematically significant films in Latin America.

In order for the reader to understand the topics addressed in this book, we first need to explain several key concepts. First, while this is a book about Cuban cinema after the Cold War, it is important to examine this time period in the context of Cuban filmmaking in general. How did Cuba's national cinema industry develop? In order to answer this question, we have to trace the main features and developments in the first half of the 20th century, as well as later productions under the revolutionary ICAIC studio.[2] Further, we need to explore the economic and cultural effects that the Special Period had on post–Cold War Cuban cinema. With this background, the reader will be able to understand how the Cuban film industry functions, and how Cuban national cinema has presented on the silver screen the island's important economic and ideological shifts.

Cuban Cinema Before the 1959 Cuban Revolution

Many film scholars used to ignore pre-revolutionary Cuban cinema because most of the films from this time period were not available for study and because they lack the esthetic quality and cultural innovations of the films produced by the ICAIC. This trend has changed recently, as some of these projects have become available on DVD and other internet venues. In addition, Cuban film historians (e.g., Luciano Castillo, Walfredo Piñera, Paulo Antonio Paranagua, and others) have recently begun to explain the industrial developments of the earlier phase of the Cuban cinema industry that took place before the foundation of the ICAIC. This new film criticism is very important because it helps researchers understand the narrative and visual connections/disconnections with the island's earlier, pre-revolutionary, national cinema and its cultural and political context.

The Legacy of Cuba's "Imperfect China"

The three most eminent pre-revolutionary filmmakers in Cuba were Ramón Peón, Ernesto Caparrós, and Manuel Alonso.[3] These directors were important in the history of the Cuban film industry, because they achieved significant for the time technical accomplishments. However, some of their output is now perceived by contemporary Cuban film criticism as problematic because of the directors' reliance on imported foreign narrative cinematic devices designed to exploit Cuban culture and submit to hegemonic interests abroad. This pre-revolutionary phase of Cuban cinema was financed mostly via Mexican co-productions, which offered a folklorist vision of the island, while relying on cliché storytelling heavily influenced by theater, sentimental literature, radio serials and nationalist musical performances.[4] Pre-revolutionary filmmaking clearly exhibited its dependence on both Hollywood (through the musical genre) and the Mexican industry where Cuban filmmakers copied the Mexican melodramas as a cinematic model to export to the rest of Latin America.[5]

All of the Cuban films from the silent period are lost with the notable exception of *La virgen de la Caridad* (1930). This film, a cinematic adaptation of the Cuban Catholic myth, is considered one of the best samples of early silent cinema in Latin America. The project was directed by Ramón Peón, one of the first successful Cuban filmmakers, who had ties to the Mexican film industry. In Mexico, he directed some commercially successful films, and garnered enough influence to become one of the founders of the Cuban national studio PECUSA (Películas Cubanas S.A.) where he directed *Romance en el Palmar* (*Romance in the Palm Grove*, 1938) and *Sucedió en la Habana* (*It Happened in Havana*, 1938). Even though his projects were successful, most of the other films made in this studio were failures, and PECUSA went bankrupt in 1940.[6] Peón tried several times to help jumpstart the Cuban cinema industry. He even offered to work with the Cuban revolutionary government and the ICAIC in 1959, but his offer was rejected, and he ended his career in Mexico.[7]

The second important pre-revolutionary filmmaker, Ernesto Caparrós, directed Cuba's first sound film, *La serpiente roja* (*The Red Serpent*, 1937), which was based on the popular radio serial revolving around a Chinese-Cuban Fu Manchu type of character. Caparrós also

Introduction

directed one of the first rumbera musicals, *Tam Tam o el origen de la rumba* (*Tam Tam, or the Origin of Rumba*, 1938). Caparrós' musical short was well received at the time because of its musical numbers' choreography and photography, but its condescending plot revolved around a slave who curses a young woman with AfroCuban witchcraft because she rejected his love proposals.[8] This is the archetype of the traditional musical plot relying on racial stereotypes that would be reused throughout most of this pre-revolutionary phase.

The figure of the third eminent pre-revolutionary filmmaker, Manuel Alonso, is currently perceived ambiguously by Cuban film historians. They acknowledge the importance of his two films, *Siete muertes a plazo fijo* (*Seven Fixed-Term Deaths*, 1950) and *Casta de roble* (*Strong as an Oak*, 1953), because of their esthetic contributions and ambitions, but scorn his monopolistic business practices. For example, *Siete muertes* was originally written to be filmed in Mexico, but Alonso adapted the screenplay to a Caribbean setting.[9] The film is very interesting from an esthetic perspective because it was shot like the American film noir B movies of the time. *Casta de roble*, in contrast, was a melodrama about the hardships of peasant life, like the ones made in Mexico. However, Alonso avoided the artificial trappings of the Cuban musicals in this film, and, by not including musical performances, made the narrative more somber and interesting. Even ICAIC's most prominent Cuban filmmaker Tomás Gutíerrez Alea considered *Casta de roble* the best pre-revolutionary Cuban movie he had seen.[10] Despite Alonso's esthetic achievements, certain Cuban film scholars criticize him for his cutthroat business approach, and his attempts to create a monopoly in Havana by trying to buy all the studios and technical equipment available in the island.[11] He was thus not a model that the ICAIC was willing to follow.

Film historian Walfredo Piñera identifies four important obstacles that marked the time period in which these pre-revolutionary directors worked. The first one was the political frustration associated with the Cuban dictatorships, and especially with Fulgencio Batista's regime in the 1950s. The second one was the appearance of new sound technology which the Cuban cinema industry was not prepared to handle. The third one was the absence of a healthy economic environment or a constant successful box office that would sustain the local studios. The fourth one was the lack of a stable national industry that would develop professional film technicians and artists.[12] These drawbacks were taken into account by the founders of the ICAIC, who then attempted to create a studio without the socio-economic, cultural, and technical limitations of the pre-revolutionary industry.

Many contemporary Cuban film historians agree that pre-revolutionary filmmaking was important in the development of the national industry, yet they also point out its reliance on and reflection of the problematic "colonial" relationships the island had with the United States and Mexico. The American industry wrestled control of local distribution from the European powers after World War I both in Cuba and the world. In addition, Mexican studios controlled the products that were being filmed for the Latin American market. Many of the pre-revolutionary films discussed above are about Cuban subjects, but were made in the exploitative and problematic industry model created by Hollywood at the time that relied on repetitive images and clichés digested for the international consumer.

Arguably the most controversial of the pre-revolutionary Cuban films was *La rosa blanca* (*The White Rose*, 1954), a biography of Cuban national hero José Martí, which was financed in large part by the Batista dictatorship.[13] According to Cuban film historian Luciano Castillo, the film is melodramatic, has exaggerated monologues, and emphasized too much the romantic life of the poet/patriot. Castillo acknowledges, however, that it should not be considered a complete failure. I concur with the author's assessment of the film, namely, that it is neither a great nor a terrible film, and that it has been criticized mostly due to its non-compliance with a strict vision of Cuban nationalism. I believe, however, that the film's flaws are the result of its being a transnational product of the traditional studio system dominated by Mexican interests. For example, Martí was played by a Mexican actor who failed to portray adequately a character of Cuban origin. Such problems exist in the Americas to this day (e.g. Hollywood films often cast Spanish actors to portray Mexican characters), affecting even contemporary revolutionary Cuba. The ICAIC itself could not escape controversy when portraying iconic 19th-century nationalist figures or texts. In 1982, the release of Humberto Solás' adaptation of the 19th-century novel *Cecilia*

Introduction

Valdés o La Loma del Ángel was met with a lot of criticism from film scholars and audiences, who had envisioned differently the revered text.

Many of the pre-revolutionary films I mentioned, such as *Siete muertes a plazo fijo, Casta de roble,* and *La rosa blanca,* are out of print and not legally available for distribution. They are thus impossible to acquire unless bought on bootleg DVDs or downloaded from illegal file-sharing websites. I do not condone the illegal acquisition of these cinematic texts, as that would mean their original creators will not receive any remuneration. However, such films rarely get an official release, and it is important for researchers to watch them, because familiarity with the pre-revolutionary cinema's esthetics and its occasionally problematic cultural values would offer a better understanding of why ICAIC filmmakers oppose or support certain types of esthetic decisions or cultural content.

ICAIC's Revolutionary Filmmaking: Successes, Failures and the Special Period

The new Cuban government that took power after the revolution of 1959 established the ICAIC with the purpose of promoting a new type of cinema for this Caribbean island, in direct opposition to the exploitative pre-revolutionary exotic images present in Cuban co-productions with Spain, Mexico, Argentina, and the Unites States. The films produced under the Institute's sponsorship were to reflect the new revolutionary ideology, and to focus on problematic issues inherited from the colonial and capitalist periods, among which were a harsh class system, sexism, and prejudice against certain races or ethnic groups. Cuban film scholar Ambrosio Fornet observed that ICAIC filmmakers wanted to make a cinema that would establish a new relationship with the spectator, where the success of a Cuban film would be judged by its capacity to launch an enriching communication with the viewer. Fornet explains that to this effect the early ICAIC filmmakers applied the Marxist concept in which the artist created new art for the viewer but also new viewers for the art.[14]

Cuban filmmakers followed their goal of politicizing creative works while experimenting with esthetics that would demonstrate their advanced cultural and filmmaking abilities. The new ideologically charged cinema that emerged in the process was admired by a number of artists, critics, and activists around the world, who applauded the ICAIC's ingenuity and optimistic social views. These were reflected, for example, in Julio García Espinosa's *Las aventuras de Juan Quin Quin* (*The Adventures of Juan Quin Quin*, 1965), Tomás Gutiérrez Alea's *Memorias del subdesarollo* (*Memories of Underdevelopment*, 1968), Humberto Solás' *Lucía* (1968), and Octavio Gómez's *La primera carga del machete* (*The First Charge of the Machete*, 1968), films which British Cuban cinema scholar Michael Chanan defines as the "four great" ones of early revolutionary Cuban cinema. International critical recognition for these films included multiple awards ranging from Latin American festivals to special prizes awarded by other countries, including the United States.

In the context of the Cold War, the ICAIC was particularly important in the 1960s and 1970s because it was the most stable leftist studio in Latin America. Revolutionary filmmakers from South America, such as Chilean Miguel Littín and Argentinean Fernando Solanas, had to live in exile in Mexico and France respectively, due to the dictatorship regimes in their countries of origin, and struggled to complete their cinematic visions. Their subversive work, however, was well respected in Cuba, whose scholars and ICAIC filmmakers encouraged social revolution and change, and provided a safe haven for alternative ideological filmmaking critical of the exploitation of capitalism and economic imperialism. The ICAIC established a support system for both Cuban revolutionary filmmakers and other leftist artists that led to the creation of innovative films throughout Latin America in the 1960s and 70s. This output in turn gave prominence to the studio in certain intellectual circles around the world and helped to promote ideas about revolutionary esthetics. The ICAIC thus became essential to the creation and dissemination of what we now know as Third Cinema, a new type of filmmaking that would defy capitalist and imperialist hegemonies.

In the complex process of establishing their new cinematic vision on the island, however, ICAIC creators had the advantage of the Institute's complete control of and distribution rights on all cinema screens in Cuba.[15] This monopoly of distribution was challenged by *Lunes*, the cultural segment of the newspaper *La Revolución*. The group of intellectuals

Introduction

that worked in *Lunes*, had sponsored the short documentary film *P.M.* (1961), the main goal of which was to present the night life in Havana. *P.M.* was first shown on Cuban television, but the ICAIC refused to allow a theater screening in Havana. Even ICAIC's former president, Alfredo Guevara, admitted that this zealous need for control led to the ICAIC's being compared at the time with the institutions of Batista's oppressive regime.[16] In his recollection of the events, however, Cuban filmmaker Manuel Pérez writes that *P.M.* was not as problematic as people thought, and that the conflict was simply that of certain intellectuals challenging the power of other intellectuals.[17] This battle led to Fidel Castro's meeting with the two opposing groups and siding with the ICAIC, hence the origin of his famous quote from the speech "A los intelectuales" ("To the Intellectuals"): "Con la Revolución todo, sin la Revolución nada" (With the revolution, everything; without the revolution, nothing).[18] This was an important event because, by having a say in the resolution of the conflict, Castro confirmed that the ICAIC was the official cinematic venue of Cuba responsible for film creation as well as distribution.

After revolutionary Cuban cinema survived its first controversy, it continued to develop and began to gain critical prominence, but many of the island's filmmakers and critics worried that ICAIC directors would set aside their political goals and become detached from their revolutionary commitments in order to pursue international accolades. In order to maintain the tenets of its founding mission, ICAIC director Julio García Espinosa wrote his 1969 manifesto, "For an Imperfect Cinema," in an attempt to promote a Third-World Socialist Cinema that would form its identity in opposition to the "vanities" of First-World filmmaking, and to assert the primary importance of a Cuban revolutionary national cinema that would capture the reality of the Cuban workers' experience. To that end, García Espinosa established a direct link between the encouragement of collective filmmaking over the *auteur* approach, and the championing of a documentary language devoid of subjective ideological manipulation. García Espinosa believed that reality could be recreated in film to the extent that it was observed through an "objective" lens, resulting in a filmed reality composed with imperfect collective esthetics that would expose the problems facing the revolution without resorting to self-conscious propaganda.

The Legacy of Cuba's "Imperfect China"

García Espinosa's essay offers an innovative Third-World Cinema discourse and a theoretical point of view indebted to other influential film writings that interrogate the nature of cinema and its photographic language, as well as their uses toward the end of representing and interpreting objective conditions with a political purpose. The notion of "imperfect cinema" is therefore linked to the relationship between Marxist theory and the Formalist approaches developed by Soviet director Sergei Eisenstein; to the realistic documentary style promoted by the French critic André Bazin; to the fear of political detachment as expressed by Siegfried Kracauer; and to the relationship of cinema with the other arts as well as with the proletariat and the bourgeoisie as articulated by Walter Benjamin and Theodor Adorno. "For an Imperfect Cinema" is a fundamental critical text that is studied around the world to this day, and the precepts of which had been consistently implemented in Cuban filmmaking of the late 1960s and most of the 1970s.

In the 1970s, the ICAIC's production stalled after some of the Institute's resources (such as funding and workforce) were redirected towards achieving the unrealistic sugar cane quota the Cuban government had ambitiously proposed. The government's economic plan ended in failure and was a source of great embarrassment. The ICAIC became one of the scapegoats blamed for the failure. It was heavily criticized for a number of reasons, including for not being sufficiently committed to the cause and for still screening "decadent" films made by the enemies in capitalist nation-states.[19] This led to a more propagandistic or "safe" ICAIC output in the seventies that is not as exciting as the material produced in the sixties. Working within these realizations, directors such as Sara Gómez and Tomás Gutíerrez Alea, became, in the 1970s and 1980s respectively, among the first to deconstruct these Cuban socialist narratives with films such as *De cierta manera* (*In a Certain Way*, 1974), and *Hasta cierto punto* (*Up to a Certain Point*, 1982). These films worked within certain parameters of imperfect cinema to criticize the gender conventions in revolutionary Cuban society, while establishing self-reflexive plots that made the audience aware of the films' narrative conventions.

The 1980s were a conflicting period for Cuban cinema because they contained the national trauma of the Mariel boatlift which deeply affected Cuban society. ICAIC filmmakers tried to retain politics and ideological messages in their narratives but they began to resort to more entertaining and conventional plots that provided amusement and attracted larger Cuban audiences than the more gloomy auteur narratives from the past. Suddenly, comedies became the local box office hits, e.g., *House Swapping, Una novia para David* (*A Girlfriend for David*, 1985), and *Los pájaros tirándole a las escopetas* (*The Birds Are Shooting the Rifles*, 1984). On the other hand, this period led to the ICAIC's expensive co-production *Cecilia* (1982), a melodramatic loose adaptation of the nationalist classic *Cecilia Valdés o La Loma del Ángel* directed by Humberto Solás. The ICAIC spent all their annual budget on this epic co-production with Spain, but after its release, the film was not embraced by critics or audiences due to its very exaggerated histrionics (which I personally find very compelling), and because many Cuban critics were adamantly opposed to some of the changes from the original novel that Solás applied to the adaptation.[20] Because of this failure, ICAIC's president Alfredo Guevara was dismissed and substituted with Julio García Espinosa, whose tenure lasted until the release of the controversial *Alicia en el pueblo de Maravillas* (*Alice in Wondertown*, 1990).

In the decade after the breakdown of the East European bloc in 1989 and the collapse of the Soviet Union in 1991, Cuban society underwent a major economic crisis that impacted the lives of all Cubans. This decade became known as the "Special Period,"[21] and it affected all facets of Cuban society, from government institutions to the most basic needs of ordinary Cuban families. One of the most important publications explaining the different aspects of the Special Period is the academic essay anthology *Cuba in the Special Period: Culture and Ideology in the 1990s*. In her introduction, editor Ariana Hernández Reguant explains how dire the situation was at the time:

> Fuel and food shortages led first to an exhortation of thrift, which included door-to-door inspections of household appliances in order to issue individually tailored saving measures. Then, a strict rationing of energy and most other necessities was imposed, and food rations—in place since 1962—were severely curtailed. For example, bread allocations were decreased to 80 grams per person per day, gas sales to individuals were suspended altogether, and the utilities' supply was limited, in many cases to a few hours a day. To address the emergence of malnutrition-related ill-

nesses, the media sought to reeducate the population's eating habits, promoting such recipes as sweet potato leaf salad, mashed banana peel, and fried grapefruit peel.[22]

Hernández Reguant also explains how the Cuban government dealt with the economic crisis by introducing a number of reforms, while obviously maintaining power and avoiding the fates of Eastern European socialist states. She writes: "Economic reforms were designed to overcome the dire situation of the early 1990s without relinquishing political power. That is, they sought to alleviate material scarcity and popular pressure for change, but only for as long as they would not subvert revolutionary governance."[23]

Cuban cinema scholar Cristina Venegas' article titled "Filmmaking with Foreigners" provides a detailed overview of the films made in that period, and discusses some of the ways in which Cuban cinema in the 1990s changed under these dire economic conditions. The first major change that impacted the ICAIC's production, as discussed by Venegas, is related to the new ways in which Cuban cinema was funded, and specifically ICAIC's reliance on foreign coproductions, and in particular coproductions with Spain.[24] As a result of these new funding channels, Cuban filmmakers had to take foreign interests into account when planning their films, which led to a lot of self-exoticism and the return of the musical genre that they had previously criticized, and that is the topic of my fourth chapter.

Another important issue of Cuban film production during the Special Period that Venegas discusses is the controversy surrounding Daniel Díaz Torres' *Alicia en el pueblo de Maravillas* and other films that represented the Cuban problems of the time.[25] While Cuban filmmakers had parodied the revolution before, the looming economic crisis had begun to create a panic among government officials, which led to the ban of Díaz Torres' film a few years before the Special Period. This controversy was very important because it almost caused the dissolution of the ICAIC, and led many artists to wonder about their role in the revolution. This polemic film is the main subject of my book's first chapter.

One could say that *Alice in Wondertown* was a controversial film, but it was among those that paved the way for more Cuban films that were critical of the flaws in the Cuban political system without being

Introduction

labeled anti-revolutionary. When renowned Cuban filmmakers Tomás Gutiérrez Alea and Juan Carlos Tabío directed the landmark film *Fresa y chocolate* (*Strawberry and Chocolate*, 1993) at the peak of the Special Period, they impacted Cuban audiences by introducing the character of Diego, a gay intellectual who represented everyone who did not fit within the conservative frames of the revolution, and by eliciting empathy toward the character through the friendship that Diego builds with David, a staunch supporter of the Cuban revolution. The film was critically acclaimed both in the island, and abroad, as it gained a wide release in a number of countries. It became the first Cuban film to be nominated for the Academy Award for Best Foreign Language Film, and it is considered among the best Latin American films of all time. *Strawberry and Chocolate* reenergized Cuban filmmaking during the Special Period by reviving international interest in Cuban cinema, something very important at the time in view of the ICAIC's diminishing funds.

Venegas also addresses in her article the shift to digital filmmaking and the rise of Cuban directors with fresh approaches and varied cinematic influences. This infusion of new blood into the ICAIC led to the emergence of a young generation of filmmakers that brought innovative film techniques but also a set of fresh cultural references that provided an original vision to the ICAIC, while maintaining the institute's social goals.[26] One of the aspects of Cuban cinema that I discuss in this book is how some of the more important films in Cuba were made with foreign funding, using new genres usually avoided in socialist studios. I examine specifically the rise of new local production companies outside of the ICAIC, the rise of independent filmmakers, and the role of festivals in showcasing the new talent to international financiers.

My book thus focuses on these and other issues, as it examines the post–Cold War cinema of some Cuban filmmakers who worked almost exclusively within the framework of the ICAIC both before and after 1991. I emphasize on the Special Period and its aftermath in an attempt to analyze these filmmakers' struggle to create a new film vocabulary that depicts more accurately contemporary Cuban reality while remaining committed to revolutionary ideals. In order to explore the changes in the Cuban film industry outlined above, I first deconstruct the cultural and visual language developed by the revolution before the Special

Period. Drawing on the ideas of major schools of criticism such as structuralism, post-modernism, Marxism, and post-colonialism, I prove that, while its revolutionary legacy is an essential part of the island's heritage, Cuban culture is too complex to be limited or reduced to a single philosophy. This supports my argument that the revolution's survival and finding its new place in the international community depends in part on an evolution from its original precepts, including an open dialogue with the different aspects of Cuban reality that constitute the fabric of its society.

Encounters with Cuban Cinema After the Cold War

During the early nineties, when I was an undergraduate student at the University of Puerto Rico at Mayagüez, my first glance at Special Period films was at festival screenings of contemporary productions such as Julio García Espinosa's *Rey y Reina* (1994), Fernando Perez' *Madagascar* (1994), and Daniel Díaz Torres' *Quiéreme y verás* (*Love Me and You Will See*, 1995). These contemporary Cuban films were very compelling to me because they specifically portrayed in an accessible and emotional manner the struggles suffered by Cubans during the Special Period. In addition, they were interesting and innovative from an esthetic point of view, following the tradition of *House Swapping*. For example, *Rey y Reina* was a moving film about an old Cuban woman, her dog, and how both survived in contemporary Cuba. This may sound like a trivial plot until one realizes that the film is an homage to Italian neorealism. Once aware of this connection, it was fascinating for me to be able to appreciate the influence of Vittorio de Sica's neorealist techniques from *Umberto D* on this particular film, and to observe how the Italian film, a product of post–World War II Italy, and many of its visual and social concepts were adapted to Special Period Cuba.

In 1995, I was also pleasantly surprised when Tomás Gutiérrez Alea and Juan Carlos Tabío's *Fresa y chocolate* was screened in several commercial theaters outside of San Juan, the Puerto Rican capital, the film's wider distribution partly due to its Academy Award nomination for Best Foreign Language Film. I was very moved by the message of the film and the gritty aspects of its narrative inside its melodramatic structure.

Introduction

The positive international reception of this film led to high expectations for Gutiérrez Alea's last film *Guantanamera* (1995), which I was able to see in its French release, while studying in Paris during the summer of 1996. This worldwide acclaim of Cuban productions made me very proud of a Caribbean national cinema that had continued to challenge and defy cultural and hegemonic concepts, while criticizing its own revolution's mistakes, even during the financial collapse of its revolutionary state.

I continued my exploration of Cuban cinema in graduate school, and I was even able to visit Cuba in the early 2000s. Despite encountering the devastating economic crisis from which the island was just beginning to emerge, I had some interesting experiences that fed my interest in Cuban cinema. I was able to visit the "mythical" ICAIC, and I was able to chat with some members of the Cuban cinématheque, and have informal discussions about cinema in general that were very helpful in guiding my research curiosity. These acquaintances told me where I could find the official VHS releases of most of the ICAIC films available on home video, and encouraged me to check out the then new Juan Carlos Tabío film, *Lista de espera* (*Waiting List*, 2000), that was currently playing at the Charles Chaplin theater. Attending a Cuban screening with a Cuban audience was a fascinating experience, as I was able to observe the audience's immediate and very warm reaction to Special Period jokes.

When I returned to the United States, I brought with me all the available VHS copies of Cuban films from the ICAIC store, as well as several books and journals printed under the ICAIC press. I then made the point of watching every single ICAIC film ever made, because I wanted to become acquainted in detail with the oeuvre of the Institute's main auteurs, such as Tomás Gutiérrez Alea, Humberto Solás, Juan Carlos Tabío, and Fernando Pérez. At the time, I had the unique advantage of being able to go to Cuba and find these official ICAIC releases. Nowadays, access to ICAIC's productions has been facilitated in the United States because more official releases with English subtitles are available both on DVD and through streaming services such as Netflix. In addition, popular Cuban films (e.g. *Juan of the Dead*) are easily available through legal web services, such as iTunes or Amazon Instant Video, and many are screened on cable channels such as Venevisión and Cine Latino.

As I watched hundreds of Cuban films and read a significant amount of Cuban scholarly writing, I realized that ICAIC's Cuban cinema during the Special Period displayed a certain continuity with themes and cinematic concepts that could be traced back to the revolutionary films made in the sixties and seventies. At that point, I realized that to understand the most important aspects of Special Period cinema, one had to study what had been done before, as the cinema of the 1990s cannot be isolated in a period bubble. This experience informed my decision to write a book that would attempt to explore in balanced ways aspects of Cuba's history and passions as reflected in its cinematic production. I thus sought to focus on the Special Period as an important historical moment in the island's complex history. However, each chapter integrates cultural and cinematic background from the previous decades of Cuban cinema in order to help the reader understand the roots of my arguments. I also cover films made after the Special Period, specifically in the later chapters, because I wanted to explore the consequences of the changes brought to Cuban filmmaking due to the economic apocalypse that Cuban society experienced in the nineties.

In my exploration of the complex development of Cuban cinema, I use a variety of industry and scholarly sources from Cuba itself. I refer to some of the criticism that has appeared in *Cine Cubano* over the years, as well some recent books published by the ICAIC to support my argument. It is important to address here my use of secondary sources that originate in Cuba, because some confusion may arise when I use these sources together with other types of academic scholarship that originates in the U.S. and Europe. When the journal *Cine Cubano* began in 1961, it was considered groundbreaking for the Caribbean to have a venue for film criticism, specifically for the new waves of ideological filmmaking that were developing at the time.[27] Of course, some scholars may have issues with the journal's objectivity because it is run by the ICAIC itself and it is possible that its peer-review process may be different to what we are familiar with in the United States. However, even though it may be ideologically biased and with allegiances to the ICAIC, the journal certainly provided a venue for the publication of Cuban filmmakers' insights about their work, and for Cuban film historians to write some excellent segments about the history of Cuban cinema. In addition, it allowed foreign readers like me to learn about the film cycles screened in Havana in the past few decades.

It is important to note that the ICAIC also has a publishing press that, since the late 2000s, has been publishing a number of books that can be of help to any Cuban cinema scholar who wants to acquire a broader view of the island's national cinema as reflected in the writings of Cuban critics. The selection of books is impressive, and it includes a wide variety of materials, such as collections of criticism by respected Cuban critics (e.g. Rufo Caballero and Julio García Espinosa), the collected interviews of some of the most important Cuban filmmakers, as well as retrospectives of famous films such as *Memories of Underdevelopment* and *Lucía*. I was fascinated by the controversial nature of some of the information divulged in these books, which makes me think that either there is currently less censorship on the island, or the government is no longer threatened by the setbacks that occurred during the Special Period.

In this book I draw on a variety of sources for information and ideas pertinent to my analysis. While I do not assign value on critical works based on their authors' country of origin, I believe that readers should try to access both Cuban works, which have an important proximity to the filmmaking process, and American and European sources, which provide criticism from outside the revolutionary framework. This is what I have attempted to do in my book. When relevant, I have specified whether the source quoted is Cuban. Almost all Cuban sources are available at various university libraries in the U.S., so those interested in further research or more in-depth background information will have no trouble accessing them.

Structure of the Book

In my first chapter, I focus on Daniel Díaz Torres' film *Alice in Wondertown*, which has gained prominence on an international scale, as it was the only Cuban feature film officially banned by the revolutionary government. *Alice* is an original film which uses European children's lit-

The Legacy of Cuba's "Imperfect China"

erature (Lewis Caroll's *Alice in Wonderland*) and detective genre elements in order to construct a critique of the restrictive Cuban revolutionary narratives trapped within their own ideological language. I trace the influence of Luis Buñuel and the surrealist movement on revolutionary Cuban cinema, and I explain how Díaz Torres crafted neo-surrealist techniques that criticized the situation in Cuba during the Perestroika era, while remaining committed to revolutionary ideals. The film provides an important criticism of Cuban society, and serves as a visual premonition of the upcoming economic collapse in Cuba. However, while it is critical of blindly following authorities, it is not a film directed against the Cuban revolutionary government per se. More importantly, it indicates the beginning of a shift in Cuban filmmaking that would later mark the Special Period.

In the second chapter, I analyze Tomás Gutíerrez Alea's and Humberto Solás' controversial redefinition of Cuban nationalism in two of their most recent works, *Fresa y chocolate* (*Strawberry and Chocolate*, Gutíerrez Alea, 1993) and *Miel para Oshún* (*Honey for Oshún*, Solás, 2001). I explore the filmmakers' new acceptance of intellectuals, emigrants, and opponents of the 1959 revolution, groups that they had previously criticized in their earlier 1968 films, *Memories of Underdevelopment* and *Lucía*. One important factor in the analysis will be how both directors used melodramatic devices in their recent projects to counter the avant-garde techniques they had employed in the sixties. One of the main theoretical concepts that I employ in this chapter is film scholar Robert Stam's application of Mikhail Bakhtin's ideas about literary dialogism in his analysis of *Memories of Underdevelopment*. I argue that Stam's line of reasoning is key to understanding the shifts in the perception of the different strands of Cuban nationalism in the Special Period films that I have selected for this chapter.

In the third chapter, I study the evolution of the Cuban workers and peasants' representation in ICAIC filmmaking, from the early influence of Italian neorealism to the more contemporary and localized approach under the umbrella of García Espinosa's imperfect cinema. I analyze the works (both before and after the Special Period) of Juan Carlos Tabío and Fernando Pérez, two Cuban directors that have been able to merge successfully avant-garde techniques, revolutionary ideol-

Introduction

ogy, and commercial success. I study the films that they made during the Special Period, and focus particularly on *El elefante y la bicicleta* (*The Elephant and the Bicycle*, Tabío, 1994) and *Suite Habana* (*Havana Suite*, Pérez, 2003). I explain how Tabío's film deconstructs the history of cinema and parodies many of the precepts of imperfect cinema while, in contrast, *Suite Habana* ambiguously reinforces and criticizes some of these precepts. My purpose is to demonstrate how the events of the Special Period made ICAIC filmmakers reconsider the role of imperfect cinema in Cuban filmmaking.

Chapter four offers a discussion of the musical genre in Cuban cinema. I first provide a brief history of Cuban coproductions with the U.S., Europe, and Latin America, and explain how the pre-revolutionary musicals disseminated racist depictions of the island in the international imaginary. In analyzing this phenomenon, I specifically apply Homi Bhaba's ambivalence theory to the myth of the mulatta and the role of race in Cuban nationalism. After explaining how many of the pre-revolutionary racist tropes from colonialism continued to be used in Cuban culture after the country's independence from Spain, I demonstrate how after the revolution the ICAIC stopped the production of potentially racist musicals, but continued to use the genre's imagery as a didactic tool to educate the masses about the decadence of capitalism.

I proceed to an overview of musical coproductions made during the Special Period. I discuss the use of ICAIC actors and directors outside of ICAIC productions in foreign coproductions that do not necessarily comply with revolutionary ideology. I focus in particular on two films, Gerardo Chijona's *Un paraíso bajo las estrellas* (*Paradise Under the Stars*, 1999) and Benito Zambrano's *Habana Blues* (2005). Chijona's film is an ironic homage to pre-revolutionary musicals set in contemporary Cuba and using ICAIC actors. However, despite satirizing the genre, the film still uses many of the traditional musical's exoticizing and sexualized gender and race constructions. *Habana Blues*, directed by a Spaniard and made shortly after the Special Period, fictionalizes and criticizes the new fetishization of Cuban music by focusing on the poaching of Cuban performers in Europe and the U.S. as a result of the economic recession. Despite this criticism, the Spanish-Cuban coproduction still promotes the idea of a sexualized Cuba. Both films were officially coproduced by the ICAIC with the main purpose of gaining access to international distribution.

The revival of the Cuban musical genre (as laid out in Chapter 4) allowed for the resurgence of other genre films and the presence of non-socialist foreign investment in Cuba. Since the 2000s, Cuban filmmakers have begun to make films that follow certain genre patterns easily marketed to international audiences. However, they still attempt to preserve the political message associated with Cuban filmmaking. This is something that happened with the introduction of the horror genre in Cuban cinema, which I discuss in my fifth and sixth chapters, where I analyze two post–Special Period films, Juan Padrón's *Más vampiros en la Habana* (*More Vampires in Havana*, 2003), and Alejandro Brugués' *Juan de los muertos* (*Juan of the Dead*, 2011), respectively.

The animated feature *More Vampires in Havana*, coproduced with Spain, is a vampire story that takes place in Cuba in World War II. The film remains anti-fascist and anti-capitalist, as befitting an ICAIC production, however, it also satirizes Soviet films about the war, with which Cuban audiences are familiar. In this fifth chapter I establish a parallel between the careers of Walt Disney and Cuban animator Juan Padrón and discuss the two filmmakers' respective struggles to balance art, politics, and entertainment. In the sixth chapter, focusing on *Juan of the Dead*, I specifically explain how the film has the nihilistic structure of some American or European zombie films, but adapts its political satire to a contemporary Cuba, and mocks both Cuban and American authorities alike. The film has a more limited participation from the ICAIC, and has gained prominence on an international scale due to its original storyline and its status as the first truly independent Cuban film. More importantly, the international success of *Juan of the Dead* demonstrates how Cuban filmmakers have adapted to the new realities of international film distribution.

My conclusion ties together all the elements discussed throughout the book (controversial subjects, genre filmmaking, new digital technology, new Cuban auteurs, coproduction financing, and the revisions of Cuban revolutionary nationalism in Cuban cinema) through a brief comparison between Juan Carlos Cremata's *Viva Cuba* and Ian Padrón's *Habanastation*. Both films are children's narratives that embody

Introduction

post–Special Period Cuban filmmaking, and both provide interesting results because of the simultaneously innovative and traditional elements that they incorporate. I argue that, even though contemporary Cuban filmmakers have tried to update the visual language and content of today's Cuban cinema, their style still follows many of the formulas established earlier by the ICAIC. Still, their films represent new realities that show that Cuban culture continues to evolve, and that its future is very exciting.

With the retirement of Fidel Castro in Cuba, new economic and cultural opportunities have opened up for the island. While the country is still officially guided by its Communist Party, it has experienced certain developments, such as the expansion of private property legislature, new foreign investments, and free Internet access. The current American government has also allowed more flexibility towards the island, e.g. scholarly access, despite the continuing U.S. embargo. I believe that Cuban culture must be studied more rigorously at this pivotal moment in history, when the possibility of Cuba's complete opening to the U.S. is within reach. I have researched Cuban cinema for more than a decade, and I am confident that my book project will provide a new perspective on the topic and bring attention to important Cuban films that have been overlooked before. Nonetheless, the post–Special Period Cuban Cinema has so many compelling films that I could not possibly cover them all within a single manuscript, especially since I have focused the book on a very limited number of texts and topics. I did not feature all the prominent ICAIC directors, but I remain hopeful that other Cuban cinema scholars will continue adding material to this fascinating topic that, I am confident, will expand and draw further academic interest in the next couple of decades.

1

Daniel Díaz Torres' *Alicia en el pueblo de Maravillas* and the Controversial Use of Surrealist Techniques and Intertextual Subjects

Throughout his entire career, Daniel Díaz Torres' astute satirical reflections on the complex and intertextual nature of Cuban film sought to subvert the stereotypes of Cuban ideological propaganda. His surrealist techniques, infused with neonoir devices and themes from children's literature,[1] attempted to construct a Cuban intertextuality that would expand earlier socialist models and their methods of self-criticism. The film *Alicia en el pueblo de Maravillas/Alice in Wondertown*[2] (Díaz Torres, 1988) played a major role in spurring the extended use of intertextuality in the Cuban cinema of the 1990s that attempted to address social changes during the controversial Special Period. In the analysis of the film that follows, I will attempt to avoid the anti–Castro sensationalism in which *Alicia* has been enveloped when reviewed in foreign and local circles, a critical reception that has thwarted the fulfillment of its original goal. My purpose is instead to elucidate the complexities of the different narratives that Díaz Torres uses and that he infuses with satiric humor and popular cultural references in order to achieve larger goals. Within the context of claims made about Díaz Torres' desire to subvert Cuba's revolutionary government, I aim to demonstrate that his films were not only critical of Cuban society, as many ICAIC films are, but also tended to promote the larger goal of recognizing and validating diversity in an ideologically homogenous society.

The Myth of the Bearded Mayor

Alice production developed under Julio García Espinosa's tenure as president of the ICAIC. García Espinosa's leadership was essential in the creation of the "grupos de creación" (creative groups) in which filmmakers discussed each other's upcoming projects. These groups represented the decentralization of power in the ICAIC, which used to be centered around the figure of the ICAIC president. The groups' independence from the typical Cuban government bureaucracy was very worrisome to some party members, who were concerned about how the filmmakers would balance ideological rigor with the cultural themes and esthetics presented in their projects.[3]

The leaders of these groups were luminaries such as Tomás Gutíerrez Alea, Humberto Solás, and Manuel Pérez. *Alicia* was conceived under Pérez's group, where other important Cuban films were developed, such as Enrique Pineda's *La bella de la Alhambra* (*The Beauty of Alhambra*, 1990) and Fernando Pérez's *Hello Hemingway* (1988). García Espinosa read all scripts and criticized some aspects of *Alicia*'s story, but he thought the film's satirical topics would create interest in the release, and therefore approved its production. Upon completion, the film premiered at the Berlin International Film Festival, as it was not ready in time to open for the Festival del Nuevo Cine Latinoamericano that takes place in Havana during the month of December.[4]

The film's premiere was followed by one of the first signs of mishandling the social message of *Alicia*. According to *Cine Cubano*, a German critic pointed out that the film's antagonist (the mayor of Wondertown) has a full beard, an undeniable link to Fidel Castro. This misconception, developed in the critic's review, was only the first misreading of the film.[5] Thereafter, it seems Díaz Torres' *Alicia* was positioned abroad as an icon of resistance against Cuban socialism.

Although the mayor in the film does not have any facial hair, Daniel Díaz Torres has become better known in some Latin American film cir-

1. The Controversial Use of Surrealist Techniques

cles precisely as a consequence of the sensationalist rumors spread about his film as an allegedly direct criticism of the Castro regime. He has directed other features[6] after the scandal that arose in Cuba with *Alicia*; however, most critical attention has been focused on this particular work since its message can be easily interpreted and sensationalized as anti-revolutionary, a situation that has led to simplistic interpretations (like the German review previously mentioned) at the cost of ignoring the director's other major contributions that merit critical analysis.

The film was groundbreaking from a political and ideological perspective, and marked only the beginning of Díaz Torres' concern regarding the construction of cinematic reality and its role in relation to ideology and authority. With *Alicia*, the filmmaker criticizes the fact that each individual's reality is constructed as a consequence of his/her submission to the discourse imposed by the segment of society and culture to which he/she belongs. These social entities' control over the masses, he suggests, can be changed through the revolutionary process of self-awareness and dialectic interaction. Critical reception has narrowed this perspective by interpreting the film as a direct attack on Fidel Castro. However, while Díaz Torres was undoubtedly inspired by Cuban issues and settings, his vision invites a more general response to the film's critical depiction of humanity's reliance on authority and ideological systems. To achieve his goal, he adapted a text like *Alice in Wonderland* into a Cuban setting, and employed surrealist and neonoir techniques to create his controversial film *Alice in Wondertown*.

Special Period Cuban cinema is often associated with Tomás Gutiérrez Alea and Juan Carlos Tabío's film *Fresa y chocolate/Strawberry and Chocolate* (1994). This film undoubtedly drew substantial mainstream critical attention toward Cuban cinema at the time, yet scholars concur that the turning point for the Cuban film industry during the collapse of the Soviet Union was the controversial *Alicia* made in 1991.[7] As documented in Michael Chanan's *Cuban Cinema*, and in the Cuban film journal, *Cine Cubano*, *Alicia* was banned by the government after being screened for only a few days, and nearly led to the dissolution of the ICAIC, one of the most prestigious social institutions of the Cuban revolution.[8]

Film scholar Diane Soles mentions that García Espinosa gave a video copy of the film to Armando Hart, Cuba's minister of culture at the time. Copies of the video were disseminated among members of the government who did not react well to the final product. Due to the overwhelmingly negative reaction, García Espinosa, Díaz Torres and Manuel Pérez met with Hart to explain their goals, and later Díaz Torres sent an official letter to Hart, written with other filmmakers, to explain their motives. After not receiving any response, Díaz Torres sent a second letter. The response came through the *Granma* newspaper where the ministry announced the merging of the ICAIC with the Cuban armed forces film division.[9]

What offended party officials and the press at the time was the fact that the film portrayed the island's decay in a nihilistic manner that emanated a current of anger against the fictional mayor of the town, without offering an upbeat message at the end. While it may be the case that *Alicia* was by no means the first Cuban film to be critical of contemporary times (another example is Juan Carlos Tabío's *Plaff*, 1988), Díaz Torres had the misfortune of releasing his film at a time when Perestroika had changed the political landscape of Eastern Europe. This apocalyptic moment for East European communist states catalyzed the Cuban government's paranoia, which led to a ban of the film after a scandalous premiere attended by a number of displeased Cuban officials. The antagonizing atmosphere was so politically dangerous, ICAIC executives deemed it necessary to issue a statement affirming Díaz Torres' commitment to the revolution but that did not help to appease the government. According to Cuban scholar Sandra del Valle, the film has only been publicly screened one time in Cuba since its original release, and it was only shown at the Charles Chaplin theater[10] to commemorate the 50th anniversary of the ICAIC.[11]

Alicia (Díaz Torres' third feature film) was an exceptionally divisive event in Cuba. Following the satiric tradition of the Monty Python troupe[12] responsible for some of his favorite movies, the director envisioned adapting Lewis Carroll's *Alice in Wonderland* to a small imaginary Cuban town called Maravillas (Wondertown). The strange inhabitants of the town, outcasts exiled there as a result of their own mistakes or corruption, all live under the leadership of a mayor, who is also the director of the local hospital. The leader constantly attempts to redeem

1. The Controversial Use of Surrealist Techniques

his outcasts, including the protagonist, Alicia, and to make them perceive the unsightly town of Maravillas in utopian and not dystopian terms. After being unable to cope with the madness of the place, Alicia succeeds in escaping; however, as she crosses the mystical bridge to freedom, she is forced to throw her pursuer, a "Cheshire Cat" figure (the antagonist mayor), into the abyss below, and therefore to his death and destruction. She then awakens from this fantasy (or dream) only to realize that reality may become like the fictional town of Maravillas after all.[13] In the final shot, the protagonist addresses the audience directly, warning them about the possibility of the island's being transformed into a place similar to Maravillas.

Cuban scholar Pedro Porbén offers a compelling interpretation of the film through the lens of Foucault's writings about the Panopticon in *Discipline and Punish*, in which the French philosopher uses the metaphor of the Panopticon to explain how authoritarian cultures regulate and normalize their citizens. Porbén writes that *Alicia* distinguishes itself from the other Cuban films of the time by focusing on the "submissive bodies" that are the result of revolutionary dogmatic teachings, rather than on the authorities that created those bodies.[14] I would add that *Alicia* uses various scenes to satirize the government propaganda and its distortions of reality in which these submissive bodies are engulfed. There are a number of examples of this satire, such as the scene in which the town's mayor attempts to convince Alice that a glass of dirty water is drinkable and that the visible particles it contains are vitamins rather than dirt, and the scene in which animated cartoons are used to teach children to resign themselves to a flawed way of life.[15] This type of humorous criticism had been used in Cuban cinema earlier (e.g. Tomás Gutíerrez Alea's *La muerte de un burócrata*) and follows ICAIC's standards of sophisticated use of irony. However, this time the authorities feared *Alicia* could be interpreted as an antirevolutionary narrative that aspires to provoke a regime change.[16]

In their official journal, *Cine Cubano*, Cuban critics have tried to defuse the political consequences of the film by consistently supporting Diaz Torres' claims that *Alicia* does not challenge the government regime, providing examples of the negative reactions of the Cuban newspapers at the time of the film's release in order to prove that the controversy was little more than a misunderstanding caused by the ambiguous nature of comedy.[17] For his part, Daniel Díaz Torres defends his position as a revolutionary, and denies the reactionary aspects attributed to his film by both anticommunist thinkers and party censors. In his view, *Alicia* neither represents Cuban reality nor promotes its destruction. Rather, he suggests, the film simply exaggerates the cultural dimensions of society with the purpose of denouncing certain elements that delay or impede Cuba's progress, or, as Díaz Torres articulates it in an interview,

> satire always implies deformation. [...] We set up situations that are, of course, exaggerated, because we're using a language that deliberately attempts to create a super-reality. A certain level of exaggeration was needed in order to have an impact on spectators, to force them to think about the causes of the problems being depicted. The town of Maravillas is not a specific, concrete town, although one can find in it many elements that are scattered throughout our national reality.[18]

The director's quest for a critical revolutionary art is supported to a certain extent by Julio García Espinosa's celebrated manifesto, "For an Imperfect Cinema," a cornerstone of academic film criticism in Cuban and Latin American cinema. While the manifesto may have become outdated since it was written (1969), it provided the foundations of a cinema of critique that would eradicate elements hindering social progress, a cinema that would not be limited to creating beautiful art for the enjoyment of the First World or the creation of useless slogans:

> We maintain that imperfect cinema must above all show the process which generates the problems. It is thus the opposite of a cinema principally dedicated to celebrating results, the opposite of a self-sufficient and contemplative cinema, the opposite of a cinema which "beautifully illustrates" ideas or concepts which we already possess. [...] To analyze a problem is to show the problem (not the process) permeated with judgments which the analysis itself generates a priority. To analyze is to block off from the outset any possibility for analysis on the part of the interlocutor.[19]

Díaz Torres took this critique a step further when, instead of focusing on a single aspect of Cuban society in his film, he defined Cuba as an imaginary place created by the amalgamation of the diverse cultures that have touched the island. The filmmaker aimed to achieve the multifaceted representation to which García Espinosa aspired, but in the process found himself constrained to deconstructing Cuban culture's

1. The Controversial Use of Surrealist Techniques

vocabularies, which in turn led to the film's controversy. Díaz Torres' *Maravillas* is conceptualized as a surrealist town that, as part of a literal dream in the film, represents the subconscious of his nation where all the characters at some point fear the Ego as represented by the mayor.

To understand this film, the viewer has to try to grasp its inherently intertextual nature. The concept known as intertextuality has a complex theoretical framework that has acquired different meanings over the course of the 20th century, and it still is much debated among cultural critics from around the word. Bulgarian critic Julia Kristeva originally coined the term in her essays "World, Dialogue and Novel" and "The Bounded Text" to expand complex linguistic and cultural concepts previously discussed by Russian critic Mikhail Bakhtin, such as his concepts of heteroglossia and dialogism, in which meaning can be affected by the multiple voices present in the text. In her article "Intertextuality: Origins and Development of the Concept," Spanish scholar María Jesús Martínez Alfaro explains that:

> the crucial step that separates every previous approximation of intertextuality from the notion that Kristeva initiated taking Bakhtin's theories as a point of departure is the view of the exterior of the text as a system (or an infinity) of other such textual structures. Thus, if a text refers to "all other texts," these are seen, in turn, as converging with history and reality, both existing only in textualized form. Likewise, both in Bakhtin and Kristeva, the subject is conceived as composed of discourses, as a signifying system, a text understood in a dynamic sense[20] [271].

Alice in Wondertown is a film that abounds in intertextual narrative devices that can provide different meanings according to the audience's perception, cultural knowledge, and ideology. In *Alice*'s case, what may have been controversial for a Cuban audience at the time is that the authority figure in this film is not the tired bourgeois archetype, a surrealist staple no longer relevant to Cuban culture, but a well-meaning revolutionary bureaucrat. The film thus links Cuban audiences' perception of the surreal town to their own reality through a variety of signifiers that are very familiar, but without directly accusing or criticizing the Cuban government. However, the meaning of the narrative and how the characters are presented in the dream sequence can vary according to what the different audiences from outside/inside Cuba bring to their interpretation based on their own cultural and ideological needs. Let us examine next the specific uses of surrealism in the film, and how its meaning/critique is intertextualized.

Luis Buñuel and the Influence of His Surrealist Techniques in Cuban Cinema

Alice's dream in the film can be linked to the work of famous Spanish surrealist director Luis Buñuel, since the dream is reminiscent of some sequences form *Muerte de un burócrata*, a film which itself was inspired by Buñuel's filmography. According to Michael Chanan, *Alice in Wondertown* was first interpreted in Cuba as following the legacy of *Muerte de un burócrata/Death of a Bureaucrat* (Gutíerrez Alea, 1965) which mocked the "sins of bureaucracy."[21] Other critics have linked *Death of a Bureaucrat* to Luis Buñuel's directing style. In his book on Buñuel's heritage in Latin America, Francisco Millán Agudo, for example, examines the film's oneiric nature as an homage to Buñuel, and all of Gutíerrez Alea's work as inspired by Buñuel in that it uses the same "subversive traits to satirize hypocrisy, bourgeois immobility (or, in Cuba's case, government bureaucracy), and religious precepts."[22] To clarify these connections and shed light on the specifics of Diaz Torres' film, I will first explain how Buñuel's ideas and his oeuvre have influenced filmmaking in Latin America in general, and Cuba in particular.

Luis Buñuel, a Spanish-born filmmaker, worked in three different countries to create an impressive amount of important films. To film studies scholars, he is best known for his films made in France, and specifically *Un chien andalou* (*An Andalusian Dog*, 1929) and *L'âge d'or* (*The Golden Age*, 1930), which are usually associated with the Surrealist movement in the 1920s in France. These two films are practically dream sequences abounding in non sequiturs which expressed inner desires of sex and violence that challenged the pretensions of the bourgeois morality of their time. They represent very clearly André Breton's idea of "sur-reality," something created by the clash between dream and reality.[23]

Because of his association with André Breton's group, Buñuel is easy to classify as a Surrealist. However, some authors, such as prominent French historian of surrealism Jose Pierre, have observed the presence

1. The Controversial Use of Surrealist Techniques

of a number of elements from different movements in his work (Gothic, pre–Raphaelite, and Surrealist). Pierre notes the difficulty in labeling any esthetic or ideological elements as purely Surrealist, including Buñuel's heavy reliance on dream sequences as expressions of unleashing desire, something which would have been censored at the time. The author notes that dream sequences are an esthetic device shared by Surrealism, Romanticism, and Symbolism. However, since Buñuel is associated with the Surrealist movement in France, his use of such cinematic devices is generally perceived as coming from that movement. According to scholar Robert Short, surrealist artists were among the first ones to emphasize on cinematic images as a link to dream constructions, and he quotes Buñuel in stating that "the cinema seems to have been invented to express the life of the subconscious whose roots penetrate so deeply into poetry. The film seems to be the involuntary imitation of the dream."[24]

After his period in France, Buñuel moved to Mexico and became one of the most influential filmmakers working within the Mexican national tradition. Francisco Millán Agudo traces the director's influence on cinema movements such as cinema novo in Brazil, as well as on renowned Mexican filmmakers such as Luis Alcoriza and Arturo Ripstein, and on ICAIC founders such as Tomás Gutíerrez Alea and Alfredo Guevara. Millán Agudo explains that Mexican intellectuals were attracted to Buñuel's work because of his link to the European intellectuals such as André Breton, Antonin Artaud, and others. However, Millán Agudo also notes the syncretism present in Latin American culture as a fertile ground for the innovative ideas Buñuel brought in.[25] This syncretism was called "lo real maravilloso" (the marvelous real) by Alejo Carpentier in "On the Marvelous Real in America," his prologue to the novel *El reino de este mundo* (*The Kingdom of This World*).

The concept of the marvelous real is constantly debated in modern Cultural Studies but is important because it establishes a difference between a perceived artificiality of European surrealist techniques vs. a cultural surrealism already embedded in the Latin American cultures. In his writing, Carpentier established that many of the forced juxtapositions in the European avant-garde came naturally to Latin American cultures that, through their colonial history, have created a diverse cultural environment where the different ethnic heritages have visually merged or appeared to be compatible with each other. Carpentier writes: "Now then, if Surrealism pursued the marvelous, one would have to say that it rarely looked for it in reality. It is true that for the first time the Surrealists knew how to see the poetic force of a window display or a market, but more often their fabrication of the marvelous was premeditated."[26] On the other hand, the marvelous real is encountered in its raw state, latent and omnipresent, in all that is Latin American. I would argue that some of the surrealist esthetics in *Alice* can be traced to Buñuel's influence on Latin American filmmaking, as opposed to being a product of a hybrid Caribbean setting. However, the marvelous real may have played a part in the film with the juxtaposition of different characters' realities that I will discuss later.

The first revolutionary Cuban film to be constructed with Buñuel's surrealist mold was *La muerte de un burócrata/Death of a Bureaucrat* (Gutíerrez Alea, 1966). This project follows the misadventures of a common man whose proletarian uncle was a famous worker who invented a machine that reproduced busts of Jose Martí[27] in an industrialized manner. After this mythical uncle who embodied the principles of the 1959 Cuban revolution dies, he is buried with his worker's card, to the great chagrin of the main character who needs this document in order to receive his aunt's pension. The nephew has to maneuver the complex world of Cuban bureaucracy throughout the entire film. When he fails to acquire the money, he becomes mad at the end of the story and finally kills the cemetery bureaucrat who has been his main nemesis throughout the film. After he commits the murder, he is taken to prison and his life is destroyed by the failures of the system he once respected.

This film follows a conventional narrative, yet it includes surrealist elements in its satire of the ways in which the new society created by the Cuban revolution could potentially devolve if social problems are ignored in order to follow authority blindly. The protagonist's submission to bureaucracy, perhaps related to his desire to be respectful to the revolutionary system supported by his deceased uncle, leads to a frustration analogous to that experienced by Buñuel's characters with the bourgeoisie and Christianity in his French and Mexican films. To establish this link, Gutíerrez Alea quotes Buñuel's *L'âge d'or*, and specifically

1. The Controversial Use of Surrealist Techniques

a scene in the French film where the main character is venting his frustrations by throwing things he hates (such as a Catholic priest) out of a window (defenestration). In *La muerte de un burócrata*, a dream sequence shows the protagonist trying to walk, burdened by heavy objects. At first, he is portrayed carrying a series of Catholic symbols such as a nun, a commonplace surrealist joke on the bourgeoisie and its Catholicism. Later, however, the protagonist is seen pulling the casket of his deceased proletarian uncle, who is sitting on top and laughing at his suffering nephew. This peculiar scene transforms the surrealist intention of Buñuel's films, adapting it to the post-revolutionary reality of Cuba, where, once in power, the proletariat becomes a new burden of authority, and is thus subject to criticism, just as the previous social entities.

La muerte de un burócrata is a classic of Latin American cinema for its esthetics and its courageous cultural criticism, having attempted to promote the idea that ICAIC could produce better films than mere propaganda pieces. The film follows a Surrealist legacy, which by no means implies that it is constructed precisely along the lines of Buñuel's films of the 1930s or even those of the Spanish director's later work with Mexican studios. Some links to these films exist, such as the depiction of repressed desires, antagonistic institutions, and dream sequences; however, a number of their aspects were adapted to the socialist context. For example, the sexuality of Buñuel's French Surrealist films is subdued in his Mexican films, and is practically non-existent in Tomás Gutíerrez Alea's film. With the exception of the irony exhibited by the character of a communist art director, an adamant anti-imperialist who cheats on his wife, in *Death of a Bureaucrat* rebellion against the system lies in misbehavior that is in direct opposition to centralized government order. Examples of this subversion include a fight that breaks out between workers, depicted in a slapstick scene, and the main character's repressed anger toward the system that ends with his committing a murder.

La muerte de un burócrata was relevant to the argument Daniel Díaz Torres proposed in 2004 in an issue of *Cine Cubano*. His article "Sobre el diablo y las liebres" ("About the Devil and the Hares") explored the role of comedy in society and in the development of revolutionary principles. Discussing (and defending) his *Alicia*, he describes it as following the tradition of Gutíerrez Alea's film, which in the 1960s was a necessary tool to fight the bureaucratic problems of the post-revolutionary Cuban government.[28] In addition, he discusses it as a film successfully avoiding the utopianization regularly deployed by socialist realist dramas. Díaz Torres saw *Death of a Bureaucrat* as an improvement over Gutíerrez Alea's *Las doce sillas* (*The Twelve Chairs*, 1962) due to its focus on the problems of the present and its avoidance of blaming current mistakes on pre-revolutionary society. In his complex argument, Díaz Torres cites passages that range from Voltaire's *Candide* to Umberto Eco's *The Name of the Rose* in an attempt to develop a philosophy of comedy as the highest form of revolutionary narrative. In his view, *Death of a Bureaucrat* constitutes one of the best examples of constructive revolutionary comedies, one that he sought to emulate in his own problematic film, *Alice in Wondertown*.

Alice in Wondertown *and Neo-Surrealism*

In *Alicia*, the film's plot structuring follows the patterns of a criminal murder mystery. Díaz Torres favors this type of storytelling, having worked as an assistant director on the Cuban noir *El hombre de Maisinicú/The Man of Maisinicu* (Manuel Pérez, 1974).[29] *Alicia* opens with its protagonist fleeing to a desolate place. She is given a ride on a truck full of workers, but as the vehicle crosses a bridge, she is attacked by a disturbing cloaked mysterious figure. Alice pushes him into the abyss and to his death (in a scene that mimics the previously discussed scenes in *L'âge d'or* and *La muerte de un burócrata*), and the other passengers accuse her of murder. The police cannot find a body, and are thus unable to press charges, but Alice proceeds to tell the viewers her terrifying story.

As the narrative moves into a flashback, the film begins to adapt freely the plot of *Alice in Wonderland*. This is not a strict adaptation of Carroll's book, and it includes only few elements from the original source (an example of such elements are recognizable figures such as the Cheshire Cat, portrayed as the mayor of Maravillas or Alicia/Alice herself). In *Alicia*, the original source's British jokes ridiculing 19th-century society are re-adjusted to Cuban reality, and as a result, the subversive

1. The Controversial Use of Surrealist Techniques

aspects of the novel aimed at the Victorian age are adapted in the film to denounce the institutions that resemble the institutions similar to the ones Cuban audiences have encountered before. *Alicia* abounds in characters derived from Cuban popular culture such as an elementary school pioneer, a corrupt produce merchant, sleazy businessmen, lazy service workers frustrated with life, and fallen priests, who all shape the setting of the film into a kind of mystical Siberia, the only sensible feature of which remains Alice's reasoning.

Since all the characters have been exiled to Maravillas as a result of making a mistake that has led to their disgrace, they are bullied by the mayor into doing everything that the system requires of them. The importance of these characters lies in the fact that they provide a Bakhtinian dialogic conflict of viewpoints,[30] which helps the narrative escape the adherence to a single, officially sanctioned point of view. Through her interactions with the other exiled characters, Cuban Alice matures, and ultimately escapes the control of the official discourse in Maravillas. Once Alice realizes how society functions with regard to power and stops believing in the authorities, she is able to return to her own reality.

Obviously, this development could be interpreted as anti-revolutionary because the characters in the film are visually grounded in current Cuban reality. Alice destroys the Chesire Cat/Mayor once she escapes his control of discourse, which allows for an interpretation of the film as a narrative promoting the destruction of the (Cuban) leader, and hence the beliefs of the Cuban people who have maintained him in power. To non-Cuban audiences whose knowledge of the island may be limited to the personality of Castro, the Mayor/Cheshire Cat would require a beard in order to be equated with the Cuban leader, even if the beard was not actually present in the film.

Once released, the production was, like all films, open to diverse interpretations by critics and audiences alike. Although influential members of the Cuban Communist Party may have resented the cynicism of *Alicia*, the film struck a nerve with other minor local authorities as well. Nevertheless, the film warrants reading not as an anti-revolutionary but rather as an anti-establishment text, since its characters are constructed according to their respective places in society and their particular traits.

This juxtaposition of different Cuban realities is very similar to the cultural devices of the marvelous real discussed previously in this chapter. The Cuban audience is able to perceive the many facets of Cuban culture which are maintained together by the Mayor. The different societal, ethnic, and political realities are blended together in a mixture that defines Cuban society.

As a Cuban fantasy, most visual references in the film allude to contemporary life in Cuba, just as Carroll's book abounds in signifiers of the British Victorian Age and Queen Victoria. It is thus useful to understand the director's views while acknowledging the possibility that Díaz Torres may have undermined his own best interests in choosing a foreign text critical of its leader. Readers of Carroll's *Alice* could link the character of the Queen of Hearts to images of Queen Victoria, just as it is easy for viewers of *Alicia* to indulge in projecting Castro in the, albeit beardless, authoritarian mayor of the film. There is certainly a subversive element in Alice's defiance of this paternal figure in the film, even though he is a version of the Cheshire Cat rather than the Queen of Hearts character.

It is important to emphasize the surrealist elements in the film, because the entire sequence in Maravillas is constructed as a dream sequence similar to the ones visualized by Buñuel. While watching the film, the audience may find many awkward elements in the narrative, such as Alice's watching a man through her bathroom mirror, characters taking a mud bath in human feces, and other strange elements that resemble the scatological humor of Buñuel's *L'âge d'or*. At the end of the film, Alice wakes up and realizes it was all a dream. However, when she sees a glass of dirty water like the one presented to her by the Mayor, it is implied that the surrealist dream the audience just experienced may be closer to reality than previously thought. This convergence of inner angst and desires with reality helps to define this film as a film with surrealist overtones.

Díaz Torres was successful in creating a surrealist dream fantasy that embodies the intertextual nature of Cuban culture. In *Alicia*, one can decode British, American, Christian, Hispanic, African, and Soviet influences that make sense in the context of Cuba's multifaceted culture. Since most of the story takes place in a dream, Alice is able to escape

1. The Controversial Use of Surrealist Techniques

from an artificial reality that unifies the different voices under the auspices of an authority that grows stale once it consolidates power. This dynamic could offer an important lesson for any state built on a particular national ideology, but in Cuba's case it mirrors the decay of the 1959 revolution which needs to acknowledge its problems if it wants to survive. While we might empathize (from a broad human point of view) with Alicia's anger toward the system in which she finds herself, the film's referential mode is undeniably specific to Cuban or post–1959 revolutionary culture. This balance between the controversial specific historical criticism of Cuban reality and the universal anti-hegemonic devices with which many around the world can identify, is the main reason for the film's controversial nature.[31]

As Cuban society began to envision its history through the lens of a specific revolutionary discourse, it also began to represent a world questioning itself, and an opening of attitudes that eventually came about with the release of *Alicia*. The film's attempt at intertextuality and its use of surrealist techniques to rupture the suffocation of the culture instantiated and reified by the revolutionary collective is a theme present in Díaz Torres' other Special Period works as well. In *Quiéreme y verás/Love Me and You Will See* (1994), the filmmaker explored the damage of the flawed past and its memories on the present through the figure of a mobster's romantic image of the Batista years that prevents the protagonist from fully engaging with and enjoying the present. In *Kleines Tropikana* (1997), that past is similarly too ambiguous to be able to define the present, thus encouraging the audience's awareness of the manipulative artificiality of narratives delivered for nationalist and individualist purposes. In *Hacerse el sueco/Becoming Swede* (2000), the present is relative to a number of factors, including class, race, and money, as well as to a variety of problematic issues that were allegedly eliminated by the revolution but in fact continue to affect the island. Daniel Díaz Torres died in 2013, but his last film, *La película de Ana* (*Ana's Film*, 2012), in which he mocks the artificiality of documentary fiction by having a professional actress performing the role of a real-life prostitute, recently won the important Caracol award[32] for best Cuban film, an honor that cemented his legacy on the island after the *Alice* controversy had almost destroyed his career.

By means of intertextual references in his films, Daniel Díaz Torres sought to prove that, as Cuba evolves, its people must acknowledge the need to maintain their revolutionary ideals while remaining aware of the world's changing realities. Díaz Torres' films often parody the distinct progression from the cinematic limitations established by a system through the esthetic and manipulative forms of narration in individual, ideological, and nationalist terms, to the artificial setups of a series of archetypes and stereotypes in which Cuban citizens begin to believe. *Alice*'s parody serves as what scholar Linda Hutcheon defines as "an important way for modern artists to come to terms with the past-through ironic recoding or, in my awkward descriptive neologism, "trans-contextualizing."[33]

These complex critical achievements warrant wider circulation of Daniel Díaz Torres' work, and a more precise analysis of its progression from the limited sensationalist interpretations of *Alicia* to acknowledging the filmmaker's subtler role as advocate of a postmodern and multitextual Cuban reality that will help the Cuban revolution survive. More importantly, *Alicia* has a significance on an international scale, for, just like its British inspiration, it promotes principles that surpass the immediate realities of a single nation. Contemporary readers of *Alice in Wonderland* can appreciate the anti-establishment overtones of the book, despite of how (un)familiar they are with Victorian England. Díaz Torres' film functions in the same manner, as its audiences are urged to transcend the limitations of the discourse in which they are entrapped.

2

Political Melodrama in the New Nationalist Vision of Tomás Gutíerrez Alea's *Strawberry and Chocolate* and Humberto Solás' *Honey for Oshún*

Cuba's most celebrated directors, Tomás Gutíerrez Alea and Humberto Solás, enjoy a legacy of cinematic masterpieces, crowned by the achievement of each director's 1968 production: Gutíerrez Alea's *Memories of Underdevelopment* and Solás' *Lucía*, acknowledged to be among the greatest Latin American films of all time.[1] Both films figure prominently in analyses of third-world and Marxist cinema; both are renowned for their esthetic achievements, as evidenced in scholarly studies of their cultural and historical impact. Contemporary screenings of these films offer viewers nostalgic memories of the exciting prospects imaginable at the dawn of the Cuban revolution because the two works embody ideals of the progressive social and artistic movements of the 1960s, the objectives of which were to improve social conditions through experimentation with conventional narratives that buttressed the institutions then in power.

More than twenty-five years later, as a consequence of the Special Period, both directors were forced to face the diminution of the revolutionary ideals they had supported through their filmmaking and the inevitability of new challenges in the post–Perestroika era. Many of the utopian socialist paradigms of the 1960s had been modified or eliminated, or were undergoing radical interrogation by the island's citizens. It thus became imperative for the two filmmakers to incorporate, within the framework of their former conceptualizations of Cuban social and artistic reality, new strategies that would appeal to contemporary viewers. In so doing, they turned away from making avant-garde didactic films that defined what an ideal revolutionary man is, offering instead harsher and more ambiguous contemporary melodramas such as Gutiérrez Alea's *Strawberry and Chocolate* (1994) and Solás' *Honey for Oshún* (2001). These works were engaging from a dramatic, narrative, and emotional perspective while attempting a degree of objectivity with regard to issues of Cuban national identity foregrounded in the debates of the 1990s. They are, however, also problematic because of their reliance on a series of culturally outdated visual signifiers pertaining to dissidents that show some of the limitations that the directors could not overcome at the time.

Strawberry and Chocolate (*Fresa y chocolate*, Tomás Gutiérrez Alea and Juan Carlos Tabío, 1994) and *Honey for Oshún* (*Miel para Oshún*, Humberto Solás, 2001) are more personal works for their respective directors. Their stance is counter to the very templates of Cuban identity that Solás and Gutiérrez Alea themselves had created over several decades. These later projects used outcast intellectual Cuban anti-heroes to represent the pre-revolutionary values that had been eradicated, but with an important difference: rather than being constructed as antagonistic or as representatives of a decaying sphere of society, in both films these characters are sympathetic, and represent an updated idea of what the contemporary Cuban national identity involves. The characters, Diego (*Strawberry and Chocolate*) and Roberto (*Honey for Oshún*), are both portrayed by actor Jorge Perugorría whose charming and popular performances led him to international superstardom and served a key role in the new acceptance of a certain part of Cuban culture that had been lost or exiled due to the revolutionary process.

This trajectory is further delineated with regard to the directors' cinematic objectives, in the sense that both position their films to promote an understanding of the conflicting Cuban factions whose ideologies separated them following the revolution of 1959. Their films, *Strawberry and Chocolate* and *Honey for Oshún*, re-established a dialogical reality, in Bakhtinian terms, that renewed the dialectical revolutionary spirit of Cuban cinema in reaction to what was then considered to be the paralysis of ICAIC's own monolithic production. This revision, with its successes and failures in the representation of culture and society, is the ultimate legacy of the island's two greatest directors.

The Intellectual and the Cuban "Dissident Other" in the 1960s

Tomás Gutíerrez Alea and Humberto Solás were part of a group of educated intellectuals who, in the middle of the 20th century, sought to critique the cultural language developed by the upper classes, specifically in the Caribbean and South America. In these regions, the Hispanic elite had been accused of undermining the workers, the indigenous tribes, and people of African descent, excluding them from the hegemonic national culture. Cinema was an essential cultural weapon used by conservative studios to teach Hispanic and Catholic values through family melodramas and musicals that recreated Latin American reality to conform to the vision of those in power, and in so doing promoted damaging stereotypes of the repressed spheres of these societies.

Both filmmakers' productions in the 1960s and 1970s represented important stages in developing a transnational revolutionary cinema that, through innovative esthetics and cultural content, would provide new voices to oppose the hegemony of Latin American commercial studios based on a Hollywood model. After returning from studying film in Italy, Gutíerrez Alea planted the seeds of revolutionary Cuban cinema before the 1959 revolution by co-directing (with Julio García Espinosa) *El mégano* (1955), an underground short film about coal workers. Solás, in contrast, abandoned high school and fought in the revolution. He became a film aficionado, who admired the European New Waves, and wrote for the revolutionary film journal *Cine Cubano*, where he made some contacts in the ICAIC.[2] Along with other directors, both filmmakers participated in recreating the history of the 1959 Cuban revolution through the socialist ideals in which they firmly believed. Their first fiction features, *Histories of the revolution* (Gutíerrez Alea, 1960) and *Manuela* (Solás, 1964), were designed and shot in an attempt to embellish the effort of the collective in an Italian neorealist manner, a strategy that today might appear outdated to many modern viewers but was certainly politically relevant at the time.[3]

Gutíerrez Alea and Solás were inclined to pursue revolutionary esthetics and goals in their filmmaking but certainly not to limit themselves to those frequently advocated in this ideological approach. Without being limited esthetically to socialist artistic practice, both directors brought to their national cinema a rich film knowledge that proved to be important in creating a cinematic alternative to the stronghold of the Latin American melodramas promoted by Mexican and Argentinean studios. They were familiar with the cinematic styles used in Soviet cinema (such as montage and socialist realism), Western Europe (such as Surrealism, Expressionism, and neorealism), and Hollywood (comedy, film noir) and adapted them to the genres popular in Cuba and Latin America at the time—picaresque comedies and melodramas. Gutíerrez Alea's more experimental films, such as *La muerte de un burócrata* (*Death of a Bureaucrat*, 1966), *La última cena* (*The Last Supper*, 1976), and *Los sobrevivientes* (*The Survivors*, 1978) were heavily influenced by Buñuel's surrealist films, while Solás' works were extravagant costume melodramas (inspired by European filmmakers such as Luchino Visconti), e.g., *Lucía* (1968), *Cecilia* (1982), *Amada* (1983), *Un hombre de éxito* (*A Successful Man*, 1986), and *El siglo de las luces* (1992). Both filmmakers stayed and worked on the island until their respective deaths, and both are considered luminaries of the Cuban cinema industry. While the two had their highs and lows in the industry, they have both always been perceived as patriotic revolutionaries who brought prestige to the island with their cinematic masterpieces.

However, this career path was not followed by other filmmakers and artists such as Spanish cinematographer Nestor Almendros, Cuban director Orlando Jiménez Leal, and Cuban writer Guillermo Cabrera Infante, all of whom fled the island over ideological differences and clashes with Castro's government's cultural policies. These new policies were implemented when, as a consequence of the Cold War, the revolutionary Cuban government decided that the transformation into a socialist state would help the island gain the protection of the Soviet Union against an American invasion; moreover, such a transformation would, they believed, better serve the purpose of eradicating the last

2. Political Melodrama in the New Nationalist Vision

vestiges of a culture that promoted colonialism, capitalist decadence, and exploitation. This choice of a particular Marxist ideology was the beginning of a split between Cuban intellectuals because of the radical changes that it would bring to the cultural infrastructure of the island.[4]

The first important intellectual split is documented by Michael Chanan in the sixth chapter ("The Coming of Socialism") of his book *Cuban Cinema*. In his account, he explores the controversy linked to the first film banned by the Cuban revolutionary Government: Sabá Cabrera Infante and Orlando Jiménez Leal's *P.M.* (1961) which was sponsored by *Lunes*, the cultural section of *Revolución*, the biggest Cuban newspaper at the time that supported the 1959 revolution. This short documentary was deemed too self-indulgent and lacking a social purpose, and, as I explained in the introduction, it led to a confrontation between the ICAIC and the intellectuals running the culture segment in the newspaper *Revolución*. Prestigious Cuban writer Guillermo Cabrera Infante, the main sponsor of the film and Sabá's brother, tried to challenge the ICAIC's control of Cuba's cinema venues.[5] However, his intellectual group suffered a defeat when Castro sided with the ICAIC and delivered his famous speech "A los intelectuales." Cabrera Infante left Cuba officially in 1965 and has since become an anti–Castro icon in certain intellectual and dissident circles. He discusses resentfully this particular event in his autobiographical book *Mea Cuba*, in which he describes former ICAIC president Alfredo Guevara in a negative light as a conservative communist enforcer, and portrays the ICAIC as a nefarious institution that banned *P.M.* while trying to establish complete control of the island's national cinema. Cabrera Infante writes:

> The Cuban Film Institute owns all the cinemas, drive-ins, and movie houses in Cuba- and you must go to them even to go to get a roll of film for a snapshot camera. On top of that, they had a long standing feud with *Lunes,* which they labeled as decadent, bourgeois, avant-gardist, and the worst epithet in the Communist name-calling catalogue, cosmopolitist [cosmopolite]. In turn, we saw them as despicable bureaucrats, a bunch of ignoramuses with artistically reactionary ideas and no taste at all. The director of the Film Institute Alfredo Guevara, was the worst Communist commissar to deal with films this side of Stalin's Shumyavsky.[6]

Cabrera Infante's account of the ICAIC's reaction to the intellectuals who worked with him in *Lunes*, and particularly its labeling them "avant-gardist," is strange, because the works of ICAIC filmmakers such as Solás and Gutiérrez Alea in the 1960s abounded in avant-garde references. I would say the main difference between a work like *P.M.* on the one hand and *Memories of Underdevelopment* and *Lucía* on the other is that, while Sabá Cabrera Infante's film emphasizes/enjoys the remnants of pre-revolutionary Havana night life, Gutíerrez Alea's and Solás' later films of the period use their modernist techniques to dialectally visualize what Che Guevara defined as "the New Man" (el hombre nuevo).

As post-revolutionary Cuba turned officially into a Marxist and Socialist state, class concepts were increasingly emphasized, and the upper class and its hegemonic culture were held responsible for most of the injustices that the Cuban people had endured under Hispanic colonialism and American capitalist exploitation. Filmmakers Gutíerrez Alea and Solás were among the first to use the upper-class antagonist as a means of dialectically constructing "the New Man" as described and promoted by Ernesto "Che" Guevara in his essay "Man and Socialism." This Cuban revolutionary sociological concept upholds the idea of a worker who would presumably not indulge in excesses (brought about by capitalism, monarchy, etc.) and who would be wary of acting only for his own benefit.[7] He[8] would, in this view, do his best for others, not out of fear of God or to support a nation-state, but rather out of conviction and care for the group of comrades or a collective that would serve as his extended family.[9]

Che Guevara was, of course, aware that the concept of the "New Man" was difficult to promote due to historical circumstances: members of Cuban society would need to be freed from the cultural education that had led them to be exploited as tools of the elite. He writes:

> The new society in formation has to compete fiercely with the past. This past makes itself felt not only in the individual consciousness—in which the residue of an education systematically oriented toward isolating the individual still weights heavily—but also through the very character of this transition period in which commodity relations still persist. The commodity is the economic cell of capitalist society. So long as it exists its effects will make themselves felt in the organization of production and, consequently, in consciousness[10] [371].

The idea of the "New Man" developed by Guevara was intended to rebuild Cuban masculinity and nationalism while detaching itself from

2. Political Melodrama in the New Nationalist Vision

the past. Guevara accused revolutionary artists and intellectuals of not always being successful in that endeavor, because they were supposedly tainted by what he calls "original sin." Guevara claims that they were born and raised in a bourgeois society, and therefore their attempts, although well intentioned, were limited and foreign in nature. He had hopes that the new Cuban society would eradicate bourgeois culture and provide a situation in which the next generation would breed more "New Men."[11] This lack of trust in intellectuals[12] perhaps accounts for why Julio García Espinosa's filmmaking manifesto "For an Imperfect Cinema" opposes the cult of the elitist director and promotes the integration of proletarian voices into the filmmaking process.

Gutiérrez Alea's *Memories of Underdevelopment* and Humberto Solás' *Lucía* were written and directed in a way that touched many people within and beyond Cuba. From an ideological perspective, it is apparent that both take a Marxist approach, and promote a dialectic class struggle that leads to the creation of an egalitarian society. This had the effect of providing propaganda for the new Cuban society that the revolution was seeking to implant, while at the same time achieving popularity in the leftist and progressive circles of the West that approved of the films' depiction of the upper classes which fit well within the goals of radical social movements in capitalist countries at the time. Although these films were not screened in the United States until 1974, they had a large and dedicated following in Western European and Latin American intellectual circles which made of them immortal classics of Latin and international cinema. These projects warrant such accolades as groundbreaking efforts, but at the same time audiences must remain aware of the esthetic manipulations the filmmakers use to criticize the Cuban bourgeoisie/elite, and inscribe it as the antagonist to the new revolutionary Cuban national identity.

The narrative of Humberto Solás' *Lucía* is modeled after the historical melodramas to which Cuban and Latin American audiences had grown accustomed during the Golden Age of Mexican cinema that ended after the 1950s. Unlike the more conventional Hispanic melodrama that served primarily to entertain with upper-class propaganda,[13] however, this film is divided into three segments, portraying the evolution of the Cuban nation from Hispanic colonialism to American capitalism, and culminating in the socialist state brought about through revolution. Solás interprets Cuban history not only as a political phenomenon but also through a detailed exposition of the evolution of the arts in each historical period. Apart from its Marxist narrative scheme, the film enables the audience to experience each historical segment through the esthetic devices that were popular in the respective periods represented. Solás thus creates a melodrama that follows the conventions established by the capitalist studios while aggressively challenging the ideology and esthetics formerly imposed on the genre. This combination of revolutionary themes and careful exploration of the evolution of esthetics and its role in politics has contributed in large measure to the status of this film as a reference point in the history of cinema.[14]

These esthetic strategies and artistic choices offer an evocative insight into Solás' dialectic approach. For not only does he construct the three stories to represent thematically the disappearance of aristocratic ways, but he also links visually the evolution of esthetics to the evolution of society. The first segment of the film depicts landowners fighting for nationalism, yet they are not necessarily portrayed as intellectuals. Lucía's brother is a revolutionary whose struggle is simply related to a nationalistic desire to defeat the Spanish. This conception makes the second segment of the film essential to any discussion of the representation of "positive" intellectual figures and the decadent elite. The archetypes of capitalist culture—the enlightened intellectual and the corrupt social climber—are respectively represented by the second Lucía's husband, Aldo, and his best friend Antonio, who take different paths: one realizes the futile efforts of deposing dictators without changing the culture, while the other is tainted by the extravagance of the times.

The split between Aldo and Antonio is visualized in two scenes: first, when Aldo, as a clerk, realizes the futility of the new government he helped to install in power. In one scene, he hears the complaints of an old man disappointed with the bureaucracy and corruption that continued to permeate Cuban society in the 1930s. In a later scene, both Aldo and his friend participate in a decadent party of government officials which makes him feel disgusted by the excesses of the former revolutionaries, now authority figures. Aldo begins to fight for the people

2. Political Melodrama in the New Nationalist Vision

again, and his eventual death signals his recognition that he belongs to a system that will never serve the national interests of the people. He must die in order to open a pathway to the proletarian government. Consequently, the utopian third segment relies on the disappearance or assimilation of the bourgeois intellectual. By the end of the film, only traces of the bourgeoisie remain in the culture; hence Tomás, the misogynistic worker husband of the third Lucía, is the sole link to the past because of his "primitive" behavior. The only intellectual figure in this section is the young instructor from the city: while he may look refined, he must work the whole day with peasants and farmers while teaching them to read during the evenings with the hope of creating erudite peasants. The decadence that led to Aldo's friend's corruption is no longer present.

Like *Lucía*, *Memories of Underdevelopment* explores the gradual historical disappearance of the Cuban upper class. This film's iconic status within Cuban filmmaking is due in large part to a nuanced presentation of socialist propaganda critical of the bourgeoisie in esthetic terms. The film's ending, albeit open, shows how the protagonist, Sergio's, world is crumbling, approaching an imminent moment of truth between the Cuban proletariat and American imperial forces. Yet the main character is not converted to the revolution, which accounts for a curious ambiguity in the face of the film's propagandistic goals.[15] The existential crisis of Sergio, the bourgeois intellectual, is intensified by the contrast between the obvious use of French New Wave self-reflexive techniques, socialist documentaries, and the film's literary source: Edmundo Desnoes' book *Inconsolable Memories*. Gutiérrez Alea's success lies in his ability to balance the three elements in his portrayal of the plight of this bourgeois intellectual whose existential dilemma focuses on his inability to choose between the bourgeois and proletarian side of the class struggle. Clearly a product of its time, the film is intertextual in construction, and has an important place in the legacy of the director.

The source novel by Desnoes explores the existentialist concepts developed by Sartre so influential to the intellectual and visual culture of the 1960s. In his *Literature through Film*, Robert Stam states that Desnoes' novel uses a narrative model similar to that of the forerunner of existentialist literature: Fyodor Dostoyevsky in *Notes from Underground*.[16] In Stam's view, the two works share intellectual protagonists who serve as unreliable narrators, and through whose unstable voices one recognizes the dialogical reality articulated by Bakhtin in his "The Discourse of the Novel" as indispensable to the novel's strength as a literary genre. Both Dostoyevsky's *Notes from Underground* and Desnoes' *Inconsolable Memories* reveal conflicting factions of thought, which increases their textual interest. The Underground Man and Sergio are conflicted masculine protagonists able to identify converging social realities and tendencies. Both protagonists despise the elites for their arrogance and the lower classes for their insignificance, whereas an ability to see beyond these different perspectives is the source of their existentialist thought. The dialogic multiple voices cross over into *Memories of Underdevelopment*. According to film scholar Paul Schroeder, the film is dialogical because "all the characters are in one way or another, disagreeing with the hegemonic discourse within the film and outside of it."[17] I believe that both characters' existence outside the parameters of their own society makes them simultaneously heroic and villainous to the cultural systems they belong.

From a cinematic perspective, in comparison with Solás' *Lucía*, *Memories of Underdevelopment* is less obviously didactic on two fronts. The esthetic strategies deployed by Gutíerrez Alea portray Sergio, its bourgeois protagonist, in a postmodern, fragmented narrative style that runs counter to the precision of the melodramatic storytelling devices of commercial cinema in its portrayal of the upper class, imparting to the film a less sentimental ambiance and a series of revolutionary ideas not dependent upon linear narrative structure. The psychology of the main character is achieved by means of innovative cinematic techniques (collages, flashback transitions, sound editing, self-reflexive jokes and irony) that allow the audience to discover Sergio in an intimate way, despite the subdued melodramatic elements. Although not the typical villain of communist/socialist films, this bourgeois character recognizes his own virtues even within his most decadent qualities, which may account for the fact that some European critics[18] continued to empathize with Sergio's character, despite the film's portrayal of his destruction as a necessary event, an obvious criticism of what the character's meaning is.

2. Political Melodrama in the New Nationalist Vision

Humberto Solás' *Lucía* is a towering achievement in the history of Latin American and Third-World cinema; nonetheless, *Memories of Underdevelopment* has greater currency because it does not attempt to utopianize the post revolutionary Cuba of the 1960s. Its bourgeois intellectual antagonist is complex; the viewer experiences events and characters through his point of view; his language is recreated by means of avant-garde techniques and camera positions that do not always claim ideological "objectivity." Instead, eyeline matches and other techniques expressing subjectivity are used in alignment with a character who does not represent the revolution. Several shots throughout the film link a presumably Cuban Socialist audience to Sergio's viewpoint through the use of point-of-view shots. Even Gutíerrez Alea interacts with him in a scene that self-reflexively connects the director to the character.

The encounter between Sergio and Gutíerrez Alea is preceded by a segment in which Sergio is trying to seduce Elena, a female worker who confesses that she wants to be an actress. Sergio does not understand her fantasy, as he sees cinema as a repetitive industrialized narrative. What follows is a collage of erotic scenes and disparate elements that do not make narrative sense. After this sequence, the audience sees Sergio and Elena chatting with Gutíerrez Alea. The director explains to the characters that he edited these images from the cuts made by the pre–Revolutionary Catholic censors. Sergio and Gutíerrez Alea bond while mocking the prudishness of these outdated "bourgeois" values, and the filmmaker assures him that he will use the sequence in a future film, which, of course, is *Memories of Underdevelopment* itself. I consider this scene to be of major importance in that it explains how the director shares a certain bond with this bourgeois intellectual character who would normally have been condemned by the new Cuban Communist culture. Gutíerrez Alea himself is not of proletarian background, a fact usually omitted in criticism written about him. His political commitment and ideals led him to support the revolution and to assimilate his rich knowledge and education into the service of the collective. This is precisely where he departs from Sergio, another intellectual, who, however, does not want to relinquish his elitist life and does not understand the proletariat and its potential for intellectualism. It is here that the film addresses the intellectual split that occurred after *P.M.*, by showing the audience the different paths the intellectual could take.

Cuban cinema scholar Julianne Burton explains that many critics in Europe and North America identify with Sergio's intellectualism even though the character is obviously criticized for doing nothing to change the society that has exploited the majority of its citizens. She explains that Gutíerrez Alea and Edmundo Desnoes are also attracted to the character because of their own upper-class intellectual origins:

> The ironic dimension begins with the fact that novelist Desnoes and filmmaker Gutíerrez Alea are both "contaminated" by what Che Guevara metaphorically termed "original sin." Their sympathetic, multidimensional portrayal of Sergio, as they collaborate to bring him to life on the screen grows out of their personal experience and is itself an expression of their own attempt to overcome the syndrome to which Sergio succumbs at the end.[19]

Gutíerrez Alea has always tried to distance himself from the identification[20] that Burton indicates. When he wrote "The Viewer's Dialectic," he specifically denounced capitalist cinema as an entertainment with happy endings that encourages the audience toward passivity. He also praised French filmmaker Jean-Luc Godard as the destroyer of "bourgeois cinema," even as he expressed disappointment in that director's lack of communication with the masses.[21] A strong relationship with the proletariat base of society, however, was crucial to ICAIC filmmakers who, as film scholar Deborah Shaw writes, believed in "Gramsci's notion that intellectuals will eventually be formed within the process of revolutionary society."[22] Gutíerrez Alea wanted his films to lead the audience to the path of socialism through the dialectical confrontation with "reality":

> The work itself must bear those premises which can bring the spectator to discern reality. That is to say, it must push spectators into the path of truth, into coming to what can be called a dialectical consciousness about reality. Then it could operate as a real "guide for action." One should not confuse openness with ambiguity, inconsistency, eclecticism, arbitrariness.[23]

When Gutíerrez Alea filmed *Memories of Underdevelopment*, it was not for the purpose of defending the anti-hero but rather to problematize his attractive ways and "decadent" class sphere by creating a dialectic

2. Political Melodrama in the New Nationalist Vision

confrontation for the audience between Sergio's fictional life and the destructive history of the island, all set up from a Marxist perspective.

Gutiérrez Alea's conceptualization of the importance of "revolutionary reality" through his acclaimed use of documentary techniques is the only aspect of the film, in my view, that has not withstood the test of time. The employment of montage with regard to the use of bourgeois imagery and its link to the brutal violence of Batista's regime may have been compelling for the generation of 1968, but now falls flat to more sophisticated practices of documentary narrative. These sequences are deployed with a specific political purpose: to demonize the upper classes and make clear to the audience that Sergio's indecision has an obvious solution. The director makes use of specific narrative methods to hint to the audience in which direction the ideological language of Cuban cinema must move, linking documentary montage to the importance of the revolution, and explaining in an obvious manner how Sergio's bourgeois ways should be eradicated.

Both *Memories of Underdevelopment* and *Lucía* were relevant in 1968 because of their masterful use of avant-garde esthetics to deconstruct the conventional cinematic language established by commercial Latin American studios. Yet both promoted a revolutionary ideology that excludes the participation of the upper class and its intellectuals, who must relinquish their bourgeois traits in order to be able to join the collective social order. The two films thus articulate a new nationalist perspective based on class and empowering revolutionary discourse. Because both films were made in the first decade after the Cuban revolution, when emigration was on a smaller scale, they were able to construct a dialogic perspective that made their dialectic message powerful. Still, both films hint at the forthcoming assimilation of Cuban culture into a worker's collective as Humberto Solás' *Lucía* makes the upper class and its intellectuals to either disappear or assimilate into the new Cuban society in the post-revolutionary segment of the film, and Gutiérrez Alea's *Memories of Underdevelopment* confronts the audience with the proposal that "bourgeois culture" may have been attractive because of its decadent values but will disappear at the hands of socialist progress.

After this "Golden Age" period of Cuban cinema in the 1960s, several events in Cuban history would affect how dissidents and intellectuals were perceived by Cuban society and open the path to Gutiérrez Alea's *Strawberry and Chocolate* and Solás' *Honey for Oshún*. Before the Special Period, the oppression of gay Cuban citizens at the hands of the Cuban revolution was linked to the "outcast intellectual" subject when many of the victims fled the island during the Mariel boatlift in 1980. This controversial topic was disseminated abroad when Nestor Almendros and Orlando Jiménez Leal (who had co-directed *P.M.*) released in 1984 the explosive documentary *Improper Conduct*. The documentary had a direct impact on the creation and release of *Strawberry and Chocolate* in 1994, one of the most debated films from the Special Period. The other important event, the Elián González controversy that took place in 2000 and became a worldwide media sensation, led to the filming of *Honey for Oshún* and its 2001 release. Both films attempted to heal the rifts caused by the ideological warfare between Cuba and its political exiles, and they are an important legacy from two of the most prominent filmmakers in the island, even if some critics disagree with their cinematic construction of emigrants.

Gay and Intellectual Issues in Tomás Gutiérrez Alea's Strawberry and Chocolate

After the 1959 revolution in Cuba, disgruntled landowners, religious figures, and people associated with the mob culture who could not reconcile their loss of power in Cuban society left the island to look for a better life in the U.S. An assortment of these figures were emphasized as antagonists in Gutiérrez Alea's *Las doce sillas* (*The Twelve Chairs*, 1962) and *Los sobrevivientes* (*The Survivors*, 1978). However, the perception that only groups associated with capitalism left the island changed with the Mariel period (1980), a shift that also affected how Cuban filmmakers saw the emigration.[24] The new cultural shift[25] became a central subject in Cuban cinema, and both Solás and Gutiérrez Alea incorporated it into their later films. It is important to point out that the two filmmakers redefined their representation of intellectuals, but not necessarily of Cubans associated with exploitative capitalist industries.

After this period of cultural rediscovery in the 1980s and during the peak of the Special Period, Tomas Gutíerrez Alea and Juan Carlos

2. Political Melodrama in the New Nationalist Vision

Tabío[26] co-directed *Strawberry and Chocolate* (1994), the first Cuban film to attract wide mainstream international audiences during the 1990s and the first Academy Award nominee in the history of the island's national cinema. Thanks to its Oscar nomination and distribution by the Miramax studio, which accorded it access to more international screens than usual, the film became popular around the world in addition to being a major success at the Cuban box office. Viewers appreciated the dynamics between the characters and were intrigued by the ambiance surrounding its taboo subject matter with regard to communism and homosexuality. Together with films from China such as *Farewell My Concubine* (*Ba wang bie ji*, Kaige Chen, 1993), Cuba provided examples from a surviving Communist state in the throes of crisis, struggling with the awareness that Marxist ideology did not contain the totality of its social and national life. Both films attempted to integrate gay characters into a society that had banished them as representatives of a forbidden bourgeois world.

Critical success at international film festivals afforded Gutiérrez Alea well-deserved moments of prominence in the last years of his life. His film helped to revive the languishing presence of Cuban cinema on the international scene. Most importantly, the film dealt with issues that had been ignored by some or superficially addressed by the filmmakers of the revolution, for, apart from its claim for tolerance toward gay characters, *Strawberry and Chocolate* explores issues of Cuban identity and the role of nationalism in the division of the Cuban people. It offers a more complex solution to the questions: What is the definition of a Cuban national? And who deserves to be acknowledged in those terms? – questions that might appear odd in view of the fact that socialist states are not meant to conceptualize themselves in terms of nation-states. Decades of revolutionary ideology had instilled a particular understanding of nationalism wherein the only true Cuban was the revolutionary who supported socialist ideals. The eradication of Cuba's former upper classes and the values promoted by ICAIC had made it difficult to fit these "lost" Cubans into the society's language, and it was time to make the Cuban revolution dialogical once again.

In films from the 1960s, such as Gutiérrez Alea's *The Twelve Chairs* and *Memories of Underdevelopment*, the elites were portrayed as leaving the island in several airport scenes. In the 1970s, many of these upper-class citizens were gone, along with wealthy intellectuals such as the ones that Sergio from *Memories of Underdevelopment* represented. Class assumptions with regard to Cuban emigration gradually evolved as many members from the working classes also began to leave the island during the Mariel exile due to economic distress and the suffocation they suffered under the Cuban regime. This proletarian/peasant dissident voice was represented around the world by prominent figures such as acclaimed gay Cuban writer Reinaldo Arenas in his novels, short stories, and his autobiography, *Before Night Falls*, which was adapted in the United States by director Julian Schnabel (*Before Night Falls*, Julian Schnabel, 2000). In his book and interviews, Arenas always emphasizes his peasant origins, so that his dissidence is not linked to tired bourgeois archetypes that dominate socialist narratives.

Arenas was one of the subjects interviewed in the very polemic documentary *Mauvais conduite* (*Improper Conduct*). This film was co-directed by the prestigious Spanish cinematographer Nestor Almendros, and Orlando Jiménez Leal, one of the co-directors of the controversial *P.M.* When they released the film in 1984, both of the filmmakers involved had already emigrated from Cuba due to the problems they had with censorship in the island. This documentary provided a voice for Cubans who had fled the island, and it focused on different groups of dissidents and their suffering at the hands of the Cuban government. The most controversial theme in the film is the collection of accounts about the persecution of gay/lesbian Cubans and their experiences with the UMAP camps designed to redeem citizens with "undesirable" habits (which included homosexuals, prostitutes, certain religious sects like Jehovah's Witnesses, and others). The way the UMAP camps are described by the speakers in the interviews make the revolutionary government look like a nefarious totalitarian regime such as the ones that operated under Stalin or Hitler.

Almendros and Jiménez Leal's film discredited the Cuban government in the eyes of the international community. While *Improper Conduct*'s anti-communist rhetoric was not new for the Cold War period, the film was innovative in that it targets an audience of intellectuals that may have previously supported Castro's government from abroad. The directors try to make their ideological case to these spectators by providing victimized critically acclaimed writers such as Reinaldo Arenas and Guillermo Cabrera Infante to support their point of view. The film certainly created dissent in the American academic sphere. Well-known scholars such as Michael Chanan criticized its esthetics and propagandistic approach to a delicate subject, while others such as Paul Julian Smith hailed its importance in defying the revolutionary discourse.

In the most recent version of his *Cuban Cinema* book, Chanan avoids dwelling too much on the subject, and only briefly describes the controversies regarding *Improper Conduct*.[27] Yet his bias against the film is reflected in the fact that he only quotes opponents of *Improper Conduct*, e.g., Tomás Gutíerrez Alea's critical thoughts of the film, and the analysis of Lumsden, a North American gay scholar who thinks that the links that Almendros and Jiménez Leal use to create parallels between Cuba, Stalinism, and Pinochet are widely exaggerated. However, when Paul Julian Smith wrote about the film in his article "Cuban Homosexualities: On the Beach with Néstor Almendros and Reinaldo Arenas," he strongly criticized Chanan for being one of the main opponents of Almendros and Jiménez Leal's film (in the original introduction to Chanan's book, available in older editions), and for using the discourse of film esthetics and Marxist dialectics to dismiss the project, while supporting the Cuban regime's propaganda. One of the main controversial statements that Chanan makes, according to Smith, is to blame revolutionary homophobia on the emerging feminism and women empowerment that threatened the control of the heterosexual man.[28, 29]

Smith writes about Chanan's criticism of *Improper Conduct* in the original version of the latter's book, then titled *The Cuban Image*.[30] Smith criticizes a biased pattern in Chanan's criticism of "dissident filmmaking" because the British critic also downplays the political problems with Cabrera Infante and Jiménez Leal's *P.M.* by providing esthetic reasons to disagree with the film, and therefore justifying the ICAIC's opposition to the project because its executives supposedly wanted to break esthetic formulas. In regards to *P.M.*, this can be observed when Chanan writes, "At ICAIC they were beginning to perceive that revolutionary change required a rupture with this equation, which meant among other things being constantly on guard against received aesthetic formulae" (136).

However, Stephen Wilkinson and other scholars have also accused Smith of being biased in his support of *Improper Conduct*. Wilkinson discusses Smith's book *Vision Machines* and analyzes the author's championing of *Improper Conduct* and criticism of Gutiérrez Alea's *Strawberry and Chocolate* as a propaganda film. He argues further that Smith is guilty of a similar "rhetoric of reversal" for it is possible to show that rather than "imagine the truth." *Improper Conduct* is more accurately read as an attempt at undermining the reputation of the revolution and, for all its "failure" as a political film, *Fresa y chocolate* can be read as a an anti-system film rather than bourgeois melodrama.[31] Wilkinson also accuses Smith of taking the film's revelations at face value, especially since many of the subjects, such as Armando Valladares, remain controversial to this day.[32] This ideological conflict between intellectuals outside of Cuba, shows the extent to which the topic has been debatable and that it is very difficult to find a more neutral point of view.

When he wrote his seminal book *Gay Cuban Nation*, scholar Emilio Bejel attempted to provide a detailed historical background to Cuban homophobia that can be traced back to the 19th century. One of the issues that scholars have with *Improper Conduct* is how the homophobia is linked to the Cuban revolution and its authorities, but it is obvious to someone with a sense of Caribbean history that the seeds were already planted in the Cuban national consciousness. Bejel explains how the pre-revolutionary beginnings of homophobia converged with the institutionalization of some conservative and nationalistic aspects of the Cuban revolution.[33]

Some Cuban cinema scholars have also been able to provide more balanced arguments. Marvin D'Lugo, for instance, argues that, while the film has a dogmatic intention, it is also very interesting because it addresses both the international audience that supports the revolution, *and* the exiled Cuban community. D'Lugo finds fascinating how Almendros and Jiménez Leal integrate queer elements into a typically homophobic dissidence, which is why he sees value in the film even though many dismiss it as ideological propaganda. D'Lugo writes:

> It [*Improper Conduct*] is addressed simultaneously to the liberal international audience that favors socialist Cuba (thus the denunciation of the persecution of gays) and to the Cuban exiled audience that needs reaffir-

2. Political Melodrama in the New Nationalist Vision

mation of its identity (thus the metaphorization of homosexuality as an "otherness," marking the shift from exiled to ethnicity). How the latter audience—itself marked by intense homophobia—is addressed and refigured as an ethnic community is the most surprising characteristic of *Improper Conduct*.[34]

This blend of queerness and dissidence in *Improper Conduct* is important to understand because sometimes contemporary viewers of *Strawberry and Chocolate* do not know how Gutiérrez Alea's film communicates with Almendros and Jiménez Leal's film. Many articles have been published about *Strawberry and Chocolate* focusing on Diego, its gay character. These critiques emphasize the values and flaws of the film, especially in relation to the charming portrayal by Perugorría, whose gay character is conventional enough for international standards of queer representation yet exceptionally daring for Cuban cinema.[35] Because of the sensationalism of this character, international audiences may have missed the film's main point, which, according to Gutiérrez Alea, was to promote tolerance in a system that had repressed certain individuals who did not conform to the standards of the revolution.

For *Strawberry and Chocolate* was not intended as a gay film; the intention, rather, was to develop a protagonist as an outcast of Cuban society who would function on several narrative and ideological levels. The role of sexuality was an important element in the character's isolation within the narrative, although it should not escape our notice that he would likely have experienced intolerance as well on other islands of the Caribbean that are not ruled by communist governments. Indeed, the key to his particular subversiveness is the character's admiration of bourgeois/aristocratic and pre-revolutionary Cuban culture, which symbolized all that the revolution opposed. Nevertheless, the film retains a certain socialist perspective, as it redeems an older type of Cuban intellectualism rather than the prerevolutionary elite.

To fully read the layers of this film, we must take into account the various sources that were combined in its creation, including the fact that the director avowedly made it to counteract the effects of *Improper Conduct*, which Gutiérrez Alea thought unfair in its portrayal of the regime and its treatment of homosexuals. In his book *Tomás Gutiérrez Alea*, José Antonio Evora asks the Cuban filmmaker to comment on

Nestor Almendros' work. Gutíerrez Alea's response is interesting because it reveals a personal connection and friendship to the exiled filmmaker that eroded because of political issues. Gutíerrez Alea mentions that Almendros was an enthusiastic film fan (more than he himself was at the time), who took him to see all types of screenings that took place in Havana, and that he learned a lot from this friendship. He also adds that, ironically, it was Almendros who introduced him to Marxism, and that he feels that the Spaniard "played dirty" with Cuba after he left the island.[36] Gutíerrez Alea also acknowledges that he felt sad when he heard about Almendros' death, because he could not see *Strawberry and Chocolate*, which was supposed to be addressed specifically to people like him, with the hopes of continuing the debates.[37]

To counter what he felt was damaging to the reputation of the Cuban revolution, Gutíerrez Alea decided to adapt Senel Paz's short story "The Wolf, The Forest and the New Man," a piece of fiction that taunted in a pleasant manner the precepts of Guevara's "New Man." The story explores the relationship between David, a communist student, and Diego, his homosexual friend with reactionary tastes. Their bond is similar to that in the film with the exception that the story explores Diego's sexuality in more detail as he narrates, in a more graphic manner, his sexual encounters with other men.[38] The short story provides an important element of the film—the relationship between the two men—but the narrative paradigm originates in previous screenplays by Senel Paz (from *Una novia para David* and *Adorables mentiras*) who, for this film, uses his earlier characters and situations to reconstruct the short story into a feature film screenplay. Contrary to his *Memories of Underdevelopment*, in which Gutíerrez Alea used avant-garde techniques to create a dialectic confrontation by juxtaposing Sergio's cynical views with the documentary segments about the struggle, in *Strawberry and Chocolate*, the director uses a more traditional melodramatic narrative structure to portray the dissenting point of view (Diego) and how it affects the hegemonic point of view (David).

The film can be considered a cinematic melodrama because it carries narrative and esthetic elements of the genre, as defined in the last couple of decades by film scholars (Elsaesser, Mercer and Shingler, Schatz, etc.).[39] Melodrama is a notoriously difficult term to define

2. Political Melodrama in the New Nationalist Vision

because it is not a clear-cut genre such as the western, or the romantic comedy. Sometimes viewers assume that melodrama is a contrived narrative for women (in the vein of soap operas or gendered narratives, such as romantic costume dramas) which is why it has acquired a negative connotation with spectators who dislike this type of storytelling. However, many of the greatest films of all time have used melodramatic devices to develop empathy, especially to characters that may function outside of hegemony. An example in Hollywood is *Giant* (dir. George Stevens, 1956), a melodrama about life in Texas, in which the white protagonist learns to care about racism against Mexicans and Mexican Americans; and in Mexico, one could point out *Angelitos negros* (Joselito Rodríguez, 1948), in which the main character struggles with prejudices against his black friends and mixed race daughter. Both films were very popular, entertaining, and used empathic devices to make audiences connect with their social messages.

In her book, *Melodrama*, Silvia Oroz traces specifically the development of the Latin American melodrama, from its origins in the sentimental prose serials published in the 19th century, through radio soap operas, to the dramatic films filled with superstars such as Pedro Infante, Libertad Lamarque, and others. Oroz points out that these melodramatic pictures sentimentally educated the masses by imparting on them values that the Western culture considered universal.[40] When José Antonio Evora interviewed Tomás Gutiérrez Alea about *Cartas en el parque* and *Contigo en la distancia*, the director acknowledged that they are his own type of melodrama and he is not embarrassed to use emotion to arrive at reason or use reason to control emotion.[41]

However, most melodramas and their plotlines in the first part of the 20th century have been linked to representing middle class subjects in capitalist societies, the main target audience for the international film industry. Because the term can be hard to define, especially since most melodrama theory is based on the Hollywood model, one has to take many issues into account in order to redefine melodrama within certain national cinemas. Under Thomas Schatz's basic model of the Hollywood family melodrama, some elements may appear in *Strawberry and Chocolate* such as its being sentimental, and featuring a family home for social interaction (Diego's apartment). Yet, the film lacks the family structure of the traditional melodrama because the characters are not related biologically to each other, and they do not necessarily represent different generations. Still, the film could be interpreted as a sort of bildungsroman where the audience identifies with David, the young revolutionary hero and with his journey, on which his experiences and interactions with other characters lead him to become the ideal Cuban man.

The characters of David and his conservative friend Miguel had already appeared in the film *A Girlfriend for David* (*Una novia para David*, Orlando Rojas, 1985), also written by Senel Paz but directed by Orlando Rojas. David was played by Jorge Luis Alvarez, a different actor, while Miguel was again portrayed by Francisco Gattorno. In this film, David has newly arrived from the fields to study in a preparatory school in the city, a typical romantic comedy plot that might be found in any country of the world: the male protagonist needs to choose between a beautiful but shallow young woman and an overweight but charming woman who in the end wins his enlightened heart. Miguel plays the macho character who encourages David to make the traditional choice of the prized trophy female, while David resists, the obvious choice that one might expect in a romantic teen comedy. Even though the viewer may recognize its revolutionary settings, the film is not readable as an ideological project, as Hollywood would have provided the same outcome.

That romantic triangle is transformed in *Strawberry and Chocolate*: instead of making a choice based on beauty and personality, the selection is between Vivian, the girl who rejects David for a foreigner, and Nancy, the prostitute who also runs clandestine operations. David again chooses appropriately according to the film's values, however, this time his selection is not pressured by Miguel, who is not related in any way to the romantic plot but is instead used as an aggressive conservative character in terms of both sexuality and politics. In this version, the character of Miguel taunts David for his friendship with Diego. This volatile conflict, in which Miguel becomes a paternal figure who represents the conservative aspects of the Cuban revolution, is not in the original short story where only David and Diego appear in the narrative.

The prostitute Nancy, portrayed by Gutiérrez Alea's wife Mirta Ibarra, had previously appeared in *Adorable Lies* (*Adorables mentiras*,

2. Political Melodrama in the New Nationalist Vision

Gerardo Chijona, 1991), also written by Senel Paz, where she plays a promiscuous secondary character in a psychological crisis due to her addiction to her sex life. Her dilemma leads her to a suicide attempt, a plot element also encountered in *Strawberry and Chocolate*. The integration of Nancy's flawed character into the plot, together with the outcast character of Diego from the short story, as well as the naïveté of David and the conservative Miguel create a pluralist vision of Cuba that resuscitates the complexity of dialogism that Bakhtin had embraced. The characters nonetheless remain types of Revolutionary cinema: the outcast roles of Diego and Nancy are sympathetic yet disappointing because they fulfill Revolutionary fantasies of the queer dissident and the exploited faithful proletarian character with a heart of gold. Nancy is a prostitute redeemed by her Marxist lover, while at the same time the film follows the tradition of Latin American cinema melodrama and its "fallen" women. Instead of conforming to types designed to bourgeois/colonial/Hispanic standards, the gender stereotype is transformed by the ideologies of revolutionary cinema to fit a Marxist framework.

The character of Diego, on the other hand, is desexualized and his mannerisms amplified to fit the stereotypes held by Cuban audiences. The character does not belong to the upper class, as he himself acknowledges in the film, but rather embraces the "decadent" culture of the past, indulging in forbidden pleasure, which would have been disapproved by Guevara's "New Man" rhetoric. Emilio Bejel points out that both Diego and David share a nationalist background although they differ in their visions of Cuban history and culture—David embodying the "good" (socialist, atheist, heterosexual) and Diego the "bad" (anti-communist, Christian, and homosexual).[42] However, Diego is sympathetic and resists assimilation, thus showing a certain sense of independence seen as heroic by both Cuban and international audiences. His strong performance as Diego made actor Jorge Perugorría an international idol, and the character of Diego provided a dissenting voice that served as a dialogic element to traditional revolutionary Cuban cinema. The film acknowledges the existence of other points of view, even though they are limited to the cinematic language developed by the revolution. Diego leaves at the end of the film, a representation of the fate of the outcasts of the Cuban revolution.

Scholar Paul Julian Smith is very critical of the film because of its sexualization of dissidence.[43] Smith's argument is important to acknowledge, even if many researchers continue to write in defense of *Strawberry and Chocolate*, because it marks one of the flaws of the film. It is a great film for Cuba at the time, but the way in which its dialectic conflict is set up can be controversial for some audience members that are not ready to accept Diego as the only possible representative of dissent. Even though the film is well intentioned, it functions primarily as a product of the Cuban revolution, and its dialectic clash or dialogism is based on the artificial construction of a dissident, whose voice is heard, but is not part of the creative process. Diego's character is supposed to give voice to the Almendros/Arenas/ Jiménez Leal type of emigrants but their discourse is interpreted through a traditional revolutionary lens. Still, the film is groundbreaking, besides its limitations, and its redefinition of Cuban nationalism sent shockwaves through the Cuban cinema industry. It was a leap, after the fiasco of *Alice in Wondertown*, that could only be taken by a great director such as Tomás Gutíerrez Alea.

The next section discusses Humberto Solás' *Honey for Oshún*, a post–Special Period melodrama inspired by the Elián González scandal, where Solás attempts to create the point of view of a Cuban American hero for the Cuban audiences. This film is less critically acclaimed and less financially successful when compared to *Strawberry and Chocolate*, but it is another very relevant example in which real events inspire the melodramatic plot, and in which the narrative attempts to open the hearts of Cuban nationals on the island as well as abroad, while still reflecting a biased revolutionary perspective.

Digital Melodrama and the Return to the Motherland in Humberto Solás' Honey for Oshún

Humberto Solás has always been *the* melodrama director of the ICAIC. His masterpiece *Lucía* was a dialectical avant-garde melodrama which portrayed its several family conflicts in various time periods and different styles. Unlike Tomás Gutíerrez Alea, who usually tried to avoid passionate sentimental performances, Solás' films became more extravagant as he developed as a filmmaker. Most of his later films such as

2. Political Melodrama in the New Nationalist Vision

Cecilia, Amada, A Successful Man, and *El siglo de las luces* were historical period dramas in which he confronted the sentimentality of the bourgeois melodramas with harsh political intrigue that would not be as visible and didactic in commercial capitalist cinema. This fusion of anti-imperialist politics and superficial sentimental storytelling make his films very interesting, although sometimes they can be difficult for contemporary audiences unfamiliar with the ways in which Solás creates his political arguments by dialectally confronting the fetishes of entertainment and melodrama with the harsh history of the oppressed.[44]

When Solás adapted Cirilo Villaverde's *Cecilia Valdés o La Loma del Ángel* with his film *Cecilia*, he tried to create a melodramatic blockbuster but failed. Critics could not figure out what he was doing with the film. The project features a wonderful esthetic execution, and its political revision of the original novel is much needed, as the literary source exhibits Eurocentric qualities despite its being an abolitionist text. Solás makes sure to include more AfroCubans into the plot and explore their point of view, and the new version is very critical of the 19th-century Cuban nationalism and its racist qualities. However, the director's use of exaggerated/outdated acting is what dooms the film for modern audiences. The adapted source is a classical bourgeois melodrama, and Solás' approach cannot distance itself enough from the outdated structure of the original.

This type of limitations of cultural and class representation are also present in Solás' *Honey for Oshún*, in which the protagonist's tragic story of a Cuban-American fictional character, also portrayed by Perugorría, relies on a different set of character types. During Humberto Solás' production of *Honey for Oshún*, the Elián Gonzalez controversy was raging in Cuba. Elián's mother had passed away while trying to cross the Atlantic Ocean and reach Florida. The child survived and was reunited with his mother's family who felt obliged to take care of him. The child's father was still alive and living in Cuba, which prompted a debate in the American media about what was best for Elián. Should he go back to Cuba with his father, as international law demands, or should he stay in the United States to "pursue happiness"? These questions also rattled the Cubans in the island, as they had just suffered through the Special Period catastrophe. Most Cubans probably knew that Elián must be returned to the father, but many also understood why the boy's mother took such a radical decision.[45]

The links between Jorge, the main character in *Honey,* and his parental figures, the reawakening of his love for his cousin Pilar, and his friendship with the local taxi driver are basic tenets for constructing a powerful family melodrama in a road movie that deals with important elements of Cuban culture. This rare, for the director, film set in contemporary times did not allow Solás to reference the "decadent" visuals of the aristocratic world previously seen in his works, but instead compelled him to concentrate on a modern grim Havana, decaying physically decades after the revolution. In an interview with scholar Desirée Díaz, Solás says that he was inspired by the European film manifesto Dogma 95 that tried to bring back certain principles of esthetic realism to contemporary filmmaking. Solás acknowledges that many of the precepts that appear in this treatise were used by his revolutionary peers during the 1960s, and he is happy that filmmakers are attracted again to these specific techniques. The Cuban director follows most of the Dogma 95 precepts, with the exception of some, such as the use of non-diegetic music and the use of conventions from genres such as the road movie. Therefore, his film cannot be seen as part of the European movement, but the latter's influences are very visible.

Using digital technology for the first time, the director conveys visually the struggles of the revolution and the Cuban people. The digital footage gives the film a more realistic look, different to that of the opulent cinematography he used in his historical epics. The film's attempt at realism is not limited to exploring the ruins of Havana: what makes the return of Jorge so realistic is the way in which the scenes are constructed to convey the atmosphere that any tourist from the U.S. or Europe might experience when visiting the island—passionate reunions between family members, con artists trying to trick naïve tourists, a city on the verge of collapse but where the population struggles to survive and get on with their lives.

The opening scene is very important in problematizing the "Cuban dissident other." The first shot is a memory of Jorge being kidnapped by his father and fleeing the country. Next, we see this flashback intercut with the protagonist's traveling on an airplane from the U.S. to

2. Political Melodrama in the New Nationalist Vision

Cuba and thinking about his father in a melodramatic way. In the dramatic close-up of his face that follows, Jorge asks his deceased father why he was taken away from Cuba. This passionate scene is scored with a very harsh string music that emotes anger. Suddenly, the music becomes more sentimental when the passengers (mostly Cuban émigrés) see the island, run to the windows of the airplane and yell "se ve Cuba" (we can see Cuba). When they arrive at the terminal, they are embraced by their families who do not see them as traitors but instead cry in extravagant ways. Jorge, the main character, is the only one portrayed alone because he has no family on the island, which makes him feel somewhat less than fully Cuban. Some may accuse Solás of an overtly passionate and exaggerated style, but the power of such scenes is undeniable as the filmmaker mixes gritty visual realism with over-the-top soap opera antics.

Jorge meets his cousin Pilar, and Tomás, the taxi driver whom he enrolls in his quest to find his mother. Apart from the somewhat trite metaphor of seeking a national identity through the figure of the mother, as the characters embark on a journey from one side of the island to the other (Havana to Guantánamo), throughout their adventures they come to understand their differences as related to social class and nationality. In this sense, the film is a courageous attempt to explore a vexed issue: are those who mimic one's culture but who are not in contact with the land part of one's national heritage? The main character is the son of an emigrant bourgeois father. He is fluent in the Spanish language, employed in the United States as a professor of Cuban culture, and a person who understands the island people's idiosyncrasies even if he does not accept them. Many Cuban Americans feel that they should be acknowledged as Cubans because they believe themselves to be Cuban, but whether or not they share the same collective experience as the Cubans from the island remains to be determined. Jorge sees himself as more unhappy than the islanders because of his identity crisis as an ethnic Cuban in the U.S., a situation Cubans on the island do not experience to the same degree, although they do experience poverty and other frustrations related to the misery suffered in the nineties. The trip helps Cubans understand the Cuban American character and vice versa, in a journey of mutual discovery.

At the film's conclusion, when the protagonist's mother (ironically portrayed by the same actress who played the third Lucía in *Lucía*) is finally located, the characters have bonded in such a way that, when the reunion takes place, their political and nationalist boundaries have disappeared in a powerful scene of sadness and happiness. The final sequence is a long shot of the beach where the encounter takes place and where one cannot recognize the faces of the characters as they have blended into a single group. The antagonist Cuban bourgeois intellectual that both Solás and Gutíerrez Alea had tried to isolate earlier has returned to the fold as a necessary part of the Cuban people. This type of character was first recognized in *Strawberry and Chocolate* through the gay proletarian character Diego, an outsider who defended the positive aspects of the forbidden elitist culture at the cost of having to leave the country. Then, through the quest of an exiled Cuban-American protagonist in *Honey for Oshún*, Cubans were able to experience empathy for the descendants of those emigrants who represented the previous system and who suffered the bitterness caused by their progenitors and the unfortunate decisions embraced by the revolution. Jorge Perugorría imparts an affecting personality to both characters that, in an ironic way, contributed to improving the image of the exiled "intellectual" Cubans.[46]

In Carlos Barba's documentary *La mujer que espera*, *Oshún* actress Isabel Santos reveals that this later Solás film was among her favorites because it gave a voice to the Cuban exile. She says that she was told that the film got a standing ovation at a Florida screening, and this was enough to please her with her work even though some critics may criticize the "corny" or imperfect aspects of the film's mise-en-scène. She herself felt that she goes to the movies to cry and have emotional reactions, which the film can provide. Another praise for the film comes from Cuban critic Rufo Caballero, who criticizes some of the dialogue, but commends Solás' esthetic reinvention of his former epic cinema, as well as the filmmaker's success at juggling road movie and melodrama concepts, with the integration of non-actors (a homage to the sixties) into the professional actor crew. More importantly, like actress Isabel Santos, he feels that Solás is very successful in portraying the new acceptance of the Cuban exile.

2. Political Melodrama in the New Nationalist Vision

Still, it is very important to point out that the film, because it was written and directed by Cubans from the island, provides a biased perspective that seeks to redeem the "Cuban dissident other" even though he/she does not need redemption. After the emotional climax at the end of the film, one can ask what the characters are going to do afterwards. Is Jorge staying in Cuba? Does finding his mother solve his psychological and cultural issues with the Cuban government and its ideology? The catharsis is all about the local audience from the island forgiving the Cuban Americans, which is why scholar Lea Ramsdell notes that "he [Jorge] has not only found his mother, he has accepted his cubanidad and has found himself, the torment of his exile has been lifted. He is healed and he is whole."[47] The ending of the film could be interpreted as a condescending view of the Cuban American plight, because it implies that the key to the emigrant's achieving happiness lies in his/her being embraced by the Cuban state and its people.

Both Solás' *Lucía* and Gutíerrez Alea's *Memories of Underdevelopment* are avant-garde films which gained international renown for their use of complex cinematic techniques to construct a dialectic vision of Cuban history in which a clear distinction was established between the class elites and their intellectuals. However, in these films both of these types of individuals needed to disappear or be assimilated in order to give birth to the new proletarian intellectuals as defined by figures like Che Guevara. After the collapse of the Soviet bloc and the downfall of Marxist prestige during the Perestroika and the Special Period, some Cubans began to realize that emigrants also could dissent or could want to simply live and work outside of Cuba, and Cuban nationalism could no longer be based on a notion of revolutionary commitment.

Solás' and Gutíerrez Alea's films in the 1990s stopped employing avant-garde methods and attempted, through the use of more traditional melodramas, to heal the rift formed within Cuban culture and to provide a voice sympathetic to the outsider intellectual as portrayed by Jorge Perugorría's characters in *Strawberry and Chocolate* and *Honey for Oshún*. The filmmakers were limited by the socialist cinematic language of the ICAIC and created stereotypes of gay and exile characters that Cuban audiences would easily understand, and feel empowered by forgiving and accepting them. Still, it is important to acknowledge that the two films are daring artistic attempts, and were instrumental in re-establishing a dialogical narrative in post–Soviet Cuba and in giving a final resolution to the two directors' evolution as filmmakers and as socialist thinkers who survived the tumultuous times in the 1990s and whose work will remain relevant to cinephiles around the world.

3

Entertainment and the Proletarian Avant-Garde in the Films of Juan Carlos Tabío and Fernando Pérez

Marxist Criticism and the Workers in Cinema

I have already outlined a number of reasons for which international scholars acknowledge the cultural and ideological importance of the Cuban cinema produced by ICAIC. This Cuban studio promoted experimental esthetics that also resulted in socially aware projects that defied certain conventions of hegemonic industrial cinema, which may explain why ICAIC's productions are considered favorably in certain North and South American intellectual circles, as well as in Europe and elsewhere. Paradoxically, the fate of being immortalized but trapped in elite intellectual circles was one of the concerns of Cuban director Julio García Espinosa, who warned his fellow Cuban filmmakers of the possibility of becoming obsessed with elitist esthetics and losing contact with the workers in his manifesto, "For an Imperfect Cinema."

Now I will turn to an examination of the development of the avant-garde portrayal of the workers in revolutionary Cuban national cinema (and the European leftist connections to its origins) as an esthetic and narrative counterpart to the bourgeois melodramas that were produced by the international commercial studio systems. I will identify the influences of Soviet montage and Italian neorealism in early works such as Tomás Gutiérrez Alea's *Histories of the revolution* (1960), and explains how the later success of Julio García Espinosa's

Cuban Cinema After the Cold War

The Adventures of Juan Quin Quin (1965) led to the creation of the imperfect cinema manifesto that adapted many European avant-garde precepts to fit the principles of the Cuban revolution. What is perceived as Cuban imperfect cinema certainly began to disappear in the 1980s, when the ICAIC attempted to invest in more commercial fare that would be successful both with the local audiences and abroad. Still, the marks of the manifesto are present in contemporary Cuban cinema, and it is important to discuss the ramifications of García Espinosa's text.

In this context, I will analyze specifically two post–Cold War films by Juan Carlos Tabío and Fernando Pérez because these two contemporary ICAIC directors still employ avant-garde techniques in their work to disrupt traditional cinematic storytelling. Their specific cinematic works, Tabío's *The Elephant and the Bicycle* (1996) and Fernando Pérez's *Suite Habana* (2004), play ironically on the revolutionary and esthetic themes promoted by imperfect cinema, and the ambiguity of their visual statements regarding the role of the Cuban worker in cinema creates a fascinating topic for discussion.

Tabío's film could be viewed as an homage to the principles of García Espinosa's imperfect cinema, and adheres to its Brechtian precepts regarding how a revolutionary culture can be developed through cinema, yet it also parodies certain idealistic notions about how the oppressed can be integrated into the filmmaking process. *Suite Habana* on the other hand, at first seems to reinforce somewhat ambiguously the didactic idea of a stoic proletarian avant-garde cinema while providing gloomy visuals that, because of the lack of dialogue, are open to multiple ideological interpretations. Still, I think that the film's originality lies in its estheticism which effectively uses old-fashioned montage to represent an ordinary day in several Cuban workers' lives, even though some could be disappointed by the failure of the film to attack directly the Cuban government (something that is done differently in *Alice in Wondertown* and later in *Juan of the Dead*). The self-reflexivity, ideological commitment, and irony of both films provide for a deep reflection about how Tabío and Pérez perceive the role of Cuban cinema in representing the workers' "voice" after the Special Period.

3. *Entertainment and the Proletarian Avant-Garde*

Italian Neorealism, Workers' Cinema and Early Cuban Cinema

It is well known to film historians that one of the most important early attempts to portray a proletarian avant-garde narrative was made in silent films produced by the Soviet government in the 1920s. These projects were influenced by early Russian formalist esthetics; Soviet directors such as Sergei Eisenstein who were engaged in these experiments applied avant-garde concepts to the creation of dialectic visual narratives that foregrounded proletarian struggle against czarist forces. The narrative strategies of this cinema included montage sequences in which unrelated images were constructed to produce a dialectic vision for indoctrinating ideological perspectives.

A closer look at films such as Eisenstein's *Battleship Potemkin* (1925) and *October: Ten Days that Shook the World* (1928) gives evidence of these formalist devices and demonstrates how the proletarian struggle is portrayed visually by connecting revolutionary images and conceptualizations in the film rather than through the subjectivity of a single protagonist. Such films offered the possibility of a collective narrative that would avoid the trappings of "bourgeois" individualism, and were indispensable for propaganda purposes during the Russian civil war, serving as an example of one of the first national cinemas that provided a cultural and esthetic alternative to films produced by international studios that promoted the values of their respective nationalist elites. Yet many of these films were difficult for proletarian audiences to understand, and prompted Soviet filmmakers, including Eisenstein himself, to modify this esthetic experimentation and to resort later to more conventional devices in order to develop a "workers' cinema."[1]

Early Soviet cinema was also significant in the development of international political cinema with its inclusion of real workers and peasants performing their own social situations. When Marxist critic Walter Benjamin singled out[2] cinematic productions of his time as examples of industrialized art that supported the élites, he saw hope in the Soviet cinema produced under Stalin's regime. The key to his embracing these works lay not in their narrative experimentation (montage editing, etc.), but in the fact that real workers and peasants participated in the filmmaking process, and that filmmakers explored their struggles rather than glorifying the upper classes.[3] For Benjamin, the sight of real workers and peasants representing themselves was transgression enough to the narratives promoted by capitalist corporations.

Benjamin's Marxist cultural and ideological statement, in which the portrayal of real peasants and workers in cinema is emphasized as a means of combating capitalist hegemony, was and continues to be embraced by many filmmakers and movements from the international left. One of the most acclaimed early examples in Western Europe (outside of official Communist filmmaking) was Vittorio De Sica's *Ladri di Bicicletti* (*Bicycle Thieves*, 1948), a classic of the Italian neorealist movement, whose narrative follows the plight of an unemployed Italian worker after World War II.[4] The protagonist was portrayed by Lamberto Maggiorani, a proletarian performer who in the film embodies the vicissitudes of his own lower-class identity. His alleged authenticity was lauded by major cultural figures as diverse as American playwright Arthur Miller and French film critic André Bazin,[5] even though the film employs the artificiality of a family melodrama. Still, the use of non-professional actors and filming on-location later inspired other filmmakers to attempt subversive filmmaking that did not conform to the corporate studios' esthetic guidelines for a glossy cinematic product and indulgence with superstars. Despite the fact that it never achieved financial success with the masses at the time, this social estheticism embedded in Italian neorealism was very influential with political filmmakers of the 1950s, including ICAIC founders Tomás Gutíerrez Alea and Julio García Espinosa.[6]

When García Espinosa wrote about *Bicycle Thieves* screenwriter Cesare Zavattini, he demonstrated the lack of mass appeal from which Italian neorealism suffered in the 1950s through an anecdote: while studying filmmaking in Rome, Zavattini and Tomás Gutíerrez Alea met Lamberto Maggiorani, the lead actor in *Bicycle Thieves*. The worker-turned-thespian had a drink with them and expressed his disappointment in Italian cinema at the time. Although *Bicycle Thieves* had become popular in film festivals, by the 1950s it was only remembered by the Italian audiences as an empty icon of popular culture. Italian filmmakers

3. Entertainment and the Proletarian Avant-Garde

such as Federico Fellini and Luchino Visconti were turning to a different type of cinema that was not necessarily "realistic," and neorealist films in the traditional sense were no longer financially viable. The only work Maggiorani himself could get was shining shoes and promoting bicycle races.[7]

The failure of films such as *Bicycle Thieves* to engage the masses, and specifically the proletariat, affected García Espinosa's and Gutiérrez Alea's approach to filmmaking. As leftist filmmakers, they wanted to integrate in their cinema many of the groundbreaking approaches that had originated in the Soviet Union and had been adapted to different situations in the national cinemas of the Western Hemisphere. It was important for them to give voice to the proletariat, peasants, and other oppressed citizens, but at the same time make films that the masses wanted to see, and therefore contribute to the possibility of social change in their culture.

Tomás Gutiérrez Alea and Julio García Espinosa studied filmmaking in Italy in the early 1950s, shortly before the 1959 Cuban revolution. As directors committed to the leftist movements in Latin America, they were attracted to the Italian neorealist films that were in vogue at the time in European intellectual circles, even though they were becoming aware of neorealism's fading presence in Italian culture.[8] When the Cuban filmmakers returned to their homeland, they followed in neorealist Italian directors' footsteps by co-directing *El mégano* (1956), a documentary critique of the Batista regime through the documentation of the real-life struggles of coal miners. The production incurred the government's wrath and the film was banned, seized, and confiscated. At the formation of the ICAIC in 1959, Gutiérrez Alea and García Espinosa were in their formative stages as filmmakers, thinking that an homage to Italian neorealism might be the best way to create a revolutionary Cuban cinema that would redefine culture.

The marriage of Italian neorealism and Cuban revolutionary cinema showed promise at the beginning, but did not yield the expected results. The filmmakers of ICAIC acknowledged the assistance provided by members of the Italian cinematic movement, especially in establishing the Cuban film institute. A post–Cold War issue of the Cuban film journal *Cine Cubano* (155) is dedicated to Cesare Zavatini, the writer of many of the Italian neorealist films including *Bicycle Thieves* and *Umberto D* (1952).[9] One of the most interesting articles in this issue was written by Julio García Espinosa, who had argued with Zavatinni on issues located at the core of his theories of imperfect cinema that subsequently had a profound influence on ICAIC filmmaking. García Espinosa acknowledges the importance of the help offered by Zavatini to Cuba, while expressing his disappointment at being assigned to direct the Italian writer's screenplay, *The Young Rebel*, believing the story to have been constructed with traditional neorealist schemes that failed to excite his imagination. The Cuban director completed the film because of its significance to Cuban cinema, yet remained dissatisfied with the final product.

Tomás Gutíerrez Alea had a similarly negative experience with Italian neorealism. His first feature film was *Historias de la revolución* (*Histories of the revolution*, 1960). According to the Cuban director, this anthology of short films about the 1959 Cuban revolution followed the model of Roberto Rossellini's *Paisà* (*Paisan*, 1946), and was heavily influenced by Italian neorealism.[10] The film is of historical and cultural value, as it was the first attempt of the new revolutionary Cuban culture to represent itself.[11] Nonetheless, the director himself considered it a failure, having simulated a dated brand of esthetic realism and narrative techniques artificially imported from Europe.[12]

Gutíerrez Alea had expressed his pleasure at having convinced Italian cinematographer Otello Martelli to come to Cuba to work on what was one of the first Cuban revolutionary films.[13] He thought Martelli, Roberto Rosellini's cinematographer in *Paisan*, had succeeded brilliantly; yet Martelli had already moved away from his neorealist origins, as his previous film had been Fellini's *La Dolce Vita* (1960). As a result, *Histories of the revolution* was constructed on the narrative model of Italian post–World War II cinema that nevertheless managed to avoid a neorealist visual esthetic.

Histories of the revolution is an anthology consisting of three unrelated segments. The first segment involves a revolutionary fugitive and takes place in Havana; its lighting sets up the visuals as an

3. Entertainment and the Proletarian Avant-Garde

expressionistic *film noir* rather than a look more typical of Rosellini's work. The artificiality of the first segment is at odds with the neo-realist aspects of the other two stories presented in the film. The second and third segment are constructed to resemble a war film, with characters played by revolutionaries who actually fought in Sierra Maestra, contributing to the film's status as a historical artifact in that viewers experience Cuban rebels playing themselves in the roles that transformed the Cuban nation. These performances comply with Benjamin's appreciation of Soviet cinema and with the leftist social principle that advocates that the proletariat play themselves in their own national filmmaking process. When studied analytically as a film text, however, *Histories of the revolution* raises the question of whether the amateur, stilted acting of the soldiers is a reflection on the (in)ability of workers to portray themselves on screen in an engaging manner or if we expect them to perform in a different manner because the studio system has influenced how we analyze what a good performance is.

Apart from the stiff acting and a failure to reproduce the look of Rosellini's early films, the most salient flaw of *Histories of the revolution* is its heavy-handed didactic approach that extends generalizations about class developed in socialist cultures born of formerly capitalist societies. The antagonists are immutable masses of police and soldiers who, whether evil or misguided, blindly follow the dictators in their quest to crush the noble revolutionaries. This polarization of representation and lack of development beyond superficial criticism has rendered some didactic films from socialist movements as passé as their fascist counterparts to the modern viewer. By attempting to counter the former authority's legacy, many directors of the time, including Gutíerrez Alea, fell into the trap of assuming their own films were realistic simply because of their political inclinations and the inclusion of actual proletarian protagonists. The proletariat's role in Cuban "imperfect cinema" esthetics was elaborated by García Espinosa in his influential manifesto. Imperfect cinema, however, differed significantly from similar European cinematic movements in the ways in which the proletariat is encouraged to participate in the filmmaking process and to engage with the cinematic text as an audience.

Cuban Cinema After the Cold War

Garcia Espinosa's Imperfect Cinema

In "For an Imperfect Cinema," García Espinosa sought to promote a proletarian cinema that worked outside of the esthetic pretensions of the European elites that patronized Third World directors, yet dictated the rules of filmmaking from within a Eurocentric perspective. When writing in 1969, García Espinosa was concerned that Cuban filmmakers' international success (with such masterpieces such as *Memories of Underdevelopment* and *Lucia*) would encourage them to pander to European movements such as Surrealism, Expressionism, and neorealism that might distance them from the Cuban proletarian audience that was the intended target of their films.[14] In his recent essay about imperfect cinema, Cuban filmmaker Manuel Herrera writes that García Espinosa's text is not an essay, neither the backbone of a cinematic movement, it was simply a call for alertness against the path that some Cuban filmmakers were opening due to their critical success.[15] Latin American cinema scholar Cristina Venegas explains further that, as an "esthetic theory," imperfect cinema is about a creative energy and a vision that insisted that artists should follow their own path and not other industrial models. She also mentions that García Espinosa urged artists to defy quality and esthetic patterns imposed by corporations that have their own agenda with the hopes that local communities could express their voice without thinking in a standard cinematic voice that is employed usually in hegemonic mass communication.[16]

Several statements made in García Espinosa's seminal text were to define the parameters of Cuban cinema for the proletarian audience in subsequent decades. García Espinosa appears detached from an auteurist position in promoting the establishment of a collective filmmaking that would favor the desires and needs of a society rather than the individualistic goals of a single director. While the author understands the need for the traditional role of a director at the beginning of the revolution, he also seeks a wide contribution from workers to be engaged in the film as performers or production assistants in order to assure that their vision directly impacts the work of art rather than being mediated by an artist who does not live in their social spheres:

3. Entertainment and the Proletarian Avant-Garde

We should endeavor to see that our future students, and therefore our future filmmakers, will themselves be scientists, sociologists, physicians, economists, agricultural engineers, etc., without of course ceasing to be filmmakers. And, at the same time, we should have the same aim for our most understanding workers, the workers who achieve the best results in terms of political and intellectual formation. We cannot develop the taste of the masses as long as the division between the two cultures continues to exist, nor as long as the masses are not the real masters of the means of artistic production. The revolution has liberated us as an artistic sector. It is only logical that we contribute to the liberation of the private means of artistic production.[17]

In defining imperfect cinema, Garcia Espinosa sought to encourage a type of filmmaking that would not emphasize hegemonic esthetics, and that would primarily address the problems of the oppressed or underrepresented from their own perspective. Some have misunderstood this idea as promoting "bad" cinema; however, García Espinosa maintains his emphasis on quality, arguing that if one expects a highly polished final product from an educated elite, the ideological elements that a non-professional could offer might be eradicated. Hence, García Espinosa insists on proletarian participation even at the expense of acknowledged failures such as *Histories of the revolution*.

In her article "Imperfect Cinema, Brecht, and *The Adventures of Juan Quin Quin*" film scholar Anna Marie Taylor establishes a link between Garcia Espinosa and German playwright Bertolt Brecht,[18] who, several decades earlier, had developed a concept of audience participation in the creation of the narrative that was a precursor to imperfect cinema:

> Without active participation on the audience's part, the art work is, for Brecht, incomplete. And if it offers a complete emotional experience or message, it will not be sufficient for people's needs intellectually or politically. Both Brecht and García Espinosa use the concept "imperfect" in a positive way. Desired audience participation has to be reached both through people's analytical distance from the representation and from their resulting political action. Brecht reverses conventional standards of artistic perfection. If a film or play succeeds politically in this way with its audience, it is necessarily and desirably "imperfect" by existing standards of artistic value. As Brecht saw it, "imperfect" art is a result rather than a goal of revolutionary practice.[19]

Cuban Cinema After the Cold War

One of the best examples of García Espinosa's imperfect cinema principle is discernible in Cuban filmmaker Sara Gómez's film *De cierta manera* (*One Way or Another*, 1974), in which documentary segments about poverty in Cuba are integrated into the narrative to explain the behavior of the fictional AfroCuban proletarian characters. A persuasive example of reality meeting fiction is the inclusion of an AfroCuban boxer who plays himself and interacts with the fictional characters played by professional actors. He had no education before the revolution; now, his life is limited in a new Cuban society in which he can no longer function as a boxer. His acting in the film is distracting and far from strong, according to the standards of traditional performance in fiction film, yet the portrayal of his real-life struggle was seen as mandatory to the plot, which suggests that workers need education to improve society and to escape from the control of a capitalist culture that formerly dominated the island. This element contributes to the status of the film as a collective effort, in which the director's vision is complemented by a worker whose participation enhances the film's "message."

Class self-identification and participation, however, are insufficient. A characteristic of imperfect cinema esthetics is the primacy of the entertainment factor. As long as a film has a social purpose, according to García Espinosa's manifesto, it should be constructed to create a pleasant experience for the audience in the theater. A dull film, it is postulated, drives away the public, while a didactic one that supports an ideology ceases to promote its revolutionary purpose. Cuban filmmakers have tried for the most part to make films that are accessible and enjoyable to the general public while incorporating workers into the narrative and introducing criticism of the system through complex avant-garde concepts in the hope of creating sophisticated worker audiences.

After the failure of García Espinosa's neorealist film *The Young Rebel*, his *The Adventures of Juan Quin Quin* (1965) combined worker participation and avant-garde techniques to become one of the most successful Cuban films of all time. It follows the adventures of a peasant who rebels against a landlord, yet with a more optimistic perspective in that it functions as a picaresque narrative, glorifying the class struggle in the very cinematic genres that García Espinosa satirizes. The battles between Juan Quin Quin and his antagonists resemble genres including

3. Entertainment and the Proletarian Avant-Garde

the western, the serial adventure, and the Mexican musical. The film is self-reflexive with regard to its flaws, including scenes of irrational images that counter narrative forms customarily associated with realist or socialist films, such as a moment when a male character looks directly at the camera and comments on the beauty of a female character. García Espinosa also assimilates techniques of "capitalist entertainment" by imitating popular, exploitative narratives (such as musicals) intended for obliteration after the revolution, and imbues them with revolutionary spirit.

The Adventures of Juan Quin Quin is more optimistic than some Latin American revolutionary movies of the same period, such as the Brazilian film *Black God, White Devil* (dir. Glauber Rocha, 1964), in that its self-reflexive aspects are associated with forms of exploitation of the Cuban past without being linked to the current revolutionary authorities. The conclusion contains a moment when Quin Quin is asked whether stealing weapons from the oppressor was difficult, to which he responds, looking directly at the camera: "It wasn't, no?" in an open solicitation to the revolutionary audience. With an entertaining homage to the Cuban revolution, García Espinosa's film was successful in Cuba in spite of its non-realist properties because it engaged its audience in support of the revolution. It is not insignificant that *The Adventures of Juan Quin Quin* has been, according to the ICAIC, the highest grossing Cuban film of all time until the release of *Strawberry and Chocolate* in 1994.[20]

After the decline of Cuban cinema in the 1970s and early 1980s, many of the imperfect cinema concepts began to disappear from the industry. Julio García Espinosa became head of the ICAIC, and after the failure of the expensive *Cecilia*, one of the most important films made to renew faith in ICAIC was Tomas Gutierrez Alea's *Hasta cierto punto* (*Up to a Certain Point*, 1982). The film functioned both as a parody and a reaffirmation of imperfect cinema: the main character is a director who seeks real proletarian participants to prepare his next film, fulfilling a goal of García Espinosa's manifesto. Marking the distance between workers and director, in a key scene, the fictional filmmaker tells Lina, the fictional female worker, that he wants to experience her life on the docks where employees are renowned for their machismo. Lina reacts with annoyance to being exoticized by the filmmaker who is unaware of the fact that no women are employed on his own film crew. This critique of the flaws of the "imperfect cinema" process and of the filmmakers' unconscious elitism imparts to viewers the realization that, despite the failings of this contact between filmmaker and proletariat, both will be transformed by the cinematic experience.

Of all Cuban filmmakers, Juan Carlos Tabío has, in my view, achieved the most complex mode of presenting the interaction between the proletariat and Cuban cinema. The following segment explores the most important films of his career, focusing on *The Elephant and the Bicycle*, with regard to this issue. The first two films that need to be addressed here are Tabío's *House Swapping* and *Plaff o demasiado miedo a la vida* (*Plaff, or Too Afraid of Life*, 1988), both of which are relevant to understanding *El elefante y la bicicleta* (*The Elephant and the Bicycle*, 1996) which I consider to be the director's major work of proletarian and revolutionary representation. In addition, understanding Tabío's view of the relationship between cinema and the revolution is essential to my subsequent analysis of Fernando Pérez's *Suite Habana*.

Juan Carlos Tabío's The Elephant and the Bicycle: *Self-Reflexivity and the Proletariat*

Juan Carlos Tabío's *Se permuta* (*House Swapping*, 1983) was the first Cuban film I saw, a film that impressed me as an entertaining romantic comedy able to deploy avant-gardist disruptions of the central narrative while critiquing classist and racist elements in post-revolutionary Cuba. Tabío is one of the most underrated Cuban filmmakers, and exploring his *oeuvre* would allow viewers to discover films that are highly entertaining, as well as sophisticated in terms of both narrative and esthetics, yet highlight worker representation. *House Swapping* may be described, in terms of genre, as a "communist romantic comedy": the plot foregrounds the struggle of Cuban seamstress Gloria Perdomo (Rosita Fornes) to find the perfect house in Havana that would assure a prosperous future for her daughter, Yolanda (Isabel Santos). The metaphor of house exchange is used to dramatize the protagonists' inability to buy

3. Entertainment and the Proletarian Avant-Garde

or own property in Cuba, leaving them no other alternative for mobility than to switch residences with other citizens.

At first, Gloria uses her negotiating ability to obtain an apartment in El Vedado, Havana's most prestigious district, moving with her daughter from the poorer district in which they had always lived. Gloria does not want her daughter Yolanda to marry a worker, as she herself once did, hoping that the new setting will enable Yolanda to meet more economically successful candidates. Once Yolanda begins to date Guillermo (Ramoncito Veloz), a business executive in a national company, Gloria seeks a more complex house swap that involves a number of people, in order finally to move to the perfect "bourgeois" house then occupied by an old woman. While Gloria exploits and manipulates people to achieve her goals, Yolanda falls in love with Pepe (Mario Balsameda), an AfroCuban engineer of lower class origins, in a plot twist that leads to the end of Gloria's plans, as her daughter finally marries a proletarian after breaking off with the corrupt and classist Guillermo. The film presents this development in a positive light: although Yolanda had been studying architecture, Guillermo wanted her to be a housewife. Her involvement with the AfroCuban Pepe, in contrast, leads her to do community work in the poorest region of Cuba (Guanabacoa), a more fulfilling life by socialist standards.

Such a narrative might be nothing more than a pleasant revolutionary romantic comedy, were it not for the fact that it includes two disruptive avant-garde scenes. In one of the scenes, a character is depicted watching himself on television on a prominent self-reflexive occasion. This scene suggests that the characters are aware of their filmic performativity, and it leads to another one, near the film's dénouement. In the second scene, the narrative is interrupted by a film critic who is reviewing *House Swapping*, and who informs the audience that the first half of the film is amusing while the second is repetitive. His comments, observed by Yolanda, influence the character's decisions and eventually the outcome of her plotline. More importantly, they serve as a self-reflexive criticism of the film, and they achieve the difficult task of making the revolutionary viewers aware of the didactic goals of the film while also helping them understand the artificiality of cinematic narratives.

Juan Carlos Tabío's next film, *Plaff, or Too Afraid of Life*, takes self-reflexivity and imperfect cinema esthetics to a more extreme satire. This film is analyzed in detail in Gilberto Moisés Blasini article "The World According to Plaff"; here, I address an aspect of his argument, namely the film's critique of the effects of socialist bureaucracy, which is typical of socialist comedies from around the world. At the time of the film's production, the East European bloc was beginning to collapse, and the effects of the collapse were being felt in Cuba. Tabío focuses on the generation gap between conservative Concha (Cuban star Daisy Granados) and her progressive daughter-in-law Clarita (Thaí Valdés), a hardworking young woman who wants to modernize the Cuban nation. While a straightforward narrative might well have made its point, according to Blasini, the film's self-conscious flaws impinge negatively on the final product, allowing for a film that is purposefully "defective" in order to demonstrate the effects of the collapsing economy both at the level of plot and on the film as a whole.[21] In this particular film, the economic chaos in the island actually shapes the physical structure of the final product.

The mystery at the heart of *Plaff* concerns the identity of a person throwing eggs at Concha's door in the form of a curse. Clarita and others who dislike Concha are suspects, each for different reasons. Eventually, each is revealed to have participated in the egg-throwing activity at a certain point. After Concha dies of a heart attack, we discover that Concha herself was to blame, having tried to implicate her daughter-in-law while playing the role of victim. Cuba's decaying revolutionary culture is, in a sense, responsible for the mystery: in the opening sequences we hear the projectionist saying that ICAIC delivered the film late, neglecting the first reel. He decides to reverse chronological order by running the second reel first, thereby omitting the initial scene, in which Concha throws an egg at her own door to initiate the curse herself, which leads the viewer to suspect the other characters instead. The dénouement portrays the projectionist locating the missing reel, thus allowing the audience to see the indiscretion that led to Concha's ultimate destruction.

Again, Tabío demonstrates that the representation of workers in Cuban filmmaking is shaped by an outside force. In *House Swapping*, the filmmaker's ideological positioning exerts an influence on the leading

3. Entertainment and the Proletarian Avant-Garde

protagonist's decision in favor of proletarian life. In *Plaff, a* decaying economy also has bearing on the outcome and meaning of the narrative. These avant-garde techniques in both of Tabío's films are essential in constructing a revolutionary Cuban cinema that avoids the trappings of bourgeois and socialist realism, and the films are able to criticize contemporary reality through the disruption of established cinematic narratives. What is important about these two films is that this deconstruction of workers' cinema was achieved through playful narratives that were enjoyed by the Cuban audiences.

In his article "Not Afraid for a Critical Space: Discovering the Post Modern in Cuban Cinema: The Case of *Plaff o demasiado miedo a la vida*," scholar Guy Baron specifically addresses the question of why *Plaff* follows a self-reflexive filmmaking legacy that can be linked to *The Adventures of Juan Quin Quin* and *Up to a Certain Point*. He also establishes the differences between the modernism in García Espinosa's *Juan Quin Quin* that tries to educate the audience about the artificiality of the narrative and the postmodern traits in Tabío's *Plaff* where the audience is already informed about the industry mechanisms.[22] Baron also uses film scholar Tim Woods' definition of the postmodern film to mark *Plaff*'s self-reflexivity as different from the older Cuban films.[23] This playful postmodern self-consciousness is used in Tabío's film to allude to various cinematic styles, breaking the line between the camera and the audience, and celebrating contemporary Cuban society and the culture it represents.[24]

Baron implies in his article that many Cubans would not see *Plaff* as a postmodern film, by specifically quoting Daniel Díaz Torres' writings about humor which the Cuban director sees more in the modernist view of "allowing the individual to free him or herself from the forces of destiny and convention, thus affirming their freedom of spirit."[25] However, Baron argues that this implies that film can project a monolithic reality, a concept that postmodern thinkers would disagree with.[26] He also writes that *Plaff* expresses multiple realities as

> this mixture of a naturalistic feel, absurdist comedy, and time compression techniques provokes this sense of the existence of the unreal within an approximation of a daily reality. This suggests that life for Cubans in the 1980s was a mixture of the real and the unreal, the quotidian and the

absurd. The film is evidently making comments both about Cuban contemporary life, and also about the nature of film-making and cinema in general. Thus, it is evident that cinematic techniques can be seen as aesthetic responses to a specific socio-political conjuncture.[27]

This is an important distinction to keep in mind, in view of the structure of Tabío's other films especially *The Elephant and the Bicycle*), and in view of how self-reflexivity is perceived in Cuba during the Special Period.

Tabío's name is usually associated during the Special Period with the films he co-directed with Gutíerrez Alea, such as *Strawberry and Chocolate* and *Guantanamera*, but his most unconventional proletarian film is *The Elephant and the Bicycle*, completed in 1996 after delaying production to help Gutíerrez Alea with his last two films. Scholar Michael Chanan has pointed out that Tabío's *The Elephant and the Bicycle* is almost an homage to Tomás Gutíerrez Alea's seminal essay "The Viewer's Dialectic."[28] This text was very important at the time of its publication (1988) because in it the director was trying to redefine the roles of Cuban filmmakers and their revolutionary audience several decades after the founding of the ICAIC. Gutíerrez Alea discussed how it was not enough to just film or capture the workers/audience on film, and argued the director had to bring something to the narrative.[29] He also established the differences between reality and fiction for the audience, as "[c]inema can draw viewers closer to reality without giving its condition of unreality as long as it lays down a bridge to reality so that viewers can return laden with experiences and simulations."[30]

The Elephant and the Bicycle begins in the early 20th century (no specific year) when "el Isleño" ("the Islander," played by Luis Alberto García) returns to his hometown after having been sent to prison for several years by the local landlord, "el Gavilán" (the Hawk). El Isleño wants to marry his fiancée, Marina Soledad (Lillian Vega) and to establish a local cinema with his portable film projector, unaware that Marina has been raped by el Gavilán in a plot not unlike those of 19th-century Latin American novels and pre-revolutionary Mexican films.

Never having seen a film before, the locals react with amazement to their introduction to cinema. The first narrative they watch is a silent adaptation of Robin Hood, in which Robin Hood, Maid Marian, and

3. Entertainment and the Proletarian Avant-Garde

the Sheriff of Nottingham are portrayed respectively by the same actors who portray el Isleño, Marina, and el Gavilán. As the melodrama of the Cuban class antagonists develops, the setting changes. El Isleño remarks at the start that he has only one film in his projector, cautioning customers that they would be watching the same film at every screening. Yet, each time the theater is packed, and the viewers see the same love triangle with the same actors, but set in a different genre that also depicts the evolution of the cinematic apparatus. Following the Robin Hood performance, el Isleño, Mariana, and el Gavilán portray the protagonists' roles in a colonial, a western, a Mexican revolutionary, and a cinema novofilm,[31] and in this order; with each successive viewing, the spectators are meant to increase their revolutionary consciousness, coming to understand the realities of oppression. Simultaneously, they begin to interact with the fictional characters, indicating ways in which they might resolve their problems, and thereby themselves playing a role in the narrative's outcome. This innovative representational mode, then, draws upon the precepts of imperfect cinema and its advocacy of workers' engagement in the filmmaking process in the interest of developing a truly revolutionary society.

When eventually el Gavilán shoots a few cannon balls into the theater, the workers bend the screen in his direction, bouncing the fired ammunition back toward his palace. When the landlord is deposed in a revolt, he flees the town (gesturing toward the flight of ex-president Fulgencio Batista), and the revolution is triumphant. Suddenly the film segues into the codes of a revolutionary musical propaganda promoting the glories of post-revolutionary society and socialist progress. This montage is interrupted when the projector breaks down and el Isleño and the other characters find themselves in a contemporary Cuban theater. As the audience complains, el Isleño apologizes for not being able to repair the machinery since real life does not imitate art. In this setting, the buildings that had been portrayed as beautiful in the revolutionary musical number now appear badly dilapidated. A worker asks why other workers are so taken by cinema if the films screened lack realism, while another responds that they provide fantasy and happy endings. Yet another replies in a speech on the need for cinematic realism in the interest of revolutionary change. As she speaks, her discourse is mocked as a sermon ignored by all. When the film projector is finally repaired, the entertainment resumes, but the viewers are bored and disappointed when what they see on the screen is themselves, and they eventually leave the theater.

Scholar Elena Adell compares Tabío's film with Arturo Sotto's *Pon tu pensamiento en mí*, another Special Period film that explores the role of cinema in constructing the Cuban revolution. Adell points out that Sotto's film is more ironic about the manipulation of revolutionary imagery and the limited role of the Cuban people in ICAIC filmmaking, while Tabío's project is more of a glorification of the development of the island's revolutionary cinema. She specifically criticizes the ending because it expresses the idea that revolutionary Cuban cinema has relinquished control to the audiences. However, she writes, these are not all audiences, as the ICAIC has consistently marginalized certain groups (such as AfroCubans and gays).[32]

While I agree with Adell's comments about the glorification of the ICAIC at the end of *The Elephant and the Bicycle*, I disagree with her interpretation, as I find the film's ending highly ironic. I think the film offers a complex critique of the ideological evolution of cinema, in which the satirized films instantiate the development of the film industry and its impact on national ideology in an homage to the role of cinema in the redefinition of the social values that would enable the masses to revolt against the "oppressor." Yet, in addition to parodying capitalist genres, *The Elephant and the Bicycle* also ridicules the ICAIC's tendency to mythologize foreign leftist cinema, as, for instance, when the films watched by the audience within the film's diegesis acquire the look and language of Brazilian cinema novo. This particular sequence resembles the Brazilian films and their esthetic devices, including hand-held camera and operatic music, which in this context appear dated, both visually and thematically. The Cuban actors feign speaking the Portuguese language, enacting a hilarious sketch of Glauber Rocha's *Antonio Das Mortes*, the protagonist of which was championed by film critics as well as by Cuban intellectuals at the ICAIC for several decades. The next narrative shift is the revolution that leads to the extravagant revolutionary musical, and ultimately to the realistic representation of the masses as depicted in the final scene with the audience looking at itself in a self-reflexive moment. The film thus invites us to reflect on whether the quest for the perfect worker representation championed for ideological purposes by scholars in the first half of the 20th century may indeed not be the "correct" way to fulfill dialectic objectives if viewers are bored by the use of cinematic realism, which makes them flee for the exits when they see themselves onscreen. Another film that addresses the imperfect/perfect representation of worker life in contemporary Cuban cinema as presented in Fernando Perez' *Suite Habana*, a Cuban film that was acclaimed by Cuban audiences and international critics alike.

Perfect and Imperfect Proletarian Homage in Fernando Pérez's Suite Habana

Fernando Pérez's *Suite Habana* is one of the most acclaimed Cuban films of recent years. Successful at the Havana local box office,[33] despite rumors that certain party officials did not appreciate it,[34] the film won first prize at the Havana film festival in 2002, as well as other honors such as the Goya award in Spain for best foreign Hispanic film. A further sign of local recognition is found in its status as the official Cuban entry for Best Foreign Language Film at the 2003 Academy Awards. Here I explore the construction of *Suite Habana* as a highly esteticized film about Cuban workers, with an ambiguous narrative and complex visuals that have created debatable readings of the film, which some could see as a glorification of the Cuban workers, and others as a criticism of post–Special Period life in Havana. Some Cuban critics, such as Rufo Caballero, have mentioned that the film had its amount of controversy on the island,[35] but it must not have reached the levels of *Alicia* if it has been so widely distributed and promoted abroad by the ICAIC.

Like Tabío, Fernando Pérez is a second generation filmmaker whose first feature, *Clandestinos* (*Clandestines*, 1988), is a conventional thriller about young revolutionary students during the 1959 revolution.[36] His next feature is an existential film, *Hello, Hemingway* (1989), which explores the legacy of the American writer in Cuba through the experiences of an overweight young woman who is bored with life and has issues with herself. At the peak of the Special Period, Pérez directed the short film *Madagascar* (1994), which was released abroad together with

Daniel Díaz Torres' *Love Me and You Will See*. Like Tabío's *House Swapping* and *Plaff!*, the film visualizes the problems on the island through the melodramatic relationship of two women (a mother and a daughter) of different generations. The mother's life is at a standstill, making her less empathic with her daughter's dreams of a transcendent experience: traveling to Madagascar. Both characters are trapped in a world of physical and mental confinement, causing their unhappiness. When discussing *Madagascar* and its portrayal of the bleak feelings that Cubans were experiencing during the Special Period, Pérez says: "I think many young Cubans have lost their illusions. It's true. And perhaps for them ideology, once converted to doctrine and reiterated, has lost its meaning. That is to say that perhaps they need a different spirit, something quite so established as the ideology of the revolution, the ideals of the revolution."[37]

Pérez's first truly great success was *La vida es silbar* (*Life Is to Whistle, 1998*), a magic realist dramedy, in which the island, personified by a young woman, narrates the story of three Cuban characters who try to find happiness and meaning in their lives: an old woman who works in a home for retired citizens, a fisherman with a subversive lifestyle, and a sexually voracious ballerina who is harassed by her boss at the ballet company. The characters' plight is captivating and culminates in their defiant resistance to conformity in a scene in which they meet in the Plaza of "La Revolución" shouting "Cuba" despite the tropical downpour.

A quite different type of film, *Suite Habana* is a fictional documentary[38] that extends and amplifies the preoccupations developed in Pérez's previous films with an auteurist imprint, following a day in the lives of several Cuban workers to demonstrate the ways in which they give life to Havana through their effort and sorrows. In his interview with Anne Marie Stock, Pérez candidly admits that at the time he was not planning to do a project like this and that the project came to fruition at the request of European producers who wanted a documentary about life in modern Havana:

> *Havana Suite* was a made-to-order film. I hadn't planned on filming a documentary about Havana, because I confess that a documentary is much harder for me to make than a fiction film. So when I was asked to work on

3. Entertainment and the Proletarian Avant-Garde

this project late in 2001 by the Spanish producer José María Morales, I hesitated [...] I wanted to make something that really motivated me, something where I felt I was leaving a part of me in what I was doing, because that is the cinema I like to work on, have done thus far, and hope to continue doing.[39]

Instead of using an extravagant narrative, as in *Life Is to Whistle*, or the tools of traditional documentaries, the film pays homage to the formalism of 1920s Soviet and other European films,[40] and especially to *Berlin Symphony of a Great City* (*Die Sinfonie der Grossstadt*, dir. Walter Ruttmann, Germany, 1927), with its focus on Berlin and its citizens, based on montage editing. This German film is considered to be one of the most important experimental films of the 1920s. As its title suggests, the narrative is envisioned as a musical homage to life in Berlin from early morning to evening. At the time of production, Germany was part of the Weimar Republic, recovering from the devastation of World War I. The economy was beginning to improve and the German nation was one of the premier industrialist countries in Europe and around the world, a situation reflected in the film's vision of a city whose citizens work hard to maintain industrial modernity while reaping the benefits of their efforts.

In terms of cinematic techniques, *Berlin Symphony of a Great City*'s narrative uses montage editing based on the principle that the language of cinema can be visualized through the link of unrelated images which, by order of appearance and rhythm, allow the viewers to decipher the story and ideas.[41] The director, Walter Ruttmann, uses such montage techniques to construct his vision of life in Berlin. In the first act, shots of a train approaching the city are edited with a fast pacing (rhythmic montage) which symbolizes the furious velocity of modernity. Once the camera switches to the empty streets in the early morning, the sequencing of images is slowed down to emphasize that the city is sleeping. These scenes include a factory not yet operational, policemen walking their beats, and a few random citizens. Once the train returns, the pace speeds up again in images of workers going to their jobs.

Ruttmann maintains this alternating rhythm between metric and rhythmic montage editing: in the former, information is provided through images of the city and its denizens' lives, while in the latter, he captures the tempo of life in a modern metropolis. In the third act, once the city is fully operational, metric editing structures an unflagging narrative pace foregrounding various visual settings, while in the fourth act, the rhythmic montage slows the pacing again, because the narrative takes place during lunch hour. One observes workers eating homemade lunches, in contrast to more affluent citizens eating in restaurants, and animals being fed. The montage speeds up in the presentation of the printing of the afternoon newspapers which leads to the citizens' return to work. Act 5 documents their evening entertainment including dining, movies, boxing matches, formal dancing and drinking in taverns.

Berlin, Symphony of a Great City differs from *Suite Habana* as an industrialist film that, while depicting the trappings of modernity in a favorable light, does not necessarily portray the proletariat as fully. We see them hard at work in Berlin while the elites indulge in modern pleasures such as fancy clothes, fine dining, and leisure time for debating. During the evening act, all citizens of all classes are seen at leisure, although the more affluent among them engage in more costly activities, while workers drink together in bars. The film clearly invites the viewer to conclude that class divisions dominate the city, yet all inhabitants enjoy the benefits of the industrial machine, as demonstrated in the visualization of its multiple stages.

Berlin, Symphony of a Great City does not need to create an emotional connection with its protagonists, as no one is developed as a three-dimensional character. The Berliners are seen as ants that feed off the mighty city which upgrades their status with its industrialist modernity. Fernando Pérez uses a different approach to montage editing by emphasizing the individuality of workers among the collective which supports Havana's life as a city. Using melodramatic devices (usually without spoken dialogue) he tries to make the audience connect with the workers. To be sure, several decades after the Cuban revolution, the city has decayed from its former glory; yet the film emphasizes that what makes Havana so vibrant is its workers with their struggles and dreams, rather than industrial modernity.

Suite Habana achieves certain goals of García Espinosa's imperfect cinema. It features proletarian workers portraying themselves and, through their lives, creating the narrative that the audience is experi-

3. Entertainment and the Proletarian Avant-Garde

encing. However, it bears the auteurist imprint of Fernando Pérez, whose previous films *Madagascar* and *Life is to Whistle* also dealt with Cuban characters' existential issues in the face of the revolution's decline (although using fictional characters and Cuban film stars). In this feature, the filmmaker's themes are achieved through a complex montage editing that can be difficult to decipher for those not acquainted with this technique, and for others who lack localized knowledge of Cuban culture. The film's warm reception in foreign academic and festival circles indicates that educated film viewers appreciate the film's formalist construction, while its commercial success in Havana may demonstrate that some locals on the island also appreciate Pérez's work. By exploring claims of its status as a "perfect" film instead of García Espinosa's imperfect ideal, one discovers the postmodern trait where esthetic enjoyment is balanced with the political features of revolutionary cinema.[42]

It is important to know life in Havana in order to understand many aspects of *Suite Habana*. The film begins with a long shot of the Havana seaport in the early hours of the morning. A slow-moving ship serves as a counterpart to the mighty speed of the train in *Berlin: Symphony of a Great City*. The camera then focuses on Lenin Park where a civilian guard is relieving another of duty. To viewers unacquainted with Cuban popular culture, this may appear odd, since the guards are there to protect the eyeglasses on a statue of John Lennon. A scandal broke out when the originals were stolen and since then, civilians have been taking turns to protect the statue. This may seem like a small detail, but it is one imbued with grander meaning in the narrative: throughout the day documented in the film, several workers will offer their free time in service of this utopian goal, a meaningful one for Cubans, for the futility of protecting this John Lennon statue may be interpreted as a symbol of their quest to protect the decaying Cuban revolution.

Suite Habana imitates the structure of *Berlin Symphony of the City*, beginning with the awakening of the city in the morning, the pauses at lunch and dinner time, and finally the evening social entertainment. Unlike the German film, however, several characters are introduced at different stages of the film; their names and ages appear on screen for audience recognition. Yet, contrary to the German film, in which metric and rhythmic montage editing is emphasized, Pérez also uses Eisenstein's concepts of tonal and overtonal montage which anchor the melodramatic situations of his protagonists. At times these constructions are more obvious, while at others repeated viewings are needed, necessitating the spectator's engagement in much the same way as in Eisenstein's films. Scholars such as Cynthia Thompkins[43] find that Pérez was successful in his use of montage editing, because, by means of these montage techniques, he removed the dialogues and interview segments (that are documentary staples), and as a result was able to make the characters more visually introspective.[44]

This does not mean that the film lacks traditional family melodrama. For example, two melodramatic plotlines that are constructed through montage, involve the relationship between the character of Francisco and his son, Francisquito who suffers from Down syndrome, and Raquel and Ivan. Francisquito is introduced as he awakens in the morning; his grandmother gets him ready for school. One assumes that she is not his mother at first because of the obvious age difference. Several segments later, she takes him to school, where he spends most of the day. His father, Francisco, is introduced later in the film while he is repairing a house. At this point, the viewer is unaware he is Francisquito's father, as several other characters have been emphasized in the crosscut editing. This storyline intersects with another as, at lunchtime, Francisco goes to the cemetery to place flowers on the tomb of someone to whom he seems closely related. This scene is intercut with another in which an emigrant bids farewell to his family at the airport. Shots of the airplane leaving Cuba alternate with those of Francisco at the cemetery, evoking the mourning typical of Cuban families faced with the departure of family members due to emigration. The pacing of these scenes is slow and solemn. Later, Francisquito meets Francisco after school; we see them bond in their family relationship. They cook dinner together; by the end of the film, Francisquito is put to bed. In the credits, we discover that the old couple taking care of him were in fact his grandparents, and that Francisco had abandoned his career as an architect to take care of Francisquito after his wife died.

Another sentimental proletarian plotline involves Raquel, a worker at a pharmaceutical factory, and her relative Ivan,[45] who is employed in a hospital laundry. He is first introduced riding a bicycle and carrying

3. Entertainment and the Proletarian Avant-Garde

a pair of high-heeled shoes. Several scenes later, he appears to be taking the shoes to a shoemaker. Raquel is introduced as a factory worker although not in relation to Ivan. At noon, instead of having lunch, she goes to visit a *santera* fortune teller. The fortune teller's words are barely audible, blurred by the intercutting of sounds from the washing machines Ivan uses to do the laundry. One barely hears the following line: "You are worried about him, but he is your ray of sun." Both characters are edited together in montage; the melodramatic connection only begins to make sense at the conclusion when it becomes clear that Raquel and Ivan are connected. After leaving work, Ivan is seen as a cross-dressing performer; the shoes he was having repaired were required for his stage performance. Raquel is in the audience proudly approving of him. Ivan sings: "déjennos vivir en paz" (let us live peacefully).

Suite Habana is an impressive esthetic achievement, and it is very appealing because it provides the opportunity for participation in filmmaking by the proletariat. The film's visuals could also be interpreted as critical of some parts of contemporary Cuban society for several reasons, and despite the absence of dialogue. For example, scholar Dara Goldman points out that when the clown Juan Carlos is performing happily for a children's party, his performance is juxtaposed with his brother leaving the island, which results in an ironic visual because the clown is performing "happiness."[46] Another scholar, Elliot Young, in turn, analyzes the scene in which the older Cubans watch a political rally on TV, and interprets it as Pérez criticizing Cuban TV stations as the mouthpieces of the government. Young writes, "By employing a visual distancing mechanism, showing Cubans watching a rally on television rather than showing the rally itself, we are made to reflect on the television not as reality but as a mediated spectacle."[47] However, in the conclusion to his article about *Suite Habana*, he argues that, even though the film has been received in both ways, it should not be labeled as "a condemnation of Cuban society or as an uncritical ode to Cuban socialism."[48]

It could be said that the most controversial part of the film from a revolutionary perspective is the ending. Despite the workers' efforts throughout the entire documentary, the final credits reveal that their dreams have nothing to do with what the revolution can provide, given their situations—dreams of becoming a famous popular singer or traveling the world. The perhaps most striking character revelation is in the final shot, when an old woman who sells peanuts admits that "she no longer has dreams." In his review of the film, Cuban film critic Rufo Caballero criticized Pérez for being manipulative with this final segment, which he deemed unnecessary.[49] He thinks that sometimes Pérez can be sentimental with his characters and that he has a need to over-explain them.[50] I would agree with this analysis of the characters, but I would counter-argue that that is precisely what makes Pérez's work so attractive, as the Cuban audience in the Special Period can identify with their plight.

I think the main issue some could have with the film is that even though the Cuban revolution is seen crumbling down, the state's presence is only visualized in the rally shown on TV. No matter how hard the ICAIC has always tried to emphasize the ideological aspect of the Cuban revolution, abroad the revolution is overwhelmingly perceived as a Castro dictatorship. Many Special Period films emphasize conservative government ideologues as the main antagonists (see *Alice in Wondertown, Strawberry and Chocolate, Guantanamera*, and others) for a reason. *Suite Habana* could be considered a traditionalist worker film, harking back to esthetic elements of early Soviet cinema that are dangerously close to estheticizing workers. It might be argued that its success in Cuba demonstrates proletarian support, which might equally be a function of its positive representation of the workers. The film's shortcomings are perhaps due to an abstract, exaggerated concept of the revolution symbolized by a decaying Havana, but also by workers who are depicted as uniformly positive, hardworking, caring, and loving. The film reveals no anger on the part of the characters toward the system (with the possible subtle exception of Ivan, who displays some resentment while cross-dressing and singing).

In this sense, *Suite Habana* only criticizes elements of the system for a nihilism limited to the lack of achieving capitalist dreams of individual success. No repression, violence, or hunger—all elements of leftist films from Latin America—are represented. Groundbreaking films such as Fernando Meirelles' *City of God* and Alejandro González Iñárritu's

3. Entertainment and the Proletarian Avant-Garde

Amores Perros used montage, as well as other techniques of Third World filmmaking, for the benefit of more exciting dramas that have earned international popular acclaim and commercial success, thereby introducing into the mainstream their subversive ideas about the world's hegemonic economic systems. Their use of montage foregrounds more visually entertaining representations of the proletariat that owe more to MTV than to Eisenstein.

The recent *Suite Habana*, however, exemplifies a filmmaking that narrows its focus to Cuban workers surviving the island's economic collapse after the revolution. The film's lack of dialogue and reliance on old-fashioned montage editing offers a vague image of contemporary Cuban culture that resists the viewer's desire to know workers' thoughts and opinions, instead deploying them in the service of the director's ideas. This makes for an interesting, worthwhile yet outdated formalistic experiment, one that is questionable with regard to its use of an actual proletariat whose lives are constructed to provide a message about the revolution in the absence of their own voices.[51]

In this chapter, I discussed briefly Eisenstein's formalist innovations and De Sica's use of neorealism in order to trace the ways in which the proletariat became part of the leftist auteurist tradition outside of Cuba. In Cuba, after the establishment of the ICAIC, García Espinosa's and Gutíerrez Alea's failed Italian neorealist adaptations prompted them to attempt more postmodern approaches to envisioning the proletariat in a cinema that is both entertaining and capable of engaging the public, despite esthetic decisions that use realism in tandem with other strategies. As Cuban cinema developed, filmmakers sought to integrate the workers into their narratives while remaining conscious of both the positive and negative aspects of this philosophy, as satirized by Gutíerrez Alea in *Up to a Certain Point*. Second generation filmmakers such as Juan Carlos Tabío promoted a proletarian avant-garde filmmaking that was self-reflexive; taking up issues of importance to a mass audience, it also taught viewers lessons on the constructed-ness of narrative in cinema. *The Elephant and the Bicycle* explored the evolution of the struggle against authority from medieval narratives, to bourgeois stories, and finally revolutionary projects that led to the workers' revolution. Once the workers acquire power, they are portrayed more accurately in revolutionary cinema, but are driven away from the theater in the process. Tabío understands cinema's revolutionary capabilities, and acknowledges that the key to maintaining audience attendance is not only the realism promoted by scholars and critics since André Bazin, but the integration of entertainment as well.

Fernando Pérez is another ICAIC director who achieved box-office success in Cuba while employing avant-garde techniques in his films. He tackles the plight and dreams of Cuban citizens in films such as *Madagascar* and *Life Is to Whistle*, as well as inter-generational conflicts in Cuba, a topic he also developed in *Suite Habana*, a significant formalist experiment with sound Marxist/Revolutionary principles. The latter film conveys the pain of Cuban citizens after the Special Period, achieving many of the precepts promoted in García Espinosa's "For an Imperfect Cinema" or Gutíerrez Alea's "The Viewer's Dialectic," while representing an esthetic peak in modern Cuban cinema. However, its social critique is attenuated by the absence of dialogue from the workers (to express their individual desires and thoughts) and by an estheticism that subdues the anger through beautiful montages that represent a more abstract melancholy. I will now continue the discussion by examining how the resurfacing of commercial genres such as musicals and horror became a way to visualize post-special period life in a more extravagant manner that is linked to global commercialism.

4

Paradise Under the Stars and *Habana Blues*

The Revival of Cuban Musical Coproductions

Before the 1959 Revolution in Cuba, musical coproductions with other countries such as Spain, the United States, and other Latin American states, consistently portrayed the island as a land of entertainment and unbridled sexuality. Cubans were often depicted as an Africanized "other," in contrast to the "white" foreign visitors to the island, which led to the sexualized musical mulatto/a archetype that is still very popular abroad. After the establishment of a revolutionary government and the ICAIC, the commercial musical genre began to disappear from the island's national cinema, as it was considered exploitative and representative of the ills of colonialism and capitalism. Nevertheless, the Cuban government occasionally used the genre's imagery as didactic tools to educate the masses about the decadence of capitalism.

During the Special Period, Cuba was in desperate need of foreign investment, and musical coproductions made during the Special Period began to revive the genre with the help of foreign investment. This revival is important, as it marks the beginning of the promotion of Cuban narratives that are not necessarily affiliated with the government or its institutions, and whose target audience includes also foreigners. Thus, after the end of the Cold War, Spain and other European states have invested in Cuban cinema, and, as a consequence, the narratives made in the island have exploited Cuba's musical heritage while adding new layers of exoticism that include a new type of primitivism associated with the island's decaying socialist economy.

A detailed analysis of two films, Gerardo Chijona's *Un paraíso bajo las estrellas* (*Paradise Under the Stars*, 1999) and Benito Zambrano's *Habana Blues* (2005), will illustrate these points. Chijona's film is an ironic homage to prerevolutionary musicals set in contemporary Cuba. However, despite parodying the genre and certain aspects of contemporary Cuban society, the film still uses exoticizing and sexualized gender and race constructions. *Habana Blues*, directed by a Spaniard, Benito Zambrano, and made shortly after the Special Period, fictionalizes and criticizes the new fetishization of Cuban music by focusing on the poaching of Cuban performers in Europe and the U.S. as a result of the economic recession. The film does not romanticize the revolutionary government, and gives voice to characters that are not happy with life in Cuba. However, despite these criticisms, this Spanish-Cuban coproduction still promotes the idea of a sexualized Cuba, thus demonstrating how even a musical that is critical of contemporary Cuban society nevertheless needs to fulfill the exploitative aspects of the genre.

The Caribbean Musical "Other" Before the 1959 Cuban Revolution: Hispanic vs. Black Otherness

Prerevolutionary Cuban cinema is often associated with the musical genre because most of the island's coproductions with foreign studios emphasized Cuban singers or *vedettes* who were popular abroad.[1] Many of these performers took advantage of the international reputation of their stage performances to co-star with famous Mexican and Argentinean stars whose names guaranteed international distribution at the time. Most of these prerevolutionary musicals are very difficult to assess in terms of quality. Viewers who admire recent Cuban cinema because of its postmodern esthetics and revolutionary ideology will be disappointed by the simplicity of their narratives, and the conservative and racially exploitative ideas presented on screen. Many Latin American scholars completely ignore this phase of Cuban cinema, which has been overshadowed by the ICAIC's excellent output after the 1959 revolution. However, these films are exceptional in that they display the kitsch traits

4. The Revival of Cuban Musical Coproductions

of Cuban culture, feature legends from the Cuban music scene such as Benny Moré, Celia Cruz, and Olga Guillot, and tend to be more entertaining to general audiences due to their unbridled displays of sexuality and decadence.

The main character archetypes in early 20th-century Cuban cinema (the black, the Galician, and the mulatta) originated in vaudeville performances in the Alhambra theater located in Havana. Many of the writers and actors who worked at this particular venue would then recreate their sketches in the Cuban films produced at the time, and would eventually become very influential in prerevolutionary Cuban cinema.[2] Among these three types of characters, the mulatta was the most popular abroad because it provided international theater and cinema audiences with sexualized racial ideas about the island.

In her article "Exotic Exports: The Myths of the Mulatta," Cuban scholar Raquel Mendieta Costa focuses her research specifically on that archetype, writing in detail about how the Cuban national myth of the mulatta[3] emerged from 19th-century racial fears of miscegenation (as represented by the iconic 19th-century novel *Cecilia Valdés*),[4] and how it evolved into sexualized vaudeville performances at the beginning of the 20th century.[5] Many of the mulatta vaudeville performers, such as Blanquita Amaro and Rita Montaner, gained international fame (specifically in Europe and the Americas) due to the exotic allure and racial otherness they exhibited in their live performances.[6] These live performances were then replicated in cinematic musicals coproduced by Cuba and other countries (Mexico, Argentina, the U.S.) and distributed on the European, American and Latin American markets which elevated the Cuban performers to the status of international superstars.

The mulatto/a figures in Cuban colonial narratives are very important to the island's nationalism, and can be understood by means of the postcolonial concept of mimicry developed by scholar Homi Bhaba. In "Representation and the Colonial Text: A Critical Exploration of Some Forms of Mimeticism," Bhaba explains[7] how the colonized tries to imitate the empire through a mimetic desire implanted into the colonial subject by the colonial power itself. Because this imitation is never completely achieved, it leads to an ambivalence in the colonial subject that tends to enhance the differences between the imperial and the colonial other.[8] Two of the most important anti-colonial Cuban nationalist novels from the 19th century, *Sab*, and *Cecilia Valdés o La Loma del Ángel*, feature mulatto protagonists who try to integrate themselves into the Eurocentric Cuban elite, but fail miserably and have tragic endings. These characters' plight was a metaphor for a Cuba that would never achieve equality under the Spanish colonial system.

After the end of the Spanish colonization, Cuba experienced a different type of economic system under American capitalism at the beginning of the 20th century. The United States had granted national independence to Cuba after the Spanish-American War but tied the island's economic interests to foreign investments. This is evidenced in the Cuban national film industry at the time, which participated in numerous coproductions with financial partners from Mexico, Hollywood, and Argentina. These films featured the island as part of a mysterious and exotic Caribbean region with African roots and subservient to the new American and Latin American foreign investors.

American cinema and television provided a plethora of exotic images of the island and its people, e.g., in the TV series *I Love Lucy*, but this exoticizing depiction was by no means limited to Anglophone productions. Cuba's African heritage also allowed Mexican and Argentinean studios to create an "African Other" for Hispanic American audiences that were both closer geographically and partially compatible with their language and culture. In this type of film, the European Hispanic side of Mexican or Argentinean culture would be seen as "civilized" in contrast to the "terrifying" and supernatural aspects of AfroCuban culture. In other words, after Spain withdrew from the island, Spanish imperial hegemony was supplanted by United States and Latin American capitalist hegemonies while Cuba remained in a position of subalternity.

The most interesting musical film from the period that explains the Cuban industry of the time is the 1956 Mexican-Cuban coproduction *No me olvides nunca* (*Don't Forget Me*). In this self-reflexive film, Mexican star Luis Aguilar and Cuban vedette Rosita Fornes play themselves in a plot about their agents' attempts to spark an artificial romance between them in order to create publicity for the mediocre film they are shooting. The Cubans in the film constantly point out how

4. The Revival of Cuban Musical Coproductions

Aguilar is the typical Mexican gentleman, while Rosita Fornes is as fiery as a Cuban woman "should be." Rosita is thus othered as a sexualized colonial object. Because the Mexican industry dominated Latin American cinema at the time, Mexican characters routinely appeared in the role of masculine civilized conquerors while Cuba was constantly feminized. It is interesting to observe, however, that in *Don't Forget Me*, this colonial-type relationship does not rely on physical markers to exoticize the colonial other. Cuban Rosita Fornes is a blonde actress, the daughter of two Catalan actors, while the "civilized" Luis Aguilar has a *mestizo* complexion. At some point in the film, a reporter asks Fornes if she would prefer blonde kids, like herself, or dark kids, like the Mexican actor. This demonstrates that the exoticism at the time was not related to the physical appearance of the actor on stage, but to the audience's perception of Mexican and Cuban culture in terms of Eurocentric civilization. Fornes is white, but Cuban culture makes her the other, while Aguilar is not racially white but represents Mexican hegemony, and hence civilization.

The musical "Africanness" of Cuba is also present in the 1951 Cuban-Argentinean co-production *A la Habana me voy* (*I Am Going to Havana*), featuring mulatto Cuban protagonists who self-identify as having "black blood," specifically for commercial purposes. In one of the first scenes in the film, these Cuban stage performers in an Argentinean theater scout the local dancers that are to perform with them, and express their disappointment in the Argentinean women's lack of "jungle" and "Afro" essence. The theater owners are dumbfounded by these comments because the Cuban performers are not that racially different from the Argentinean dancers, until a Cuban female dancer (portrayed by famous Cuban vedette Blanquita Amaro) demonstrates what it means to be "Afro" through her wild and sensuous hip movements. This "Africanness" is visually portrayed by her dance mimicking the ones associated with African cultures, and by switching the musicians playing for her with AfroCuban performers. Instead of performing on European instruments such as pianos and violins, they play African drums. This has an effect on the music which was previously played in a perceivably dull manner. Impacted by the Cuban dance, the Argentinean audience goes wild, and hints are made that the dance enhances their libido. The Argentinean producers end the scene by shouting "we love the jungle."

The same type of racialized musical representations of Cuban performers were predominant in Latin America, in the United States (e.g., *I Love Lucy*, and the film *Weekend in Havana*, 1941), and Spain (e.g., *El negro que tenía alma blanca*).[9] Concepts of race in Latin America, however, work differently from the U.S., which is why it can sometimes be confusing when Latin American films try to imitate ideas imported from Hollywood. The ideals of racial *mestizaje* are an important part of Latin American nationalism, and, when they appear in Hispanic films, they probably do not seem as controversial to Latin American audiences. Still, many Latin American intellectuals, such as Angel Rama or Antonio Cornejo Polar, have debated *mestizaje* as an idealist concept that, however, is not always applied in practice when the inclusion of certain racial, ethnic, and class groups into a particular national hegemony is concerned. In Cuba's case, due to historical and geographical realities, African heritage represents the nation's non–Eurocentric other, and thus provides for a different perception of the island in comparison to other Latin American countries which are more concerned with indigenous groups. It is important to explain here that certain racial ideas about the Cuban performers in musicals were widely accepted in a variety of national cinemas, and that the racist perceptions about the island circulated in different regions and among different cultures. A discussion of how Cubans were perceived on an international scale will help us understand why later, in the 1990s, they were forced to return to this type of representation that, albeit problematic and racist, is certainly profitable.

Sexuality, Cuban Revolutionary Nationalism and the Rebirth of the Musical

After the 1959 Cuban revolution, the new government charged ICAIC with the task of eradicating images of imperial, colonial, and capitalist culture. The Institute quickly discarded production of superficial and offensive musicals, shifting its coproductions with Latin America and Europe to promote socialist ideology instead of sex, tourism, and

4. The Revival of Cuban Musical Coproductions

exploitative propaganda. However, Cuban and foreign socialist directors continued to use the metaphor of sex between foreign male and Cuban female characters but with a new purpose: to denounce rather than celebrate the brutality and metaphorical rape of the island. A number of films were made to reflect that shift, including *I Am Cuba*, *Lucia*, and others.

This shift from the predominant low-brow, exoticizing coproduced musical comedies to serious revolutionary drama, and to a certain point nationalist propaganda, is evidenced in *I Am Cuba*, a Cuban-Soviet coproduction, which maintained aspects of exotic visuals (e.g., musical numbers typical of earlier Cuban co-productions) for its Soviet audiences while condemning the American sexual exploitation of the island as a symbol of imperialist decadence.[10] Directed by Soviet filmmaker Mikhail Kalatozishvili (already critically acclaimed for *The Cranes Are Flying*, 1957) as a Soviet response to the nuclear missile crisis that nearly launched World War III, *I Am Cuba* was criticized by both Cuban and Soviet audiences for its dated narrative style that bore the imprint of Mosfilm Studio in the 1950s. As noted in the documentary *I Am Cuba: The Siberian Mammoth* (2005), Soviet viewers considered the film to be a passé Communist epic, while disdainful Cuban critics and filmmakers found it inferior to the more innovative Western European movements such as Italian neorealism and the French New Wave.

To communist audiences in Eastern Europe, Cuba symbolized the frontier in the battle against capitalism. Consequently, in *I Am Cuba*, the excesses normally associated with the island's African heritage were transferred, in the first segment of the film, to Cuban upper-class protagonists and the image of American investors. When a black prostitute is introduced in the segment, she is walking with her boyfriend, a fruit seller who smuggles weapons for revolutionaries in Havana. Their love is depicted as a chaste one that could only be consummated once they are married, and only later is the female character revealed to be a prostitute. In the brothel, an American tourist is interested in her, and, despite her initial resistance, she finally succumbs to the seductive beats of American swing (symbolizing decadent, capitalist, American music), the African beat (as a remnant of a "primitive" culture), and alcohol in one of the film's few musical scenes. This is a departure from the norms of the period in that it is the white male character who imposes decadent sexuality rather than himself being seduced by a Cuban black or mulatta woman.

In the scene of the female character's "perversion," the camera situates the viewers within the narrative by filming the action from a first-person point of view, and simulating the dancing and chaotic inebriation through hand-held camera movements. This portrayal continues to depict sexuality (outside of conventional marriage) as dangerous, evil, and African, while transforming Christian and capitalist prejudices into a variant of communist puritanism and Cuban nationalism. The "decadence" that finally destroys the prostitute remains associated with African culture (when she becomes sexually aroused, it is to the beats of AfroCuban music). This is contrasted with the director's portrayal of the second segment's naïve Caucasian/lighter-skinned *mestiza* Cuban female peasant as innocent and pure. She also performs a musical number, but, contrary to the first segment, where the African beat doomed the AfroCuban girl, the peasant music in the second segment is portrayed as something innocent. The difference in portrayal between the peasant and the black Cuban women demonstrates the ways in which the Soviet director shared an apprehensive attitude toward the Cubans' African otherness with other Mexican and Argentinean directors, despite the fact that his is a "socialist gaze."

Initially, Cuban filmmakers attempted to use imperfect cinema techniques to represent authentic Cuban music without exoticizing it. As early as 1964, Rogelio París' documentary feature ¡*Nosotros, la música!* (*We Are the Music*) used a fragmented narrative that integrates the worker audience as part of the performance, and presented the different types of popular Cuban folk music without exoticizing them. Among the film's more interesting aspects is the inclusion of the point of view of the AfroCuban performers that were often exoticized in pre-revolutionary Cuban cinema. Through interviews, they are able to communicate directly with their audience, thus downplaying the AfroCuban exoticism. AfroCaribbean rites (e.g., Santeria) are also shot and presented in a respectful manner.

The first Cuban director who tried to achieve the most "imperfect" Cuban musical was Julio García Espinosa himself (writer of the "For an

4. The Revival of Cuban Musical Coproductions

Imperfect Cinema" manifesto) with his *Son o no son* (1978), a fragmented fictional essay with several musical numbers. This film followed many of the precepts of García Espinosa's imperfect cinema, as performers from the music and film industry deconstructed the genre and created practically a movie essay that educates audiences about musical films while entertaining them. The film has a fragmented plot but is able to sustain its disjointed narrative through remarkable random musical numbers. These numbers are entertaining, yet they are shot with simple techniques that made *Son o no son* an unattractive film, the main goal of which is to inform, and not to serve as an esthetic fetish.[11]

In his discussion of *Son o no son*, film critic Michael Chanan points out several important details about the film. First, the movie was never released in theaters, but due to the director's dissatisfaction with the final product, and not because of censorship. Second, according to Chanan, the film has a cult status because "it thus led a kind of underground existence as García Espinosa showed it to people who visited ICAIC, through which, in fact, it reached its intended audience."[12] Third, Chanan frames it as an essay about mass culture created by García Espinosa and addressed to his fellow practitioners of radical cinema in Latin America, thus defining the film as a narrative that could not be consumed by the masses.[13] I agree with Chanan's assessment of the film, yet *Son o no son* remains a film unlikely to appeal to wide audiences.

In one of the film's segments, a film critic talks about why the musical genre is not respected by revolutionary thinkers. He states that the narrative structure of the musical usually leads to simplistic plots due to its reliance on a few great numbers on the program. The critic also compares Hollywood musicals with their foreign counterparts to establish their similarities (even though he admits American products are always unfairly perceived as superior) and to assert that most of them are part of the repetitive industrialist capitalist machine. This segment also establishes the association of the musical genre with Cuba's decadent past, and a few allusions are made to the prerevolutionary gambling hotels and the American mob. However, the critic also points out that after the Cuban revolution removed these exploitative aspects of capitalism, the genre and the music still remain, and it is time to think about how they can be used to convey important political messages.[14]

Cuban Cinema After the Cold War

With *Son o no son*, García Espinosa recognizes that the musical genre has its narrative flaws and limitations as a political tool, but also acknowledges that it is very entertaining to worker audiences. The film clearly demonstrates that proletarian viewers need the fantasy of these musicals to disconnect from the realities of work, however, the revolutionary filmmaker's goal is to avoid returning to the fantasies of prerevolutionary filmmaking. For the director, these musicals had to include the workers, and be a representation of true popular culture. The film is thus an attempt to provide a view of music as art created by the people, and not as something imposed by the state, even if that state is post–1959 Cuba. The workers, an angry voiceover asserts, will always express themselves through music outside of what the state is willing to produce for them. Bertold Brecht is referenced as inspiration for these thoughts in one of the intertitles, together with a brief black-and-white clip from an old film featuring German workers singing together in a beer saloon.

In 1985, the ICAIC made its first musical employing revolutionary conventions. *Patakin*, directed by Manuel Octavio Gómez, is a full-fledged fictional musical with a revolutionary message and setting. This film stands out with its proletariat setting and its glorification of Yoruba myths, as it remakes the Oshún and Oggún myths into a worker narrative and a love story. The narrative contains several fun musical numbers, specifically the second showstopper song, in which Oggún is introduced as a revolutionary agrarian manager. The number is full of farmers and tractors, and it comes out as amusing communist kitsch. The film is very important for its positive recognition of AfroCuban *santería*, especially because prerevolutionary Cuban musicals had a history of constructing the African other as an exotic and dangerous non–Eurocentric aspect of Cuban society.

Still, *Patakin* displays a series of problems related to the musical genre. The abundance of songs in the film is fun for the audiences, but does not allow sufficient time for character development. The film features some funny jokes against socialist bureaucracy and corruption, and against the misogynistic attitudes of Cuban men, however, this type of criticism was characteristic of ICAIC cinema at the time, and is quite subdued when aimed at the authorities.[15] In addition, since the narrative abounds in vaudeville-type sketches, the characters are simplistic types.

4. The Revival of Cuban Musical Coproductions

The shallowness of the main character Oshún (named after the Yoruba god) is particularly problematic because the actor who plays him is an AfroCuban actor, and the film portrays him as lazy and sexual. Oggún, his antagonist and another Yoruba god, is a responsible white worker.

Although the film makes fun of Oggún for being too reserved, it somehow sets up a problematic black-white binary where Africa represents desire and Europe is civilization. Oggún's companion Elegúa (another Yoruba character) is portrayed by an AfroCuban actor but his portrayal is dangerously close to outdated vaudeville minstrelsy. In other words, this revolutionary musical is still very similar in its depiction of race to the previously criticized prerevolutionary musicals and sometimes contradicts the progressive racial aspects of the narrative by mimicking prerevolutionary racial genre tropes. In her article "Multic-ubanidad," scholar Ariana Hernández-Reguant points out how the Cuban revolution improved the living conditions of Afro Cubans, but by "sweeping some 19th-century racial concepts under the rug," it retained a number of questionable ideas in contemporary Cuban culture.[16] Nevertheless, the ICAIC continued making musicals, and, with the financial help of Spanish institutions, they were able to make *La bella del Alhambra* (*The Beauty of the Alhambra*), one of their best musicals and most critically acclaimed films from the 1980s.

Alhambra is a historical musical directed by Cuban filmmaker Enrique Pineda. It is an adaptation of a historical novel, written by the prestigious Cuban novelist Miguel Barnet. Barnet tells the life story of a fictional cabaret dancer who achieved national fame by performing in the legendary Alhambra theater before the 1959 revolution.[17] The book is carefully researched, and offers a lot of minute detail about the music in Cuba at the time and the venues where it was performed. Barnet cowrote the screenplay adaptation with Pineda, and focused the plot on the turbulent period during the Machado dictatorship to make the staging of the story more manageable. The novel is more complex than the film and features more characters, historical events, and journeys abroad undertaken by the protagonists, but the adaptation achieves a careful balance of dialectics, entertaining musical performances, and old-fashioned melodrama.

One interesting aspect of the female protagonist, Raquel, that the novel explores is the fact that her mulatta stage character is a performance and not necessarily a racial trait. In the novel, it is revealed that her father was German and her mother Hungarian, and she specifically acknowledges that she plays "the role of the mulatta."[18] This is important to point out because, in the international imaginary, prerevolutionary Cuban musical coproductions racialized Cuban performers and inferred that their talents were a biological product of racial miscegenation. Both the novel and the movie adaptation, however, construct Raquel as a white woman who is able to dance because of her hard work and training, and not because of her racial heritage. In addition, she is able to perform AfroCuban and mulatto sketches because of the syncretic ethnic nature of Cuban society, and not because of her specific racial makeup.

The main reason *Alhambra* succeeds over *Patakin*, is because its historical context allows the filmmakers to present more controversial elements of Cuban history such as the Machado dictatorship, while using Pineda's research for the novel to offer an accurate representation of the influence of the Alhambra theater on Cuban narratives and popular culture. *Patakin*'s contemporary revolutionary world is too tame and boring in comparison, and in a way it represents the status quo. *Alhambra* was one of the first Cuban films to render a nostalgic view of the past, providing a dialectic contrast between the decadent pleasure in which the island used to indulge, and the terrible political reality of the 1930s. The homage musical numbers are fun to watch, and the film was successful both abroad and on the island. In Spain, it won the 1988 Goya award for best foreign picture in Spanish, and the film was also submitted for consideration to the 1990 Academy Awards for Best Foreign Film.

During the Special Period, many of the coproductions began to be more sexual, melodramatic, and musical, and less political. It seems foreign audiences were more interested in watching the poverty of the island in that period as well as displays of Cuban sexuality, rather than being lectured about historical materialism. Foreign funding from Western European countries such as France, Spain, Germany, and Italy made sure that these new Cuban musical coproductions depicted a fusion of two different types of Cuban exoticism: racial (AfroCubanism) and ideological (the Cuban revolution.)

4. The Revival of Cuban Musical Coproductions

Paradise Under the Stars: *Coproductions During the Special Period and the Rebirth of the Exploitative Musical*

After the collapse of the Eastern and Central European bloc and the decline of socialism in Latin America and Western Europe in the early 1990s, Cuba was faced with the need to refocus its cinema, now intended for international audiences. European producers invested much-needed capital, which allowed for political films such as Humberto Solás' adaptation of Alejo Carpentier's *El siglo de las luces* (1992), and important projects such as Tomás Gutíerrez Alea's *Strawberry and Chocolate*.[19] Still, critics such as Michael Chanan have observed that many foreign investors were primarily interested in filming exotic locales and attractive Cuban characters that fulfilled stereotypes[20] of what I would call a Caribbean version of the "noble Communist savage." Cuba had not completely disposed of its Africanized, eroticized image that permeated the visual culture of other countries. Its otherness was also amplified by the fact that audiences in the Western Hemisphere were intrigued by Cuba's status as the only communist state in the region. Thus, in the 1990s, when Cuban filmmakers lacked the funding to sustain Cuba's cinema industry, they had to employ a mélange of versions of the other (sexuality, African heritage, and communism) in their projects in order to be funded from abroad. The resulting films again foregrounded sexual encounters between Cubans and foreigners in order to satisfy both left- and right-wing European audiences, and practically marked a return to the schemes of prerevolutionary cinema.

The conflict between the desire to pay homage to the musical past on the one hand, and the precepts of revolutionary culture on the other are emphasized in Gerardo Chijona's musical *Paradise Under the Stars*, a Cuban film that embodies the contradictions of the musical in the Special Period, as filmmakers working in that genre tried to satisfy the demands of foreign investors. When *Paradise Under the Stars* was released in 1998, I was surprised to see that Chijona had directed such a straightforward musical. The plot follows the struggles of a young Cuban woman named Sissy who wants to star in the Tropicana cabaret.[21] She has to avoid the advances of Armando, her AfroCuban boss, and the overprotectiveness of her father Candido, while dating a young man who is her true love. In the end, all the characters discover that they are related, and become a family that represents Cuban hybridity. At first glance, this sounds like the plot of a prerevolutionary film, and one wonders who the main target audience is: a Cuban audience that has seen this plot a dozen times, or a foreign audience that wants to see in its national theaters a vaudevillian performance it could otherwise only see in Cuba.

Paradise Under the Stars is an unusual movie because it feels like a prerevolutionary genre film with its political incorrectness and shallow plot, yet it is also a product of ICAIC filmmaking. As in many Cuban musicals, the melodramatic plot of the film is superficial and features the slapstick comedy that one would have found in the Alhambra theater at the beginning of the 20th century. Sexual innuendo jokes and satires of Cuban machismo abound, and, while entertaining, the film does not exhibit the social depth associated with ICAIC filmmaking. *Paradise Under the Stars* is also problematic in terms of race representation, since it still relies on the two AfroCuban stereotypes that appeared in the previously discussed *Patakin*, namely, the sexual fiend and the minstrel.

There are two types of AfroCuban characters in the film. The first one, represented by Armando (Santiago Alonso), is a sexualized figure. Since the very first scene of the film, Armando dances passionately with Sissy's mother at the Tropicana theater, which eventually causes the divorce of Sissy's parents. Throughout the movie, he is also a sexual threat to Sissy, until the final segment when he is revealed to be her biological father, and finally backs off. His sexual allure is explained by Sissy's Cuban mother, played by Spanish actress Jacqueline Arenal, when she reappears toward the end of the movie, and explains on multiple occasions how good it is to have sex with Blacks when in the Caribbean, a comment I believe is an ironic wink to Spanish audiences, since they hear it from a Spanish actress. The second AfroCuban character type is just a comic relief. It is represented by Promedio, played by comedian José Litico Rodríguez (in practically the same comedic role he had as the protagonist's companion in *Patakin*). Promedio is Sissy's father's companion, who is able to unravel the mystery of the film through comic relief. He suspects that Sissy's boyfriend is really her father's long-lost son, because the two share a huge mole on their buttocks. This particular

4. The Revival of Cuban Musical Coproductions

character functions as a remnant of minstrel theater and provides nothing but physical humor.

Paradise Under the Stars is a funny and entertaining film but a bad musical with a shallow racially problematic narrative. Many of the main actors are from the ICAIC studio troupe and most of them fail in the musical numbers. With the exception of Thaí Valdés, who performs a wonderful dance number during her audition at the Tropicana, most of the actors can barely sing or dance. Enrique Molina plays Sissy's father Candido, a very talented singer whose nickname is the Havana Nightingale. When he sings, everyone appears to be in love with his voice, yet the actor is completely out of tune. This is a musical in which good dramatic Cuban actors try to recreate musical performances but are incapable of executing great numbers, unlike the prerevolutionary films in which the actors were good singers and dancers but failed to give credible dramatic performances. Nevertheless, the main value of the film is that in its superficiality and simplicity, it offers entertainment that avoids the suffocating ideology of Cuban revolutionary projects. In this case, the shallowness of the film could be interpreted as subversive because it avoids the didacticism customarily addressed to Cuban audiences already overwhelmed with the revolution's pervasive dogma.

The simplistic plot of the film is infused with at least some of the revolutionary ideas about race in Cuba. When Sissy is auditioning at the Tropicana at the beginning of the movie, the performance director, Armando, is one of its legendary AfroCuban dancers, and does not represent the aristocratic white Cuban owners emphasized in prerevolutionary films such as *Tropicana* (1957) and *Never Forget Me*. This fulfills the revolutionary idea that the worker is the person in charge, and not the bourgeois. This social change is also reflected in the character of Sissy's father, Candido, who was a famous singer but, because show business destroyed his marriage, has become a proletarian truck driver, and has abandoned his decadent ways. In a way, he represents the revolutionary Cuban society which transformed itself from a musical tourist land to a worker state.

Sissy herself, however, resists attempts to be inscribed into the new social order by insisting on following her dream of becoming a dancer. Despite Candido's warnings about how the music industry is superficial and exploitative of women (obviously ideas embraced and promoted by the Cuban revolution), she continues to follow her dreams, and rejects this paternal authority figure. When at the end of the film it is revealed that Candido is not, after all, Sissy's real father, her desire to be part of the music industry is legitimized, and becomes biologically defined by her newly found racial makeup.

Another interesting aspect of the film is that one of its main plotlines involves incest, as it is discovered that Sissy is her husband Sergito's half-sister. This incestuous storyline is very similar in nature to the plot of the novel *Cecilia Valdés* with which Cuban audiences are well familiar. At the end of the film, Sissy has a baby with Sergito, and everyone is worried it will be a deformed creature. To everyone's surprise, however, the baby is simply a perfectly healthy black girl, a fact which the film points to as something equally terrible. Eventually Sissy's mother reveals that the black dancer Armando was Sissy's biological father, thus eliminating the possibility of incest, but racially linking all the characters.

In terms of race, the narrative is constructed to promote some of the stereotypes one would find in a Tropicana theater vaudeville performance mostly attended by foreign tourists. Critics such as Ariana Hernández-Reguant have expressed concern that *Paradise Under the Stars* is problematic because its characters embody the return of the "voracious mulatta" and "the criminalization of the black man."[22] Sissy's dancing abilities and her desire to work in the music industry, for example, are linked to the fact that she has African blood.[23] This is a very limiting view of performance, and it was already rejected in the character of Raquel in *Alhambra*, where the performer's abilities are linked to talent, hard work, and syncretism, but not to race. However, the embracement of mulatto culture and the linking of performance to race are essential in view of the fact that the film is a coproduction, and it needs to offer a simple message that can be easily digested by foreign audiences who just want a good AfroCuban performance like the ones they used to enjoy before the revolution.

In addition to these problematic racial representations, the film places a lot of emphasis on sexuality, and one could say that the actions of all the characters are linked to sex. There is even a sex scene between the handsome actors Thaí Valdés and Vladimir Cruz, which is obviously

4. The Revival of Cuban Musical Coproductions

choreographed for the enjoyment of the audience. This could be perceived as an effect of the new coproduction phenomenon, since the ICAIC had avoided graphic apolitical sex in its productions, but the representation of erotic sexuality made a comeback with foreign studio coproductions.

A final problematic aspect of the film is the intrusive appearance of Spanish actress Jacqueline Arenal that shows how the financial contribution from Spain has affected Cuban cinema. In her brief appearance, Arenal's character, Sonia (Sissy's mother), is presented as Cuban but it is obvious she is not due to her thick Spanish accent. The characters try to justify her speech patterns by saying that she has lived in Spain for a long time, which could happen, but is somehow hard to believe, especially in view of the fact that she emigrated as an adult. What is particularly interesting is her position of power in the film, with which the Spanish audience can identify. For example, once she shows up, all the Cubans begin asking her for gifts, which situates her in a more financially powerful situation. All the Cuban characters look up to her, and she practically resolves all the plotlines in the film in a very paternalistic manner. Thus, even though she is Cuban in the plot, she behaves like a Spanish citizen.

Some of these problematic coproduction elements in *Paradise Under the Stars*, also appear in Spanish director Benito Zambrano's *Habana Blues*. However, this coproduction was able to modernize certain aspects of the musical genre, and, while still presenting the typical Afro-communist exoticism to international audiences, succeeded in reconstructing the musical by means of some interesting narrative choices.

Habana Blues: *Moving the Musical Beyond the Special Period and Neocolonial Spain*

One of the important contributors to the rebirth of the Cuban musical on the international market was the popularity of the German-American production of Wim Wenders' *Buena Vista Social Club* (1999), a documentary foregrounding a group of older, charming and engaging Cuban musicians. The film was commercially successful for a documentary, with good distribution on several American and European markets. While this project is commendable for reviving the reputation of forgotten Cuban musicians, leading to their wide popularity outside of the island, it remains a victim of paternalistic superficiality in part because of the role of Ry Cooder figured as a benevolent "civilized and foreign" producer.

Several elements of the film suggest it is constructed as a patronizing Cinderella narrative created for a foreign audience, such as the assumption that the music it features is completely Cuban, a debatable premise because the soundtrack also includes songs from Mexico and Puerto Rico (e.g., Rafael Hernández' "Silencio"), of which most Latin American viewers with a basic knowledge of popular songs would be aware. Moreover, contrary to what the film suggests, these songs have not been completely forgotten, as they are still played in various Hispanic countries.[24] While Wenders appears to construct producer Ry Cooder as the benevolent capitalist rescuing the songs from Cuba's isolation, he is merely introducing and repackaging them to a European and American market through an exoticizing Cuban lens. Finally, although Cubans are not sexualized as they were in the 1950s features (the musicians portrayed in the film are elderly Cubans), the documentary nonetheless exploits them as "free spirits."

This kind of representation is evident in a scene where Omara Portuondo sings in the streets, walking like a diva while ordinary passersby watch her. The other singers, Compay Segundo and Ibrahim Ferrer, smoke cigars, talk about women, African magic and other topics that conform to stereotypes of 1950s musical productions. Wenders intercuts the musicians' performance on stage with close-ups of Ry Cooder observing them in a paternalistic manner. Not only is this producer their "savior," but he plays along them on his electric guitar, as if he were a member of their band. It is quite obvious that he is undermining the Cuban performers' music with dissonant sonorities that do not belong to the genres they are playing.[25] He appears to use his economic power to impose his style onto the music, as none of the musicians are seen complaining about the obviously dissonant sounds.

Another problematic scene in the film is when Cooder takes the musicians on a tour to New York City, which the audience appreciates

4. The Revival of Cuban Musical Coproductions

because talented Cubans are finally allowed to leave the island. Yet this leaves the impression of a well-intentioned but sensationalistic "noble savage" strategy, such as the image of Pocahontas being brought to England as a primitive curiosity: the primitive and naïve citizens of a communist state parading through the streets of the powerful nation that opposes it. The success of *Buena Vista Social Club* opened the doors to more European musical coproductions by providing a market that allowed the creation of economically feasible low-budget projects feeding the First-World nostalgia for tropical musical adventures. I believe this helped the revival of the prerevolutionary exploitative films from the 1950s that I discussed earlier. The difference is that Cuba's communist culture is now integrated into the exoticism of its AfroCuban heritage.

Buena Vista Social Club has been the target of very harsh academic criticism. Rufo Caballero, one of the most important Cuban film critics, wrote a scathing article, "La excusa: Semiosis, ideología y montaje en *Buena Vista Social Club*," about the film, in which he practically defines the project as neoliberal racism and attacks Wim Wenders for essentializing Cuban culture for capitalist entertainment. Along Caballero, scholar Román de la Campa criticizes the portrayal of Cooder as a benevolent figure who rescues Cuban music from oblivion, and Tanya Katerí Hernández even sees Cooder portrayed as a "discover conqueror of native resources that have gone unappreciated."[26] The role of the foreign capitalist producer looking for Cuban talent that has existed since before the revolution, became popular again in Cuba during the Special Period, and has been harshly criticized in more recent films such as *Habana Blues*.

Habana Blues, directed by Spaniard Benito Zambrano, is a coproduction between ICAIC, Spanish, and French institutions and partners. An evocation of the Cuban underground music scene rarely treated in official ICAIC productions, which more commonly feature pre–1960s musical numbers,[27] the soundtrack abounds in punk, heavy metal, reggaeton, and other contemporary musical genres with lyrics that deal with the lives of contemporary Cuban youth. This automatically goes against the foreign assumption that the only music produced in Cuba is the old-fashioned tunes (such as son and rumba) featured in Wim Wenders' *Buena Vista Social Club*. It also defies the idea that Cuban music is rooted only in the Hispanic and AfroCaribbean traditions, and features instead a selection of songs that are very influenced by musical traditions from the United States.

In her book, *Cuba Represent: Cuban Arts, State Power, and the Making of New Revolutionary Cultures*, scholar Sujatha Fernandes writes a comprehensive account of the Cuban rap/hip hop scene of the 1990s. She mentions that the Cuban state has realized that it could harness various sectors of these movements as a way of recapturing popular support in the Special Period.[28] This statement is criticized by Cuban music scholar Geoffrey Baker, who states that Fernandes does not provide evidence about the machinations of the Cuban government. Baker does not approve of the vision of the Cuban government as a monolithic body either. He writes: "[the Cuban government] incorporates divergent ideological tendencies, and this lack of uniformity is reflected in its cultural policies, including those relating to rap."[29]

In a different analysis, the article "*Cuba Rebelión*: Underground Music in Havana," Baker studies the rise of underground music in Cuba and how these alternative musicians expressed their discontent in the Special Period with sporadic support from the government. He writes:

> I do not set out to deny the existence or the importance of censorship. It is common knowledge that the Cuban state controls the dissemination of information in various ways [...] What interests me, in my view, merits further discussion is that de jure restrictions are rarely if ever applied to underground musicians and that the vast majority of such musicians do not face the kinds of repression experienced by political activists; in fact they receive a certain amount of support from the state.[30]

Baker specifically wrote this article to counter the dissemination of the documentary *Cuba Rebelión*, which portrays negatively and criticizes the repression and imprisonment of "punk" rebel Gorki Águila (who leads the Cuban punk band Porno para Ricardo) by the Cuban government. This scandal was controversial in Cuban music circles, and it certainly influenced the creation of Zambrano's *Habana Blues*.

Habana Blues is dialogic in nature because it contains Cuban musicians and other characters who are not happy living on the island, and who clash with the ones that support the revolutionary society or simply do not want to emigrate. Other films in the Special Period had reflected

4. The Revival of Cuban Musical Coproductions

this unhappiness (e.g., *Strawberry and Chocolate*), and Spanish director Benito Zamabrano was able to capture it in a passionate manner. Protagonist Tito and his friend's (Ruy's) wife, Caridad, want to leave Cuba; their melodramatic speeches express their intolerance of the island's mediocrity and isolation, in a marked departure from the silent suffering of workers in *Suite Habana*. Zambrano avoids ideological overtones in Tito and Caridad's departure, instead visualizing them as emigrants who love the Cuban nation but are in dire need of better economic opportunities than what the revolution is able to provide, not unlike the proposition of the later films of Gutíerrez Alea and Solás.[31] The film concludes with the musicians' final concert before they are separated forever. Fearing exploitation abroad, Ruy remains in Cuba, an idealistic position unattainable for many Cubans searching for a better life, including Tito and Caridad.

Having studied filmmaking in Cuba, Zambrano is intimately aware of the tensions endemic to Cuban life, as the film makes apparent. Like Diego in *Strawberry and Chocolate,* Ruy and Tito are outsiders to the revolution, although their extravagant lifestyle is subdued, and their excesses limited mainly to Ruy's sexual escapades with a French photographer and a Spanish producer. Although the characters' behavior resembles the sexualized mulatto archetype, Zambrano transcends at times the cultural tourism of the modern Cuban musical by emphasizing Tito and Ruy's ability to function both outside and inside the system. Con artists by day and bohemians by night, they are sympathetic enough to attract audience cheers for their success, despite the fact that the characters do not necessarily share a revolutionary audience's ideological point of view. ICAIC's recent attempts to make Cuban characters more sympathetic to international audiences by portraying them as ordinary people with good values rather than militant communists is a significant manifestation of the industry's efforts to reach a global audience.[32]

Habana Blues is thus at once a commercial and entertaining film in keeping with both Cuban and Spanish nationalist visions that merged in these coproductions. Its representation of the Cuban government is nuanced because some officials support Ruy and Tito's music while others do not. Nonetheless, its rather paternalistic view appears in the portrayal of the Spanish producers as benign figures willing to help financially, and contravening the constrictions of the American embargo by taking the musicians' product to Europe though Spain. The film does not invite opposition to the Spanish producer Marta's sexual escapade with Ruy (a handsome mulatto somewhat less racially threatening as an AfroCuban). Marta is shown scouting different types of Cuban music in a montage sequence, and the eroticism and alcohol she stumbles upon lead to her having sex with Ruy. The way this scene is shot, however, might lead foreign audiences to misinterpret it as a consequence of the island's perceived sexual nature.

The explicit scene between the two characters promotes a reading of Cuban masculine sexual prowess while emphasizing Spanish neoliberal attitudes of the post–Almodóvar era in that it graphically portrays a Spanish woman's orgasm. The scene is thus an attempt to defy Spanish nationalist gender conventions in that it involves a Spanish woman with a mulatto Cuban man (something unthinkable in the 19th and first part of the 20th century). It is, however, also exploitative, since, despite Marta's assurance that she is giving Ruy a contract because of his musical talent, and not because of his sexual performance, the film suggests that Ruy is with her only because he is hoping to get that contract.

When in the dénouement the Cuban musicians are divided over the contract terms, the Spanish characters blame the Miami producers' animosity toward the island for the unfavorable proposal. Although they are partners in crime with the Americans, the Spanish producers do not hesitate to express their displeasure with the contract. In an earlier scene, Marta complains of having to meet "those evil people in Miami." The character thus justifies Spain's neocolonialist attitudes by transferring the responsibility for the neocolonial process to the U.S. Ironically the character that defies both Cuban revolutionary values and Spanish capitalism is a fictional punk musician named Gorki that the Cuban audiences may intertextually associate with the real Gorki Águila who was in prison at the time. The fictional Gorki's adamant refusal to bow to the Cuban revolution or the Spanish producer's tactics, drives a wedge between the protagonists Ruy and Tito that almost destroys their friendship. This leads to the emotional but bizarre climax of the film where

4. The Revival of Cuban Musical Coproductions

Zambrano had to provide a satisfying resolution to both Spanish and Cuban audiences.

The convergence of Cuban communist culture and Spanish neoliberalism in *Habana Blues* is discernible in the portrayal of the black proletarian protagonist and the queer crossdressers who live in Cuba in what appears to be an Almodovarian cinematic corporate device.[33] From a revolutionary perspective, the heroes are aided by an AfroCuban stage manager and a crossdresser who helps Ruy and Tito stage their final concert: the former tells the Cuban musicians his story of how he had been put in charge of the theater by the revolution without prior training. This comment seems ironic, for, although the theater in question is in poor condition, the manager's worker spirit is praised for it allowed him to make the necessary repairs. The crossdressers, who seem very affluent, in turn save the day when they lend money to Ruy and host the concert presentation.

It may seem that after my criticism of Spanish neoliberal fantasies, I am dismissing *Habana Blues*. I actually believe this is one of the best Cuban musicals ever made because it features a new type of musical with alternative characters and music. In addition, it has a compelling plot that humanizes the Cuban characters, and it criticizes the neo-exploitation of the Cuban music industry at the hands of European producers brought by the phenomena of *Buena Vista Social Club*. However, it also has a complex plot that uses adequately the musical numbers to specifically develop the characters. For example, some of the songs sung by Tito and Ruy deal with life in Havana, and the director uses montage sequences to illustrate the hardships of their lives. When Ruy sings the song "Caridad" to his wife just when she is announcing her departure for the United States, the audience feels the pain of the couple's failed marriage. The music in this film is not frivolous, and the final song that Ruy sings in his concert is intercut with images of his friend Tito leaving for Spain, and Ruy's family leaving for Miami. The sequence is edited like a music video which makes it a more poignant way of expressing the message of the movie about how Cuban society is splitting up due to the Cubans' desires for a better life abroad, and how no one is at fault with the exception of the imperial powers in Europe and the United States, and perhaps a revolutionary government that is failing to help and protect its people because of its economic failings and ideological overzealousness. *Habana Blues* remains significant to post–Cold War Cuban cinema, as it was able to reinvent the Cuban musical for the 21st century by mostly overcoming the esthetic, racial, and formalistic limitations of the genre, and by being self-aware of the neocolonial European attitudes and perceptions on the island even if it has to still indulge in certain parts of the film for commercial purposes.

5

Ideology, Realism and Fantasy in Juan Padrón's Animated Franchises *Elpidio Valdés* and *Vampires in Havana* Before and After the Special Period

One of the most pleasant surprises I had while researching Cuban cinema was when I became aware of the rich history of Cuban animation. It is often difficult to sustain a stable animation studio in any country due to the complexities of this type of filmmaking, the necessity of procuring big budgets, and the challenges involved in competing with the highly polished esthetics and elaborate marketing of animated films made and distributed by studios and corporations such as the Walt Disney Company, Dreamworks and others. Avoiding this trend, Cuba's ICAIC animation studios have been active since 1960, and have produced hundred of shorts, as well as long feature films, and even franchises such as Juan Padrón's *Elpidio Valdés* (1974–2003) and *Vampires in Havana* (1985–2003). These two series have been successful with both children and adult audiences, while gaining local and foreign critical acclaim. The popularity of the original features has allowed the Cuban studio to produce several sequels that have even gained international distribution in the United States, Spain, Mexico, and other Hispanic markets.[1]

There are three reasons why it is important to study both of Padrón's animated franchises. First, Padrón has established himself as one of the top Hispanic/Latin American animation auteurs whose authentic style can be recognized by transnational Hispanic audiences. Second, the revolutionary/nationalist ideology embedded in these Cuban animated films is designed to use entertainment as a vehicle to address Cuba's political history and exploitation at the hands of European and American institutions, while using many of the esthetic devices that had been previously used by artists such as Walt Disney to disseminate capitalist propaganda. Lastly, after the Special Period, Padrón uses interesting metaphors in his work that subtly visualize the social changes happening on the island during and after the 1990s.

In order to explain the complex relationship between animation esthetics and Marxist ideology, I will examine certain filmmakers' and critics', such as Sergei Eisenstein, Theodor Adorno, and others, writings on early Disney films. This will demonstrate why groundbreaking animated projects such as Padrón's *Elpidio Valdés* function as culturally significant counter-narratives to Hollywood animation esthetics and ideology. One of my main goals in this analysis is to explore the visual language of animated film (and its openness to multifaceted readings) as not simply a recreation of "reality," but as a signifier that represents the consciousness of a certain culture, as presented in Padrón's second franchise, *Vampires in Havana*. The suggestion offered here is that the spectator's visual pleasure of this kind of animated realism derives at least partially from an audience's recognition of intertextuality and of a given filmmaker's art and its underlying national ideological narratives.

Realism, the Marxist Avant-Garde School and Disney

Viewers tend to take for granted their ability to differentiate between animated and live-action films. While the two are similar as visual mediums, their languages differ in that their respective vocabularies consist of drawings and photos. In *Understanding Animation*, scholar Paul Wells defines animation in the following way:

> To animate, and the related words, animation, animated and animator all derive from the Latin verb, animare, which means "to give life," and within the context of the animated film, this largely means the artificial creation of the illusion of movement in inanimate lines and forms. A working defi-

5. Idealogy, Realism and Fantasy and the Special Period

nition, therefore, of animation in practice, is that it is a film made by hand, frame-by-frame, providing an illusion of movement which has not been directly recorded in the conventional photographic sense.[2]

The most significant part of Wells' definition for the purposes of this chapter is its assertion that animation is not photographic in nature. While both animated and live-action films function by means of the same mechanics (a number of frames are attached together to create movement), the difference between them lies in animation's use of drawings and live-action's use of "real life" photographic images in the frames. This difference is indispensable to understanding how the concept of realism is applied to animation. For, although a large corpus of theoretical works on realism in film does exist, a substantial portion of it is based on live-action filmmaking and its capacity to depict "real life" through photographic images.

André Bazin was among the first film scholars in the first half of the 20th century to emphasize this critical approach, developed in his seminal essay "The Ontology of the Photographic Image," in which he asserts that, prior to the age of photography, the visual arts were based on drawings. Despite claims to realism in the representation of the depicted object, these works of art were infused with the artist's own sensibility, offering a subjectively skewed representation of reality. With the invention of the camera, however, the "true essence" of life was captured, as human mediators between art and reality were no longer needed, thus allowing the audience to perceive objective and not subjective reality.[3]

For Bazin, since live-action films are photo-realistic in nature, they are esthetically superior to other visual arts, as they present a "pure" view of reality rather than a substitute.[4] This argument may have been supported to a certain extent by Aristotle. Although he saw neither photographs nor films, the Greek philosopher believed that audiences needed to identify at some point with the visuality of a narrative in order for mimetic pleasure to be linked to familiarity with the object,[5] with the assumption that the spectator may also enjoy other elements such as style, colors, and social class identification. We can only speculate whether his opinion might have been modified had he witnessed the phenomenon of photography.

Cuban Cinema After the Cold War

I bring Aristotle into the discussion because, while I agree with Bazin's view regarding the power of the photographic image, audiences may, it seems to me, seek mimetic identification or pleasure in different ways. Animation has an important place in our society as it brings an alternative type of enjoyment to the viewer. According to Scott McCloud, a renowned theorist of comics, the language of comic books and animation abounds in icons that visually mimic real life while remaining abstract representations. He considers that, when compared to that of a photograph, the meaning of an object or theme depicted in a drawing is amplified.

> McCloud notes that when we observe a realistic image of a face, we perceive it as the face of another person, but when we see a cartoon face, we identify with it because we are observing the essence of the image, and can perceive ourselves in it. This leads him to conclude that such abstract simplicity is a key factor in children's admiration of cartoons in general.[7]

Debates on the value of the ambiguous nature of drawings as opposed to the alleged realism of photography have occupied cultural studies since the 1920s. As cinema attempted to find its voice in international art communities, German Expressionism was among the early influential movements that challenged ideas regarding photographic realism. German expressionist cinema was the focus of endless Marxist discussions because the artificiality of its mise-en-scène, set construction and extreme imagery endeavored to counter the purity of realism[8] that photography would achieve, a realism championed by Bazin and other film critics of the time. Marxist philosophers tended to scorn German expressionist narratives' desire to withdraw from "reality" in order to maintain the status quo and entertain audiences, believing that this development undermines photography's potential for ideological change.[9]

The employment of fantastic elements, bourgeois melodrama, and artificial sets for the glorification of capitalist industrialization in the worlds created by German studios led Siegfried Kracauer in *From Caligari to Hitler* to link expressionist films such as Fritz Lang's *Metropolis* to Hitler's rise to power. For the purposes of this chapter, I am interested primarily in the ways in which certain intellectuals perceived these

5. Idealogy, Realism and Fantasy and the Special Period

incursions into the fantastic as propaganda and their expressionist devices as "bourgeois," and thus championed a documentary realism as the only locus of subversive esthetics. This viewpoint has led some to ignore animation's potential to defy hegemony, and has limited the scope of their criticism to a condemnation of the Disney Studio's exploitation of other cultures.

Throughout the 20th century, Marxists scholars have linked expressionist films (both animated and live action) with bourgeois esthetics, opening a path to socialist realism such as that produced in the Soviet Union, and to Italian Neorealism. While both types of realist cinema are valued and analyzed in Film Studies, they do not necessarily always engage non-academic audiences. To remedy this disparity, and despite his position as a Marxist critic who disagreed with the goals of German Expressionism, in "Realism in the Balance" György Lukács articulates his belief in realism that is more than a quest for perfect mimetic or "true" documentary representation, theorizing that realism must also be present in the construction of characters and narrative structures.[10]

When in the early 20th century animation was introduced into the realm of cinema through short films from around the world, avant-garde Marxist theorists were fascinated by these shorts' ability to function as visual narratives outside the domain of photographic realism. They admired animated shorts that avoided the tedious frames of photographic realism which could allegedly display "reality," but could also easily be transformed into "bourgeois" realism. In *Hollywood Flatlands: Animation, Critical Theory, and the Avant-Garde*, scholar Esther Leslie traces the thoughts of Sergei Eisenstein, Theodor Adorno, Walter Benjamin, and others who were captivated in particular by Walt Disney's short films and their cultural and esthetic implications for the modern narrative.

From a formalist perspective, Sergei Eisenstein admired Disney's abilities to use sound and images in order to construct ideas that achieved perfection in terms of narrative structure and montage. This was evident in the American animator's 1920s and 1930s cartoon shorts currently known as *The Silly Symphonies*. Marxist scholars might be surprised by Sergei Eisenstein's effusive comments enthusiastically praising Disney's works,[11] in which he finds Disney's esthetics to be dialectic abstractions of reality that liberate audiences from the yoke of photography, reality, and society. In his own words, Disney's works were revolutionary.[12]

Other Marxist critics such as Adorno and Horkheimer did not trust the purposes for which Disney's animation was intended; suspicious of the Donald Duck cartoons that preceded Disney's fairy tale adaptations, they claimed that these animated shorts promoted "complacency with the harsh aspects of life" to the audience.[13] According to Esther Leslie, this marked the beginnings of the split between Disney and the avant-garde Marxist school. The American animator entered the full-length feature market with his fairy tales, and thus conformed to the industrialized narratives that, according to Adorno and Horkheimer, were used to create fascist cultures.[14] In a chapter on the culture industry, Adorno and Horkheimer explore the notion that art has become the product of capitalist corporations. This, they suggest, is a development particular to animated films because of the large staff and budgets they require, thus enforcing the monopoly of the studio infrastructure. Further, the critics associate the culture industry's "simplistic morals" with animation's reliance on fairy tale narratives, suggesting that, no matter how tragic the story, its entertainment value is designed to support the status quo:

> The morality of mass culture is the cheap form of yesterday's children's books. In a first-class production, for example, the villainous character appears as a hysterical woman who (with presumed clinical accuracy) tries to ruin the happiness of her opposite number, who is truer to reality, and herself suffers a quite untheatrical death.
> The masses, demoralized by their life under the pressure of the system, and who show signs of civilization only in modes of behavior which have been forced on them and through which fury and recalcitrance show everywhere, are to be kept in order by the sight of an inexorable life and exemplary behavior. Culture has always played its part in taming revolutionary and barbaric instincts. Industrial culture adds its contribution.[15]

After the success of *Snow White and the Seven Dwarfs* (1937), his first melodramatic fairy tale adaptation, Walt Disney turned to esthetic experimentation with *Fantasia* (1940). This ambitious film does not feature a central melodramatic narrative but instead consists of a series of

5. Ideology, Realism and Fantasy and the Special Period

musical vignettes. Disney had grandiose plans for the project, including presentations in specialized theaters, as well as the incorporation of new shorts in the film on an annual basis. The film's abstraction, however, was not as successful with general audiences as *Snow White* or *Pinocchio*'s well-defined plots, and *Fantasia* was a commercial failure that led Disney to limit future attempts to adaptations of fairy tales.[16] Forced to emulate Hollywood strategies in order to remain financially successful, he "betrayed" the expectations of his contemporary avant-garde and Marxist scholars such as Eisenstein.

Walt Disney would not use avant-garde esthetics again until the "drunken sequence" in *Dumbo* (1941). This film was criticized by Siegfried Kracauer for its protagonist's submission to the system. After his mother is nearly beaten to death by circus employees for defending her son, Dumbo remains in the circus, and is ultimately redeemed, as he proves to be a financial asset thanks to his extraordinarily large ears that allow him to fly.[17] In Esther Leslie's view, "[f]or Kracauer there is a connection between this ideological turn and the move of cartoons away from slapstick and gags to feature-length productions."[18]

Despite the ideological controversies surrounding his work, Walt Disney was consistent in following a rigid financial agenda. He succeeded where German Expressionist films had failed because, by constructing an animated world, he was able to integrate more seamlessly characters with exaggerated backgrounds. The genre of fairy tales suited his global commercial goals as the incongruities of the fantastic seem at home in the abstract iconography of animation. Moreover, fairy tales evoke psychological elements that allow for a certain universality, which may explain why many cultures have their own version of the Cinderella story but still accept Disney's corporate version. Through this kind of abstraction of reality, a trait particular to animation, and the manipulation of the emotional layer that underlies fairy tales, Walt Disney discovered the formula for success by creating films with which international audiences could identify without surrendering their own national identity.

Disney encouraged audiences to care about his cartoons by giving them a sense of reality inside the "fantastic nature" of animation as an art form. In other words, because the cartoon characters were not human beings, Disney tried to endow them with human characteristics, and hence melodramatic elements by means of realistic gestures and actions that, to a certain point, mimicked those of Hollywood actors of the era. For his first full-length animated feature, he insisted that his artists observe live-action actors and replicate their movements, which goes far toward accounting for why *Snow White and the Seven Dwarfs* became a groundbreaking event from an esthetic perspective. The film was an expressionist fantasy that moved the audience to tears, despite the fact that not a single photographic image was used in the entire film. To this day, the Walt Disney Company continues to use realistic human motion in order to create an illusion of animated realism. Replicating reality in animation through melodramatic fantasies thus took priority over avant-garde exploration.

Walt Disney is an acknowledged master of the melodramatic genre within animation: while Disney's audiences may not be aware of the difference between animated and photographic mimesis, they are likely to be emotionally seduced by the compelling narrative, which compensates for the absence of photographic images. These melodramatic elements may be more powerful in animation because their sentimental effect is amplified by the expressionist nature of cartoons. While Disney's esthetic achievement and success lie in embedding this type of content within basic principles of mimetic representation, the studio's politics and the nature of its representation are problematic.

Walt Disney and his corporate empire have been the object of criticism for assimilating stories from around the world[19] and repackaging them into a corporate product oriented to propagating American bourgeois values. Although this may be a common Hollywood tactic, Disney animation has arguably applied it more effectively: unlike live-action films, its drawings are not determined by the temporal or precise cultural definitions that may hinder photography. In his influential article, "The Work of Art in the Age of Mechanical Reproduction," Walter Benjamin defines the difference between painted art and live-action film, emphasizing the painter's ability to withdraw from reality. Thus, if animation can only simulate the physical world, Disney nonetheless retains the power to shape its representational world. After Walt Disney's death, the Disney Corporation's hyper-universe became yoked to corporate

5. Idealogy, Realism and Fantasy and the Special Period

reality. Parents buy Disney products that range from bed sheets to films and videogames, while children internalize the company's version of sanitized amusement fun, fantasy, and middle-class values. The mass production of American values embedded in these Disney corporate products provides a homogenous world that assimilates and reshapes other cultures in its own image, making Disney films the critical target of cultural studies scholars.

When Chilean scholar Ariel Dorfman published his book *Como leer el pato Donald* (*How to Read Donald Duck*) in 1972, he adapted this previous criticism that had been targeted toward Walt Disney and his Disney company since World War II to a Latin American context. In this long critical essay, he tries to explain to a South American audience how some corporate Disney products, such as Donald Duck comics, hide a fervent imperialist and exploitative capitalist ideology where the heroic anthropomorphic animals, led by the iconic Donald Duck, constantly have adventures where they trick Third-World communities in order to steal their resources. He explains this idea in the third chapter of the book and links it to the imperialist discourse that has been implanted in the Americas since colonial times.

Dorfman specifically abhors the infantilized idiotic depiction of the "natives" and the ways in which a lot of the suffering caused by imperialism is whitewashed by means of the clean and proper Disney esthetic. This Dorfman manifesto has some outdated aspects, e.g., the author's failure to analyze the creative significance of the prominent auteurs of some of these comics (such as Carl Barks and Don Rosa), because he sees their work as simply the product of a soulless corporate machine. Still, his writing was important at the time to remind Latin American audiences about the danger of letting children see the world through the subtle capitalist dogma embedded in Disney's version of culture industry. Dorfman's native Chile could not sustain its socialist government due to the coup that installed Augusto Pinochet as a dictator, but Cuba has been able to maintain a revolutionary state for many decades and its artists have been able to create comics and animation that locally defy the control that American hegemonic entities such as the Walt Disney Company have had over the international market.

The history of Cuban animation is marked by the establishment of the ICAIC animation studio, and by Juan Padrón, who became the face of the Cuban animation industry. Padrón's revolutionary narratives differ ideologically from Walt Disney's works, but his *Elpidio Valdés* character, while defying imperialist hegemony, can still serve as both a problematic didactic tool and a progressive alternative to capitalist entertainment.

Animated Realism and Its Political Use: Juan Padrón's Elpidio Valdés

In his article "Juan Padrón et l'animation," Cuban scholar Roberto Cobas provides a very comprehensive history of Cuban animation that can be traced all the way back to 1937. Among the most interesting tidbits of information he provides is the fact that many of the original ICAIC animators used to work (before the 1959 Revolution) in private companies that provided animated content for commercials, the fact that Jesús de Armas was the founder and head of the ICAIC animation department in the sixties, and that some of the ICAIC's first cartoons were heavily influenced by American institutions such as the Hanna Barbera studio, and the irreverent and anarchic humor of *Mad Magazine*.[20] The article mentions specific examples, such as the short "El Cow-Boy," in which revolutionary ideology is expressed through the mockery of American characters and the Western genre. Cobas specifically mentions that in the mid-sixties, the ICAIC's animators began to be heavily influenced by European cartoons (from both sides of the Iron Curtain) and suddenly began to produce bleaker material that reflected certain nihilistic ideas from the sixties such as the atomic bomb.[21] Cuban scholar Azucena Plasencia confirms that most of the Cuban animated works of the 1960s were targeted to adult audiences, and that they were heavily influenced by Czech artists such as Karel Zeman, Jiri Trnka, and Zsevenk Miller, and Polish filmmakers who used surrealist techniques in their animation.[22] These new influences helped to produce interesting revolutionary material, however, Plasencia notes that in the early 1970s, content was prioritized over form, the ICAIC's animation decayed, and the animators lost the interest of Cuban audiences.[23] It was when cartoonist/filmmaker Juan Padrón entered the scene in 1972, that ICAIC animation began to

5. Idealogy, Realism and Fantasy and the Special Period

achieve new heights of popularity with the nation's young audiences and set up a formula that would later achieve international success.

Juan Padrón was a cartoonist who in the 1960s used to do work for the Cuban national army where he was enlisted. He used to draw short comic strips for the children's magazine *Pionero*, where he began to publish his comic book serial *Elpidio Valdés*. He was not too interested in joining the ICAIC because he liked to create adventures, and did not find much appeal in the experimental filmmaking that was being produced by the Cuban studio at the time.[24] In the documentary *Hasta la próxima aventura* (*Until the Next Adventure*, 2013) he mentions how he was raised before the 1959 Cuban Revolution with American comics and animation, and how he could draw anything related to the United States, but could not visualize what the Cubans and Spanish looked like in the 19th century because the visual material was not available or disseminated in Cuban popular culture. He decided to use all the available historical material to create the character of Elpidio Valdés, and present Cuban kids not only with a local hero with whom they could identify, but also with an opportunity to learn more about their national history. He finally arrived to the ICAIC, and created two Elpidio shorts, *Una aventura de Elpidio Valdés* and *Elpidio Valdés ataca el puente*, that were released in 1974, and became instantly popular among Cuban children. Scholar Roberto Cobas describes the shorts as historical and political narratives, in which Elpidio's character was portrayed as a comedic prankster because it was heavily influenced by American cartoons. In 1975, Padrón turned a corner with his Elpidio short *El machete* that featured a more serious story and achieved dramatic depth while also becoming more didactic.[25] By the end of the franchise in 2003, Padrón had created over a dozen Elpidio shorts and three feature-length films, *Elpidio Valdés* (1978), *Elpidio Valdés contra dólar y cañón* (1983), and *Elpidio Valdés contra el águila y el león* (1995) which was later edited as the longer television series *Más se perdió en Cuba*.

In a relatively recent interview with Cuban critic filmmaker Arturo Sotto, Padrón candidly revealed that his rise in the ICAIC animation department was not an easy process, and that his work was not immediately embraced by the older animators who saw him as an outsider. At present, however, Padrón has become a Cuban institution, since he has achieved national and international fame with his *Elpidio* and *Vampires* series, and he has been awarded prestigious prizes such as the Havana Film Festival's Coral Award and the ICAIC's national film award in 2008. However, he maintains that the Cuban studio has never been too interested in animation, and that they never provided him with the best materials (paper, pencils, colors etc.) he needed for his work. He also states that before his two animated series gained popularity, they received a lukewarm reception from ICAIC executives. The Institute disapproved even of the first two 1974 Elpidio shorts because they contained too much of the slapstick found in cartoons such as *Mighty Mouse* (Sotto 152). The ICAIC halted the production of the *Elpidio* shorts, and only resumed their production once they were embraced by Cuban children.

Padrón went on to create more "didactic" material in the form of educational shorts. His shift from sheer entertainment to a more didactic approach is evident in the *Elpidio* shorts and films that he created subsequently. Still, although it promoted a Cuban nationalist ideology, the *Elpidio* franchise is entertaining because it portrays the rebels as characters who bring about anarchic disorder against the Spanish colonial authorities, much in the way that successful American animated characters such as Bugs Bunny did against grumpy Caucasian characters such as Elmer and Sam. The first long feature film of the franchise, *Elpidio Valdés*, was released in 1978, and it sold over one million tickets. The Cuban public embraced the entertaining and action-packed didactic historical narrative, which became one of the biggest triumphs achieved by the ICAIC.

The *Elpidio* shorts and films are significant for a number of reasons. They construct Cuban nationalism from a post-colonialist perspective, as they trace the seeds of the 1959 revolution back to the struggle for independence in 1898. This development differs substantially from the portrayal in animated features of exclusively aristocratic characters, a trend established as a result of Disney's hegemony on the international market. Padrón subverts ideologically the Disney fairy tale narrative style by means of a Marxist historiographic depiction, as many of his protagonists are peasants, and not royalty. However, the franchise offers a pluralist vision of Cuban revolutionaries that includes Cuban nationals from the elite, and peasants, who work with members of other races,

5. Idealogy, Realism and Fantasy and the Special Period

countries, and social classes to oppose exploitation. The enemies are imperial Spain and the capitalist United States (not its citizens), and Padrón inverts/parodies some of the Disney stereotypes that scholar Ariel Dorfman had pointed out before: his oppressed heroes are smart and cunning, while the imperial characters are flawed and idiotic. In the documentary *Hasta la próxima aventura*, Padrón points out that some Spanish audiences have complained about how the Spanish characters are portrayed in his narratives, to which his response was: "better clumsy idiots than genocidal villains."

In addition to offering a different view of colonialism, Padrón's Elpidio films also diverge from Disney in their featuring of specific national markers. The first segment of the first film is a blend of an homage to Disney and the live-action Cuban historical epics produced by the ICAIC. The animated depictions of the forest in the opening of the film are expressionistic in nature; a passing storm serves as a symbol of the tumultuous times of the war of Cuban Independence. Immediately, the audience is introduced to Captain Valdés from the rebel army, who has returned from a mission to meet his newborn son (also named Elpidio), and to embrace his wife who is singing a song to the baby. This peasant lullaby functions like the musical numbers in Disney films, but its countryside origin offers a twist on the theatrical Broadway-type performances usually associated with American animation. The idyllic family reunion is interrupted by the attack of the Cuban counter-guerrillas who support Spanish colonialism. The leader of the antagonists, a "traitor" nicknamed Media Cara (half-face) because his hair covers half his face, has gold teeth (perhaps a symbol of capitalist greed), and is drawn to be ugly and distorted, like a Disney villain.

The subsequent scene could be interpreted as a musical performance because, moving in synchronization with the sounds of the score, Elpidio Senior kills several of the counter-guerrillas with his machete. The depiction of the violence in the scene is bloodless and softened by the comical style of Padrón's drawings, but its rapid pacing serves as a counterpoint to the next scene in which the family are shown hidden in the forest where they are comfortable with the tropical surroundings, a nationalist vision of attachment to the land. The local fauna play with the child Elpidio, and even bring him food, as if he were the prince of the land. This is an approach similar to the one employed in Disney's *Bambi* and most recently in *The Lion King*, in which the baby deer and lion respectively are visited and admired by the other animals. Padrón undoubtedly appropriates the Disney model of pleasure and bourgeois melodrama but infuses it with a revolutionary and nationalist ideology. Throughout this film franchise, young Elpidio becomes a captain of the armies fighting for Cuba's independence from Spain, thus continuing the legacy of his parents.

In his depiction of Elpidio, Padrón rebels against Eurocentrism by making the character speak in a peasant slang which is not easily comprehensible to foreigners (including native speakers of Spanish). In addition, many of the jokes in the film rely on a thorough understanding of Caribbean colonial culture and its history to the extent of excluding those unfamiliar with the region. However, while this approach is successful with Caribbean and specifically Cuban audiences, it could sometimes be difficult for international audiences because of its complex cultural and historical references. In contrast, even though Disney studio films can afford to make references to U.S. popular culture because of its worldwide pervasiveness,[26] they avoid specific historical references that would bind their narratives to an exclusively American reality. In other words, with the exception of films such as *Pocahontas*, Disney studios usually avoid direct nationalist references in their quest to appeal to a global audience. The American-ness of their product is embedded in their narratives' message, and this message excludes history, a concept crucial to Marxist ideology which cannot be ignored in revolutionary Cuban animation.

The *Elpidio* franchise's nationalist ideology may even distance the mainstream audience (including both children and adults) from other Caribbean cultures, such as Puerto Rico, a neighboring island whose population would otherwise not have difficulty understanding the film because of a shared history and familiarity with Cuba's language and humor. In the second film, *Elpidio Valdés contra dólar y cañón* (*Elpidio Valdés vs. Dollars and Cannons,* 1982) a Puerto Rican sea captain helps the Cuban rebels because he dreams of Puerto Rico's independence from Spain. In the end, he heroically sacrifices his life as he leads his ship to crash Kamikaze-style against an antagonist American Navy battleship

5. Idealogy, Realism and Fantasy and the Special Period

aptly named The Imperial Eagle. The scene promoting Puerto Rican nationalism would probably be applauded by the relatively small Puerto Rican nationalist groups, in whose reality the captain's hatred of American imperialism would be seen as 'the truth' and therefore realistic. Yet, for many other Puerto Ricans, who are familiar with American colonialism, scenes in which the Cubans portray them as consumed by nationalist hatred that ends in violence against the empire are likely to be perceived as Cuban revolutionary fantasies of Puerto Rico's culture.

Elpidio Valdés is a fascinating character because, from a Cuban Revolutionary perspective, he becomes what Adorno and Horkheimer despised in Donald Duck cartoons, a teaching tool for ideological conformity, even though he represents the revolutionary forces against imperialism. As ICAIC's platform for the promotion of revolutionary ideas, the character maintains that all is well in Cuba, because the 1959 revolution supposedly achieved total independence from foreign powers as well as class equality, the two goals that Elpidio had been pursuing at the end of the 19th century. Portraying Cuban reality in this manner is particularly problematic in the context of the Special Period when audiences suffering from poverty and shortages were bombarded with nationalistic discourse and reassurances that the 1959 revolution was successful.

In the 1990s, Spanish cultural institutions and private businesses began investing heavily in Cuba, also influencing the Elpidio films made at the time. Thus, the *Elpidio* television miniseries *Más se perdió en Cuba* (1996) offers a revised view of Cuban history that includes more sympathy for Spanish characters, a questionable approach considering that the project was financed by Spanish Television. The series and the film on which it is based link 19th century Cuban nationalism to the later revolutions in the 20th century by refocusing the antagonism to the American villains instead of the Spanish colonial army. In this animated television miniseries, which is an extended version of the third film *Elpidio Valdés contra el águila y el león* (*Elpidio Valdés vs. The Eagle and the Lion*, 1995), the Spanish army is seen as more benevolent than the American army led by Theodor Roosevelt. Padrón portrays the Spanish as more amicable and receptive than the Americans (who are racist), thus softening his stance against the Spanish colonial army.

This revitalization of the island's Hispanic heritage is constructed through the character of a Spanish soldier who marries a Cuban, and remains in Cuba after the Spanish army leaves the island in 1898. In the last ten minutes of the last episode, the action moves to 1933, when the now older Elpidio and his Spanish counterpart exact vengeance (thus redeeming Spanish nationalism as well) upon the old American sugarcane plantation owner, who has been their antagonist throughout the series. Their murder of the American is crosscut with scenes portraying Elpidio Junior's involvement in the political struggles of this turbulent historical period. Through the link of the different Valdés family generations, Padrón establishes a connection between the War of Independence at the end of the 19th century to the events in the 1930s which culminated in the 1959 revolution that eventually brought about the revolutionary government still currently in power. This connection is reflected in Elpidio's final words, "We will triumph one day." The link between the three revolts and the different Cuban generations make Cuban children aware of their own roles as revolutionaries, since they will inherit the revolutionary struggle from their ancestors, as did Elpidio.

The most problematic evidence of the use of the character of Elpidio for this purpose was when the Cuban journal *Cine Cubano* (no. 147) published a letter allegedly written by Elpidio himself to Elián González, a Cuban child who was then the epicenter of an ideological and legal battle between Cuba and the U.S. Elián's mother had taken him to the U.S. but died en route. The ensuing legal battle for custody over Elián, between the child's Cuban father and his relatives in Florida, achieved international notoriety when it transformed into an ideological dispute between the United States and Cuba. Elpidio's letter, written by ICAIC's animators from a 19th-century perspective, assures Elián that the other Mambí (historical Cuban rebels against Spanish colonialism) discuss his suffering daily, and are eager to crush with their horses those who have dressed him like a bat and wrapped him in an American flag (a reference to Elián's trip to Disneyworld where he wore a Mickey Mouse hat). Elpidio asserts that the rebels will wage war on and defy the people who are taking Elián away from his homeland.[27]

The message abounds in nationalist rhetoric, as Elpidio practically

5. Ideology, Realism and Fantasy and the Special Period

states that Cuban children should be with their Cuban families, and that they should fear their assimilation into American culture. His discourse references revolutionary violence which will offer protection and allow Cuban children to "feel safe" under the armed forces of the Cuban government. They may not have access to the commodities and resources that Elián's Cuban American family was publicizing (e.g., the child's visits to Disneyworld), but they have the comfort of being among other Cubans, and of sharing a legacy that dates back to the 19th century. In this case nationalism was used in an attempt to limit Cuban children to Cuba's reality, and to encourage them not to aspire to anything outside the national boundaries. This stance is in direct conflict with ICAIC's 1990s and 2000s cinematic live-action productions (such as *Alice in Wondertown, Strawberry and Chocolate, Habana Blues*, and others), one of the main criticisms of which targets the existing outdated conformity with Cuban revolutionary culture.

One example of how Elpidio Valdés can be interpreted as an ideologically charged character can be found in a sketch from an American television show hosted by Cuban exile Carlos Otero.[28] In this comedic segment, an actor dressed as Elpidio Valdés mocks the Cubans that visit the United States as cultural ambassadors, by presenting Elpidio as a loser who has lost everything, and whose wife has become a prostitute and married a Spanish citizen. What is interesting about this segment, is how the writers assume that the exiled Cuban audience knows all the Elpidio references, and how they bitterly desecrate this icon of the Cuban revolution. One of the most interesting parts of the segment is the inclusion of a fake trailer for an upcoming film that shows how Elpidio will escape Cuba. The footage from the animated films is dubbed, and its discourse changed by means of added lines which express the character's criticism of the Cuban revolution and his desire to leave the island. From the point of view of the Cuban exiles, this would be a more ideologically accurate version of the character.

My analysis of *Elpidio Valdés* demonstrated the ways in which Cuban revolutionary ideology limits the abstract nature of animation in order to create a product to teach audiences how to defy imperialist hegemony, but also to manipulate children audiences to conform to revolutionary ideology. Thus, Juan Padrón's estheticization of historical reality functions in a way similar to the Disney films criticized in Marxist and Cultural studies. Disney's films achieved worldwide recognition due to three factors, their magnificent esthetic execution, their adherence to a triumphant capitalist ideology, and their employment of U.S. popular culture references that are universally understood because of American cultural hegemony. On the other hand, the *Elpidio* franchise attempts to counter the imperial ideological discourse criticized by Marxist thinkers since the late 19th century, by providing a carefully researched historical and national approach that attempts to disrupt the "fairy tale" devices used by capitalist narratives to hide imperial agendas. However, once the character of Elpidio Valdés becomes an icon representing Cuban revolutionary ideology, it also becomes a tool for implementing political discourse in the minds of Cuban kids. In the following segment, I will discuss Padrón's *Vampires in Havana* franchise, another didactic and fun series that, through the use of intertextual genres, is able to function as a dogmatic tool while presenting a more ironic version of Cuban historicism than what the filmmaker presented in his Elpidio series.

More Vampires in Havana *as a Satire of Official Historical Discourse*

Juan Padrón's *Vampiros en la Habana* (*Vampires in Havana*) franchise is an animated film series beloved in Cuba[29] that also has a cult following outside the island. The films are made using the eclectic style developed by Padrón in his previous *Elpidio Valdés* franchise, in which he successfully mixed slapstick entertainment with nationalistic dogmatic messages, and some interesting animated depictions of Cuban history and the War of Independence against Spain. The *Vampire* series differs from the *Elpidio* movies, since it targets an older demographic and, in addition, satirizes and indulges in more archaic cinematic genres, such as horror and gangster narratives, that were used less frequently in Cuban revolutionary cinema. Padrón claims, however, that the only aspects criticized by the studio before *Vampires in Havana* was officially released were the adult tone (with a lot of depictions of sex) of the film, and the fact that it used too much Cuban slang.[30] When the film was about to be released, the ICAIC asked for two separate versions: the original, and a more subdued version for Cuban audiences. Padrón had an argument with the executives, and he suspects this is the reason why the film never had a premiere or a press conference presentation.[31]

Vampires in Havana exhibits features typical of Padrón's filmmaking style, mixing slapstick entertainment with dogmatic messages and some historical elements. The film is popular with certain international audiences in Spain and Latin America because, although it is focused exclusively on Cuba and its revolutionary history, its vampire theme makes it more accessible, providing something international audiences understand regardless of the film's Marxist and nationalist context. *Vampires in Havana* takes place during the Cuban revolution against the Machado dictatorship that was in power in the 1930s. Pepito is a European immigrant (formerly Joseph Amadeus) who has forgotten his vampire heritage because his vampire uncle, son of the legendary count Dracula, gave him a potion that allows him to go outside, even in direct sunlight. When the vampires from Europe and the U.S. find out about the potion, they come to Cuba to obtain it for their own economic ends.

Naturally, Pepito's uncle does not wish to participate in the exploitation of his fellow vampires, preferring to share the potions with all the vampires of the world (a revolutionary Marxist concept). Pepito finally succeeds in fulfilling his uncle's utopian goals, while bringing down the tyranny of Machado. He is an anarchic free spirit throughout the film, defying his vampire heritage, the Cuban government, and even his own rebel allies; in the end he conforms to the 1930s Cuban revolution and the establishment of a new government, both of which mark the end of his sexual and violent needs. Conformity is re-established as his vampire talents are concealed so that he can mix with the crowd and remain a Cuban national among his friends.

The vampire myth[32] works well for class ideology narratives such as *Vampires in Havana* because of the original *Dracula* novel by Bram Stoker. The novel was published in 1898, and focused on the heroics of the British middle class against the fading aristocracy. Dracula represents the "bloody" aristocrats from Eastern Europe who are defeated by the wits, science, and Christian morality of the English clerk Jonathan Harker, his middle-class wife Mina Murray, and the Dutch scholar Abraham Van Helsing. Other Westerners such as American Quincy Morris and British aristocrats Lucy Westenra and Arthur Holmwood are ineffective against the orientalized monster who preys on British society. Only a mixture of rational science, adherence to Christianity, and middle-class morality allow Harker, Murray, and Van Helsing to survive the experience and defend British nationalism while inserting metaphorically their colonial presence in the East by liberating Eastern Europeans through the destruction of Dracula, a monstrous feudal lord. Padrón twists Stoker's original ideology by transforming his vampires from orientalist non–Western others into nationalist bourgeois characters (obsessed with their economic national hegemonies) whose monstrosity lies in their efforts to re-conquer Cuba, but whose plans are foiled by revolutionary Cubans. The film provides the Cuban audience with a horror fantasy, the main transgressive aspect of which is its depiction of capitalist hegemonies as the monstrous other.

Contrary to the *Elpidio Valdés* films' attempt to mimic certain aspects of live-action historical films from ICAIC, *Vampires in Havana*'s visual and narrative language mirrors the musical comedies made before the revolution that were later revived and promoted in the 1990s through Spanish-Cuban coproductions. Pepito, the film's protagonist, is a picaresque character who plays exotic Latin music (like the stereotypes of the time) but also fulfills communist standards by being a revolutionary conspiring against a Cuban capitalist dictatorship. Animation's expressionistic qualities thus allowed Padrón to merge pre- and post-revolutionary narratives in *Vampires in Havana*.[33] The film is also distinctly intertextual, as it replicates genres such as vampire and gangster films. This gives the film an edge over the *Elpidio* franchise because of the deconstruction of the narrative in which Cuban cinematic styles from different ideological times clash to produce a more complex representation of Cuban reality.

A comparison of *Vampires in Havana* with the first *Elpidio* film produces a notable difference in the construction of Cuban nationalism. *Miradas*, the online Cuban cinema journal edited by filmmaker and critic José Luis García Espinosa, recently published an article by Dean Luis Reyes, which outlines the disparities between the two franchises. Reyes states that Pepito's nationalism is not constructed by birth and

5. Ideology, Realism and Fantasy and the Special Period

connection to the land, an element clearly present in Elpidio's case. Pepito is an immigrant who assimilates into the culture and forgoes his evil European vampire heritage to finally become "native" and produce a new Cuban generation. Moreover, unlike the glorification of the revolutionary assistance of peasants and AfroCubans in the *Elpidio* films, the idea of ethnic and underprivileged groups being key to destroying the foreign forces is mocked in *Vampires*, according to Reyes, through scenes in which drunks and AfroCubans help the revolution against Machado not through their nobility but by coincidences linked to their mediocrity. Interestingly, Padrón uses a number of demeaning stereotypes dating from before the revolution in order to represent the oppressed while empowering them by making them important in the struggle against the imperialist vampires, and at the same time parodying the seriousness of communist propaganda. This clash of cultural signs, minstrelsy, and intentions works well in the juxtaposition of images, colors, and sounds that is unique to the genre of animation.[34]

Padrón knows his film is not supposed to represent reality but rather to mimic it. An important self-reflexive moment occurs when the European vampires follow Pepito and his girlfriend to a cinema. The animated audiences are mystified and frightened by a live-action vampire film ironically inverting the live-audience's experience when watching cartoons. The vampires cheer for their live-action counterparts and boo when a priest in the film interrupts the drinking of blood. Their link to the screen was the Dracula-like character who mimicked their actions and intentions despite the fact that he was photographed and not drawn. This scene is Padrón's attempt to invite the audience to realize that it is watching an abstract representation of reality, a brilliant ploy that indicates that animated reality is related to certain signifiers with which audiences identify, including physical appearance (being a European vampire) and philosophical concepts (women had to be seduced and drained of their blood).

After the Special Period, Padrón's sequel, *More Vampires in Havana*, was eagerly awaited by fans of the original film. Completed and released in 2001, 15 years after the first film had become an icon of Cuban popular culture that was quoted in live-action Cuban films, the sequel sports more advanced animated techniques due to the implementation of computer effects, and a higher budget that was sponsored by several European institutions, mostly from Spain. The most significant difference is that this is the first Padrón film to reflect clearly the cultural changes brought by the end of Eastern European socialism. An analysis of *More Vampires in Havana* will demonstrate how these historical events changed the way in which Padrón originally approached the story and how the film creates a third space for Cuban nationalism and class ideology.

The first few minutes of the sequel retell the plot of the original *Vampires in Havana* in the broken Spanish voiceover of legendary American writer, Ernest Hemingway. This is the first reference to Cuban popular culture, as this literary figure has been an icon of the revolution, even if he was also parodied for his colonial attitudes in Tomás Gutiérrez Alea's *Memories of Underdevelopment*. The involvement of Hemingway in the narration is doubly ironic because at this point the Cuban revolution uses his past association with the island to sell *mojitos* to the tourists in what was his favorite bar, "La bodeguita del medio." It is also amusing to observe how Padrón involves him in a ludicrous story of Cubans and communists fighting vampires during World War II.

While the first *Vampires in Havana* film was a metaphor for revolutionary Marxist ideals, it did not make direct references to this ideology. After the introduction by Hemingway, the sequel follows an attack of a Nazi compound at the hands of Soviet soldiers. Vanya, a Czech communist officer, leads the attack which is visually represented as a parody of World War II Soviet films. When the military offensive begins, a Soviet soldier plays famous Soviet anthem "Sacred War" (Svyashchennaya Voyna) on a phonograph, and the action is scored to these diegetic sounds. When one of the brave men is shot by Nazi fire, he poses patriotically for the camera for a moment, then says "I am kidding," and continues to march. In the first film, the pre-revolutionary cultural past and its narratives were rescued by constructing a story that paid homage to fondly remembered Cuban narratives that did not fit the revolution's ideological climate. The post–Soviet era sequel incorporates the communist popular culture from the past that, while outdated today, remains an important part of Cuba's heritage.

After discovering that the German army was mutating Nazi soldiers

5. Ideology, Realism and Fantasy and the Special Period

into monsters with Pepito's anti-solar formula for vampires (*vampisol*), Vanya brings the news to Moscow and his boss, Joseph Stalin. The Soviet dictator is portrayed as an affable old man who sends the Czech soldier as a spy in Cuba after explaining to him that Pepito's *vampisol* comes from this tropical paradise controlled by the American mafia, one of the epicenters of the evils of capitalism. This scene's ironic tone offers an outdated representation of Stalin in communist terms, as the Soviet leader had already been condemned in socialist states since the 1950s arrival of the new Soviet regime under Nikita Krushchev. Yet Stalin's violent legacy is ignored here, much in the same way that it might have been in World War II Soviet films from the 1950s.

The story shifts to Cuba where Pepe (formerly Pepito) is part of the Cuban middle class and owns a dance club where he plays along with his orchestra. The struggle against Machado ended in the first film, but the struggle against president Batista has already begun. Pepe's AfroCuban friend from the prequel is still part of the struggle alongside a new Chinese character who wants to expose Batista's aid to capitalist and fascist forces. Pepito saves both from the police by hiding them, indicating that, even though he is doing well financially, he is still committed to the revolution. The AfroCuban and Chinese characters are constructed as politically incorrect (for American standards) "blackface" stereotypes, so outdated that one may justify their use as ironic. They belong to the blackface and oriental performing tradition of the 1940s (the black character is sexualized and violent, while the Chinese does not discriminate between "l" and "r" sounds). Still, since this film uses animation to capture Cuban popular culture, it cannot completely eradicate the characters present in pre-revolutionary live-action Cuban cinema, which would require ignoring an aspect of the island's heritage, however offensive it may be. A similar debate exists in American cultural studies in which academics argue whether these stereotypes should be remembered, if only in ironic, post-modern fashion.

The problematic representations used to reconstruct the narrative of the 1940s and World War II communist culture are supported by a melodramatic device concerning generational differences between Pepe and his son, Pepín. Pepe has abandoned his vampire ways, and has been assimilated into Cuban culture and nationalism. His son, however, has been in contact with his deceased vampire uncle's spirit, and wants to be a vampire because it is a legacy that will make him more interesting than other Cuban children. Pepe tries to convince his son that vampire ways are evil; his arguments are based on the fact that Pepin should enjoy Cuban life, which includes playing music and baseball, and going out in the sun. He cries as he explains this to his son, who in turn replies that he will not be a vampire and that he has even made a stronger *vampisol* mixed with guava, called *vampiyaba*. This scene could be interpreted as a metaphoric representation of the way in which the current generation of Cuban children and youth is attracted to seductive but dangerous ideas of capitalism. This is important for the development of the relationship between Pepin and his deceased vampire uncle Amadeus' spirit, which Padrón tries to portray in a fair manner that, in the end, provides a representation that transcends ideology.

Pepín ultimately understands his father's point of view, as the sequel provides him with an adventure in which he experiences personally his father's fear of capitalism, vampires, and the First World. This suggests that the film is targeted to Cuban youth who did not face the fight against imperialism and may be losing faith in the revolution. The fascist Europeans, comprised of German vampire squads, clumsy Italian navy officers, and an obtuse Spanish scientist come to the island to steal the *vampiyaba* created by Pepín, and are fought by a collective that includes his father (Pepe) the revolutionary Cuban ethnic minority characters already mentioned, a Slavic communist soldier, and intellectual historical figures such as Ernest Hemingway. The American forces are insulted in such a way that the film would likely offend many in the U.S. Al Tapone from the prequel is elevated from mobster to U.S. Army officer, implying the mob control of the American forces in World War II. Tapone sends American vampires to Cuba to obtain the *vampiyaba* (for the government) through the base at Guanatánamo, which contains atomic bombs that the mobsters reveal will be used against the Japanese a few years later. In these brief scenes, Padrón is able to summarize a great many stereotypes about Americans.

Another minor villain in the film is ex-president Fulgencio Batista whom the 1959 revolution deposed. As the film opens, the Chinese character says he wants to link the president to the imperialist forces of fas-

5. Idealogy, Realism and Fantasy and the Special Period

cism and capitalism, which the film certainly manages to do. Batista only appears at the end, but his emissary is an unattractive Captain Dumigrón who is, ironically, voiced by the handsome Cuban superstar Jorge Perugorría. Dumigrón helps the Germans and Americans obtain what they need and accuses Batista of selling fuel to Nazi submarine operations in the Caribbean. In the end, Batista is not deposed; in his only scene, he utters the same words he had said before abandoning Cuba in 1959: "salud, salud, salud." At the end of the film, although the Nazis and the Americans are defeated, one of the last drawings shows how the AfroCuban and the Chinese characters are using the *vampiyaba* to gain powers and fight the dictator in the 1950s, foreshadowing the impending revolution.

More Vampires in Havana's ambiguous nature lies in the fact that the film functions as a propagandistic communist World War II film, but its heroes are drawn in racist, classist, and nationalist pre-revolutionary visuals that parody elements of communist popular culture. When Vanya, the Czech spy, sends a message to Stalin telling him that Germans now have the ability to transform themselves into animals using *vampiyaba*, the dictator sends all animals into the gulag where they are interrogated. This scene is amusing for its mockery of Soviet paranoia, as the animals do not understand what is happening. Nevertheless, at the end Stalin is redeemed (unusual in a communist society) because Hemingway states, in his closing narration, that all the German spies were caught because of the interrogations, thus justifying the stupidity of the act.

Socialist culture is also parodied through Vanya, portrayed as a well intentioned but incredibly dull Slav who is culturally far removed from other Cubans. In the final scene, while celebrating victory with the other Cuban animated characters at Pepe's club, he talks to Cuban music legend Benny Moré (in a cameo) and tells him flatly how Ukrainians dance. This dull conversation inspires the musician to copy Vanya's words and turn them into the famous song: "pero que bonito bailan el mambo las mexicanas." This scene is amusing in its ironic reconstruction of history to demonstrate that Cuban music was inspired by Eastern European lines instead of AfroCubanism, and may be interpreted as a gag mocking communist revision of history and cultural development.

Cuban Cinema After the Cold War

Padrón's contradictory representation of Cuban culture through the visual language of animation deconstructs the clashes of ideas that the island experienced after its isolation from and flirtation with European capitalism. With animation, Padrón is able to make the point that pre- and post-revolutionary Cuba are one by using iconic images that represent the split of ideology, while fusing them into one narrative. The Cuban heroes in *More Vampires in Havana* are as sexually attractive and delightful as colonialism imagines them, yet also committed revolutionaries who fit the ideals of socialism and multiculturalism. With their flaws and strengths they become embodiments of the contradictions of their nation.

The relationship between Pepín and his uncle is crucial to understanding the self-reflexive aspects of the film. Pepín learns to hate imperialism and capitalism through his encounters with Nazis and American mobsters, but also becomes a scientist thanks to the positive influence of his uncle's ghost, which affirms his European heritage. His vampire uncle Amadeus trains Pepe to be a stronger vampire and to defeat the Nazi vampires because the repercussions of these battles are important in the future. Uncle Amadeus understands that Pepe needs his vampire heritage to overpower the enemy, and this attitude responds to the postcolonial nationalist debate regarding to what extent ignoring or rejecting the empire's culture leaves one at its mercy. The uncle's *vampisol* had made Pepe a human Cuban national; he returns to train his nephew to use his vampire powers for good instead of simply avoiding them and consequently risking destruction.

Uncle Amadeus' spirit is powerful: he is not held back by temporal boundaries, and he drops hints of an intertextual knowledge of the future which the protagonists cannot understand because they partake of an older version of Cuban culture. The uncle refers to himself as the Obi Wan Kenobi mentor in *Star Wars*, quotes the Beatles, and tells Vanya (the Czech spy) that the Soviets will collapse due to Perestroika and not because of the Nazis. At the end, this "positive" European figure who sees beyond nationalisms and ideologies departs, as Pepe's son Pepín yells to him: "I love you, uncle." Hemingway tells the audience that professor Von Dracula's last words are "The future will always be better," an ambiguous line that can be read as a link to the 1959 revolution or, simply, as a statement

5. *Idealogy, Realism and Fantasy and the Special Period*

that Cuba's post–Soviet struggles will improve either by upgrading the socialist government or by the collapse of the Cuban revolution. This ambiguity about the future and what is ideologically right for the Cuban nation serves as an interesting metaphor of the uncertainty of post–Special Period Cuban reality.

Even though I find the themes in *More Vampires in Havana* very exciting, the sequel is considered to be a failure in comparison to the success of the original. In her book *On Location in Cuba: Street Filmmaking During Times of Transition*, scholar Ann Marie Stock quotes an undisclosed Cuban animator on the failure of the film, but she is vague about the shortcomings referred to, and it is unclear if the film is perceived as an esthetic disappointment, a commercial one, or both. Padrón himself addresses the failure directly in an interview by saying that he felt he emphasized adventure over slapstick in the sequel, and it seemed the audiences wanted more comedy than action.[35] I still insist that, even if its box office numbers might not have been as impressive as those of the first *Vampires* movie, the film is successful esthetically. It is also innovative, and has been officially distributed in various European and Latin American countries, which attests at least partially to its popularity outside of Cuba. Hopefully, both films in the franchise will continue to boast a cult status around the world.

The visual language of animation differs esthetically from live action features, and this creates different perceptions of reality. Many of the Marxist thinkers of the 20th century acknowledged that the medium provided a different vision of reality that could be transcendental and liberating for the masses but that could also be used to manipulate ideology in the service of the culture industry, usually embodied by figures such as Walt Disney. The theoretical background in this chapter illustrates how the ICAIC animation studio tried to counter the hegemony of Hollywood, but was not completely successful until Juan Padrón entered the scene. This Cuban filmmaker and cartoonist simply used the narrative devices of American commercial entertainment to create two ideologically charged animated franchises: the *Elpidio Valdés* saga and the *Vampires in Havana* films.

The *Elpidio* adventures are interesting from an esthetic and narrative point of view because they provide the perspective of the oppressed, and because the stories aggressively teach political history, something usually avoided in American animation. However, when used to embody the Cuban revolution, the character of Elpidio becomes as propagandistic and manipulative as the Walt Disney Company cartoons. In his second franchise, *Vampires in Havana*, Padrón uses animation in more interesting ways to entertain and educate Cuban audiences, because, through the use of genres such as horror, crime, musicals, and others, he is able to deconstruct and illustrate the contradictions of the Cuban revolutionary language. The post–Special Period sequel is of particular interest because it offers an ambiguous ideological narrative that can be interpreted as committed to the Cuban revolution, while allowing the Cuban kids to realize that it is okay to think about other alternatives and to remain confident that "the future will always be better."

6

Juan of the Dead and the Ideological Evolution of the Caribbean Zombie

When I attended the French Canadian premiere of *Juan of the Dead* at the 2012 Fantasia Film Festival in Montreal, I had mixed expectations for the film. I had enjoyed the trailers, and read very positive reviews from horror aficionados, but I was worried that this production would mark the end of Cuban revolutionary cinema, as the new independent filmmakers from the island attempted to create more commercial projects. The screening surprised me because it was a resounding success, and the audience visibly enjoyed the jokes presented on the screen. The Canadian audience understood the physical comedy and sexual innuendos, but for the most part missed the astonishing critique of the incompetence of the Cuban revolutionary government, and other subtle intricacies of life in Cuba after the Special Period. Just hearing the protagonist Juan mention ironically the Special Period would make me laugh out loud but, sadly, I was the only one in on the joke. Some ask me if this is due to the audience's being Canadian, but the truth is that often even Latin American or Spanish native speakers lack the experience with Cuban culture and its cinematic references to truly appreciate the genius of this film. Clarifying how the events that happened after the collapse of the Soviet Union and the Special Period and its aftermath affected Cuban filmmakers and the way they made their revolutionary films, and understanding these themes will provide the reader with a better grasp of the meanings embedded in the new crop of Cuban films currently being made.

The success of *Juan of the Dead*, which includes broad international distribution, good local box office, warm reception by both film critics and horror fans abroad, and a victory at the prestigious 2013 Goya awards in Spain for the category of best foreign film in Spanish, shows how Cuban filmmakers, such as *Juan*'s Alejandro Brugués, were able to adapt to the new realities their industry had to face after the collapse of the Soviet Union. This particular film works well in representing life after the Special Period, and it reflects the monumental changes in Cuban filmmaking that occurred in the 1990s.

Some of the most important debates in post–Cold War Cuban cinema (as outlined so far) concern the role of the filmmakers in criticizing the Cuban government regime, the integration of the "non-revolutionary" into Cuban revolutionary nationalism, the fair depiction of workers and ethnicities and whether it can be achieved with moderate success through revolutionary esthetics, and, finally, how the lack of funds in Cuba after the Special Period and accepting investments from abroad affected modern Cuban narratives in terms of esthetics and ideology. It is interesting to explore where Brugués' *Juan of the Dead* is located within these debates. The filmmaker intertextually reproduces some of the narrative conventions of the zombie genre such as the melodramatic dissolution of the hegemonic family and the mockery of social institutions, while at the same time rewriting the rules because of Cuba's unique ideologically revolutionary setting. Through the use of certain elements of horror/fantasy, Brugués was able to express an ambiguous message that reflects the conflicted political nature of the Post–Special Period Cuban society. Some of these ideas would have been considered anti-revolutionary in the past (e.g., when they appeared in *Alice in Wondertown*,[1] but the evolution of thought in Cuban society after the Special Period and the much changed economic climate has allowed Cuban filmmakers to criticize the flaws of the Cuban revolution while reaffirming their commitment to its precepts.

The Cinematic Zombie: Colonial Fantasies About the Caribbean Other to Apocalyptic Capitalist Metaphor

In order to explain the relevance of *Juan of the Dead* from a Cuban industry and narrative point of view, it is important first to consider the

6. The Idealogical Evolution of the Caribbean Zombie

Western cinematic zombie genre, which is key to understanding Alejandro Brugués' film. First, there is an important distinction between the original Caribbean zombies (a racialized European and American colonial fantasy) that were the subject of early horror films such as *White Zombie* and *I Walked with a Zombie,* and the more contemporary version linked to a viral disease that became popular with George Romero's *Night of the Living Dead* (1968). It is important to address the differences between these types of zombie films because their setting and political space is different even though the two share criticisms about the ruling elite and its hegemony. This juxtaposition will allow me to explain the evolution of social criticism in zombie films, from decaying Caribbean colonial settings to collapsing capitalist economies, in order to conceptualize the way in which *Juan of the Dead* parodies certain aspects of the Cuban government through a horror genre that has traditionally mocked hegemonies and social structures.

First, one has to understand that the concept of the undead is a universal myth rooted in humanity's fears about death, and that numerous variants of it exist throughout the world, e.g., zombies, vampires, ghouls, mummies, ghosts, and many others. Some of the earlier zombies that appeared in American popular culture during the first half of the 20th century are a version of the undead that was geographically linked to the Caribbean or other regions in the Americas influenced by African culture and religious beliefs. These zombies embodied "Africanness" through their link to what was perceived at the time as AfroCaribbean witchcraft, and therefore represented a specific threat to the Eurocentric hegemony.[2] The first two relevant Hollywood Caribbean zombie movies, Victor Halperin's *White Zombie* and Jacques Tourneur's *I Walked with a Zombie*, are important in my analysis, for they embody different perceptions of "The Colonized Other" and the monstrous Caribbean zombie figures, thus showing how the same settings and genre conventions could convey different political messages in regards to the oppressed. In addition, in order to appeal to a mainstream audience, the films use melodramatic narrative devices centered around the family structure. This approach was highly influential in the modern zombie films that range from George Romero's *Dead* saga to Brugués' *Juan of the Dead*.

One of the elements that tie together Halperin's and Tourneur's

Caribbean zombie pictures is that their story is roughly based on two different American non-fiction travelogues about Haiti and its culture. *White Zombie*'s sensationalistic script is based on William Seabrook's book *The Magic Island* (1929), and *I Walked with a Zombie* was inspired by an article with the same title written by Inez Wallace in *American Weekly*. The two films freely adapt the original sources by adding fictional characters, such as the white couples who represent the classical hegemonic family. These protagonists are threatened in the colonial territory when the Caucasian female spouses in both films are turned into zombies, thus providing material for conflict and melodrama.[3]

In *White Zombie*, an American couple (Madeleine Short and her fiancé Neil Parker) visiting Haiti are threatened by both an evil voodoo master called Murder Legendre (played by Bela Lugosi) and a landowner, Charles Beaumont (who wants to seduce Madeleine away from Neil). In *I Walked with a Zombie* the main plot revolves around nurse Betsy Connell's trip to the fictional Caribbean island of Saint Sebastián where she has to unravel the mystery surrounding the white and aristocratic Holland family while taking care of Mrs. Holland, who is either mentally insane or a zombie. In both films, two Caucasian women are turned into zombies, although not by black voodoo priests, but by characters in power within the colonial system who have learned to use the drugs that are part of the AfroCaribbean religions and rites. However, beyond these narrative structure similarities, the two films are perceived differently by contemporary scholars in their depiction of race and the colonized Caribbean. The main difference between the films is that Halperin's *White Zombie* portrays African culture and miscegenation as part of the threat because it corrupts white hegemony, while Tourneur provides a more ambiguous take on the subject and actually uses the family melodrama structure to make the Holland family more monstrous than the AfroCaribbean characters.

William Seabrook (author of the book on which *White Zombie* is based) was a popular pseudo ethnologist at the time, and his book sought to present Haitian culture to his contemporary American audience. Through his otherwise problematic and exoticizing writing, he provided at least some critique of the United States' occupation of Haiti. Seabrook was also critical of American attempts to import into the island certain

6. The Idealogical Evolution of the Caribbean Zombie

aspects of racial segregation similar to the Jim Crow laws.[4] In *White Zombie*, Halperin distorts Seabrook's critiques of American colonial policies in Haiti by redirecting the source of the crisis to both Afro-Caribbean culture and a decaying European colonialist system that has been obviously influenced by "blackness." The zombies are controlled by a fictional voodoo master of ambiguous racial origin called Murder Legendre, who commands the walking dead with his knowledge of Afro-Caribbean pharmacology and potions to which only a voodoo priest would have access. These local zombies are enslaved in Legendre's sugar mill, which represents the economy of old-fashioned European colonialism and veers away from Seabrook's criticism of modern American imperialism and its exploitative industrial factories. The film illustrates how threatening the creole and the concept of miscegenation were at the time for an American society that was racially divided. The character of Legendre is a European colonial syncretic model, and serves as an attempt to mitigate American colonial anxieties in Haiti.[5] This is why the greatest horror in the film is the white female protagonist's zombification, and thus the importance of the title of the film *White Zombie*.

In contrast, Tourneur's *I Walked with a Zombie* is considered esthetically superior by film critics because the filmmaker enhanced Wallace's travelogue with some narrative elements from Charlotte Bronte's *Jayne Eyre* to provide a more solid dramatic structure. Tourneur's narrative has some exploitative elements related to the genre, and his ambiguous depiction of the events does not directly blame AfroCaribbean culture for the threat against the white female protagonist. The filmmaker portrays the white colonial civilization as the one that is decaying, while the black/native population is vibrant.[6] Scholar Gwenda Jones observes that the dysfunctional melodrama and the threat in the film are embodied by the aristocratic family, whose white matriarch has learned the ways of voodoo in order to curse her son's wife for having an affair with her other son. As a counterpoint, the black families are presented as having a more harmonious family structure.[7] Jones adds that Tourneur's ambiguous depiction of his female white zombie and the source of her plight (which could also be interpreted as a mental breakdown) may be open to the interpretation that the zombification of the characters (black and white) included in the film may be intended more as a metaphor of the colonial system's attempt to control its people rather than as a demonization of the otherness of the AfroCaribbean heritage.[8] Contrary to *White Zombie*'s happy ending where the white American couple is redeemed at the end and the racial status quo is preserved, in *I Walked with a Zombie*, the Holland matrimony is not restored and the female white zombie and her lover are destroyed towards the end of the film.

AfroCaribbean zombies have continued to appear on the silver screen with a more recent example being Wes Craven's *The Serpent and the Rainbow* (1988), another horror film based on a non-fiction American travelogue with the same title (written by Wade Davis). However, this type of film has become more scarce in Hollywood, which has embraced George Romero's revised zombie model since his 1968 masterpiece *Night of The Living Dead*. This particular film was groundbreaking and influential in the genre in many ways, such as refocusing the source of zombification from AfroCaribbean ritual drugs to some sort of alien virus. In addition, the film became famous due to its politically charged use of the African American protagonist, Ben Huss.

One could argue that the main difference between the early zombie films set in the Caribbean and the ones made by Romero is the political space in which the plots develop. In the films with colonial settings, the zombification occurs at the hand of hegemonic figures influenced by "blackness," and it is easy for an American audience to blame the conflict on outdated European models of colonization and the threat of miscegenation. Romero's films from the second half of the 20th century, however, take place in the United States, the heart of the most powerful Eurocentric society at the time, and the zombies have no hegemonic origins, nor are they limited to a certain ethnicity or social class. They emerge out of nowhere, are multicultural, function as agents of chaos, and destroy American "civilization," a representation which at the time served as a metaphor for the social revolts that were happening after the 1950s. Unlike the Caribbean zombies, these zombies do not obey authority figures, but instead fulfill basic animalistic desires of violence and hunger.

Tourneur deconstructs the colonial white hegemonic family in *I Walked with a Zombie* by using family melodramatic devices, while Romero, in his original film *Night of the Living Dead* (1968), uses similar

6. The Idealogical Evolution of the Caribbean Zombie

melodramatic devices, but to portray different types of middle-class white families in more modern industrial settings as self-destructive. More importantly, both filmmakers portray black characters as positive counterparts to the white characters. In *Night of the Living Dead*, African American character Ben Huss is the only rational being. The film begins with white siblings bickering in front of their father's grave, and, even though the sister Barbra survives the initial zombie attack, she is destroyed by her zombified brother at the end of the film. The nice young couple (Tom and Judy) that try to help Ben pump gas at a station also perish because of the lovers' obsession with each other. The main antagonist (Harry, another Caucasian character), by trying to protect his family, betrays the group at a very dangerous point in the narrative which leads to his being killed by his zombie daughter. Romero's depiction of the white family is that of a diseased national institution that is a dangerous element in the zombie apocalypse. Ben, however, survives all zombie attacks only to be killed by a police officer from an all-white zombie-hunting party.

It is interesting to explore how the African American character was perceived as an "other" in relation to the Caucasian characters in the film because, as film scholar Ben Hervey has observed, Ben Huss' character is clean-cut, does not speak African American ethnic dialects, and his race is not addressed at any point in the movie.[9] No background is provided about the character in the film, including elements such as social class, education, or profession. He is visually (albeit not culturally) a "racial other" but not necessarily a threatening figure for the audience. Romero's most important social criticism thus comes towards the end of the film when Ben is killed by a white mob that resembles the extremist right-wing groups lynching blacks during the Civil Rights struggle in the 1960s. This ironic plot twist sends an important political message, since the zombie outbreak is never linked to blackness in Romero's film unlike the earlier zombie films set in the Caribbean.

Romero continued his social criticism in the sequels to *Night of the Living Dead*, most importantly in the acclaimed capitalist allegory about zombies in the mall (*Dawn of the Dead*, 1978) and in the denunciation of military jingoism in *Day of the Dead* (1985). Romero's original zombie trilogy is an explicit commentary on the dead ends of the American family, post–Fordist consumerism, and the barbarism of the military-scientific complex.[10] I would add that the films successfully ridicule the hegemonic system's refusal to accept change and delay the inevitable evolution of society and the changes brought about by the social movements in the 1960s.[11] Romero's films assert that these monsters are not going away, and it is up to the survivors to pick up the pieces and adjust to their new reality, while admitting that their previous status quo is never going to return.

The 2013 documentary *The Birth of the Living Dead* explains how many of the scenes in Romero's *Night of the Living Dead* depict visual metaphors that audiences at the time would understand as allegories of contemporary civil unrest. For example, one visual quote that may be lost on American audiences nowadays is that the zombie hunters that kill Ben utter the phrase "Search and destroy," an expression then commonly used by American soldiers in Vietnam. Another visual reference is that the police officers' dogs in the film were similar to the ones often unleashed against African Americans in race riots at the time. The fictional newscasts presented in the film were also constructed to resemble their real-life counterparts, which showed documentary footage of people rioting in the streets and destroying the city in a manner similar to how the zombies do it in *Night of the Living Dead*.

In the 2000s, two of the most politically subversive post–9/11 zombie films were Danny Boyle's *28 Days Later* (2002), a British production, and Robert Rodríguez's *Planet Terror* (2007). As I explain in detail in my article "Miscegenation and Family Apocalypse in Robert Rodríguez' *Planet Terror*," both films feature heroic ethnic protagonists (black British heroine Selene in *28 Days Later* and Latino hero Elwray in *Planet Terror*), who are initially presented to the audience as shady and violent, but who eventually help the Caucasian characters, while having interracial romances, to build new family structures in place of the flawed ones that were dominant before the zombie apocalypse. Racial miscegenation in the films is key to rebuilding society, especially in Rodríguez's *Planet Terror* where the birth of the baby of a Latino (Elwray) and a Caucasian (Cherry Darling) character is portrayed as some sort of Messianic event.

Unlike the ambiguous origins of Romero's zombie outbreaks, in

6. The Idealogical Evolution of the Caribbean Zombie

these films, the cause of the plague is explicitly linked to hegemonic social structures. In *28 Days Later*, the virus was created by a corporation, and in *Planet Terror* it was a biological weapon deployed by the American forces in Afghanistan. In both films, the survivors' final battle is not with the zombies but with post–9/11 British and American military squads that were supposed to represent the best their country had to offer but that are now more terrifying than the zombie monsters themselves.[12] In the modern "political" zombie genre, danger comes not from the racial other (Black or mixed-race Latino), or from the monsters themselves, but is embodied in the Western hegemonic structures (corporations or armies) of modern capitalism which are typically supported by the bourgeois family structure.

In his book *History of Sexuality*, Michel Foucault asserts that the family structure is the key to regulating sexuality and the manner in which society establishes order. He writes:

> The family, in its contemporary form, must not be understood as a social, economic, and political structure of alliance that excludes or at least restrains sexuality, that diminishes it as much as possible, preserving only its useful functions. On the contrary, its role is to anchor sexuality and provide it with a permanent support.[13]

This quote is important because in the zombie genre the family structure is the last remnant of civilization. In *I Walked with a Zombie*, the zombification of the female protagonist occurs when the matriarch of the Holland family attempts to control her sexuality in order to maintain the colonial status quo. In post–9/11 films like *Planet Terror* and *28 Days Later*, the family has collapsed, but capitalist hegemonic structures continue to attempt to re-establish the pre-zombie status quo by controlling female sexuality. That is why the climactic battles in these films are not with ordinary zombies but with soldiers who want to dominate women through rape. The female protagonists' refusal to return to previous gender roles that they had forsaken with the advance of the zombie apocalypse is what leads to these final destructive battles in which the last remnants of hegemony fall.

Certain narrative elements of these zombie films from the 2000s may be interpreted as subversive because of their criticism of traditional societies. However, not all recent zombie films follow the same pattern.

To provide a balanced perspective on the genre, I can also quote a number of films that attempt to pander to mainstream audiences and therefore rely on racist tropes or simplistic family melodrama. For example, Zach Snyder's *Dawn of the Dead* (2004), a remake of Romero's film, downplays the anarchist political elements of the original. In the opening credits, after the protagonist barely escapes the attacks of her zombie family, the apocalyptic montage of destructive images begins with footage of Muslims praying. The use of this image in the film is very irresponsible at the time because it links Islam to the apocalypse even though the film does not contain any Muslim characters or plots. The film also features an interracial baby with an African American father and an Eastern European mother. A grotesque birth scene depicts the baby coming out as a zombie from the mother's womb. Contrary to Rodríguez's *Planet Terror* where the racially mixed baby is to represent the future of mankind, in Snyder's film it is visualized as a monster that is killed by the white protagonist. Another example of a conventional Hollywood zombie project is the Brad Pitt vehicle *World War Z* (2013). In this film, Pitt's character protects his family and uses his United Nations credentials to provide them with safe heaven on an American battleship. He embarks on a round-the-world adventure in an attempt to find a cure for the zombie outbreak, but his only motive in saving the world is to maintain alive his own family unit.

As this brief history of the politicization of the zombie genre shows, many directors working in capitalist countries have used zombie films to criticize colonialism and the capitalist system with its racial segregation, worker exploitation, and use of heterosexual family structures to establish order. When I heard a zombie film was being made in Cuba, I wondered if Brugués could add political overtones to the film, even though it is set in Cuba, a leftist society that had already fought against colonialism, imperialism, racism, misogyny, economic exploitation, and other types of social injustice. When I first saw *Juan of the Dead*, the film surpassed my expectations, as it provided an alternative take on the topic that was much more interesting than the nihilistic fantasies created in Europe and the United States. The film shows a Cuba that had already lived its own apocalypse, and thus the plot lacks the shocking revelations about the fall of civilization. Unlike the American and European zombie films that represent the collapse of traditional society as a traumatic experience to which the characters cannot easily adjust, the Cuban film refers to the zombie apocalypse as just one of a series of social and economic changes that have affected the island for centuries. This is a calamity that Cuban characters will survive not because they subscribe to a certain ideology but rather because of their ability to evolve and modify their lifestyles in accordance with the times.

Juan of the Dead *and the New International Film Markets*

Los cien caminos del cine cubano, a history book about the Cuban film industry published by the ICAIC, contains a small blurb about the director's cinematic formation, which mentions that he received a degree in screenwriting in the Escuela Internacional de Cine y TV de San Antonio de los Baños (EICTV). He began working in the industry as a screenwriter in films such as Manuel Herrera's *Bailando chachachá* (2005) and Humberto Padrón's *Frutas en el café* (2005). (126) Brugués' first long feature film as a director was *Personal Belongings* (2006), a film that screened at several festivals, and was distributed in the United States with a DVD release.

In her article "Resisting Disconnectedness in *Larga Distancia* and *Juan de los muertos*: Cuban Filmmakers Create and Compete in a Globalized World," Cuban cinema scholar Anne Marie Stock provides more details about Alejandro Brugues' career as a director, and the important role of his producer Inti Herrera who was able to secure private financing outside of the ICAIC through his own production company *La 5ta Avenida*, which produced Brugués' two films *Belongings* and *Juan of the Dead*. Stock describes the working relationship between Brugués and Herrera, who first met in film school. The role of Herrera as a producer is very important because his parents, Carlos Herrera and Eslinda Nuñez,[14] work at the ICAIC,[15] which means he has met many of the creators at the Institute, and has been familiar with how the Cuban industry works since he was a child.[16] Brugués and Herrera's first film together, *Personal Belongings*, was a modest success, winning prizes at festivals, and gaining international distribution. This particular film is not a genre film like *Juan*, but its plot and setting are reminiscent of the existentialist

Special Period films. The project was not produced by the ICAIC yet is quite influenced by what ICAIC filmmakers were doing at the time.

Personal Belongings is a love story between a nurse named Ana and Ernesto, a young man who wants to leave Cuba. It is a very timid romantic film that hides complex political rifts by means of basic melodramatic tricks, and by downplaying Cuban ideological debates. For example, Ana's family leaves Cuba at the beginning of the film but the narrative is never too clear about why they did it, or why she is the only one who wants to stay on the island. Further, Ernesto is presented as living an unhappy life in Cuba, but in a twist later in the film the source of his pain is revealed to be family and not the political system. Ernesto's estranged father is coincidentally also Ana's boss, who reveals to her and the audience that Ernesto's issues are related to losing his mother in an accident caused by his father while driving under the influence of alcohol. Some Cuban critics, such as Frank Padrón, commend the film for attempting to avoid traditional political messages. Padrón sees the film as an intimate narrative about feelings rather than politics. He thinks the screenplay is well-polished, but does not approve of the soap opera twist with Ernesto's father.[17]

The film has a slightly ambiguous ending because the two main characters meet dramatically at the exit of the foreign embassy where Ernesto is being interviewed for a visa, but it is unclear whether they stay together or not. Despite the ambiguity, the revelation about Ernesto's parents leads to the extremely conventional resolution of the film, where in his exit visa interview, Ernesto tells the interviewer that he does not care about the interview's result because he has found true love. This ending is disappointing to a seasoned viewer, as the characters make ideological decisions in the name of love. The sentimentalism of the story surprised me because this type of ending had already been ridiculed in earlier ICAIC productions. For example, Juan Carlos Tabío had already mocked this type of Cuban romance in the first segment of his underrated self-reflexive film *Aunque estés lejos* (*So Far Away*, 2001).[18]

Visually *Personal Belongings* looks a lot like an ICAIC Cuban film, and it is very traditional from an esthetic point of view. The main character lives in his car, which gives him the opportunity to travel around Havana to show some of the city staples. The credit sequence, like in

6. The Idealogical Evolution of the Caribbean Zombie

Brugués' next film, *Juan of the Dead,* shows a montage of Havana which is beautiful, but has become a common and contrived visual device in most ICAIC films. Some of the scenes belong to conventional romantic films, such as when Brugués manipulates the mise-en-scène to express the feelings of the characters. In one of the scenes where the protagonists are fighting, for example, Brugués uses a rain sequence, a cliché narrative convention highlighting the characters' emotional suffering for the audience. The film is disappointing because it both conforms to the esthetics of commercial entertainment, and is very ideologically tame from a Cuban perspective. However, one has to acknowledge that this was Brugués' first film, so the filmmaker probably had to navigate between making a film that could work on the international scene because he was using other types of financing, and one that would make him remain in good standing with Cuban institutions. Despite these shortcomings, *Personal Belongings* showed that Brugués is good with actors, and that he had a distinct visual style. In addition, the film contains cameos by some of the actors who would later be part of the cast in *Juan of the Dead.*

After the festival success of *Personal Belongings*, which was commercially released in the United States, Brugués and Herrera decided to work together again to create a zombie picture. They secured private funding from foreign institutions such as the Spanish company Zanfoña films, because they could not assume any financing from the ICAIC infrastructure.[19] However, they made sure to procure the ICAIC's participation[20] in the project because the Institute could provide them with technology, and could exercise influence on local distribution.[21] This allowed them to use several iconic ICAIC actors and filmmakers in the movie, e.g., Herrera's parents, Carlos Herrera and Eslinda Nuñez, as well as famous Cuban actor Luis Alberto García. Herrera played the government's TV presenter that repeatedly announces in the local news that everything is fine and that the zombies are nothing more than subversive Cuban dissidents. Nuñez acted the role of the conservative revolutionary citizen from the Comité de defensa de la Revolución (CDR) that is harassing all the neighbors at the beginning of the film, and García portrayed the police officer that represents order and is slain by Juan at the end of the film. In a brilliant move, Brugués and Herrera put their ICAIC stars in the most controversial and antagonistic cameo roles, something that worked to the film's advantage because these performers had become institutions in themselves for the island, and thus function as shorthand intertextual references to the more traditional Revolutionary Cuban cinema.

After the film was completed, it premiered at the Havana Film Festival in 2010 and immediately won the audience award. The trailer of the film featured "zombies" in Havana, and gained the attention of film fan websites in the U.S., such as aintitcoolnews.com. I followed the film's facebook page, and was able to track the film's international distribution. It screened at the prestigious Toronto Film Festival in 2011, created hype with its screening at the Fantastic Fest in Austin, TX, and was officially released in Mexico, Spain, Germany, Japan, and other profitable international markets. In the United States, *Juan of the Dead* signed a distribution deal with Lionsgate which released the film on DVD, and in HD in many online stores such as amazon.com. This means the film is widely available and easy to acquire in this country and other international markets. This type of distribution success, despite the American embargo, shows that new Cuban filmmakers are able to achieve international success by exploring genres that have inbuilt audiences, which have the tools to interpret the basics of the movie, even if they are unfamiliar with Cuban reality.

The following more detailed analysis of the film will allow me to explain its intertextual homages to the zombie genre. It will also demonstrate how Brugués reinvented the zombie narrative in order to ridicule certain aspects of the post–Special Period Cuban society, as well as the models provided by both Spain and the U.S.

Zombie Intertextuality: Cuban Melodrama, Zombie Antiheroes and the Rebirth of the Cuban Family

Juan of the Dead is a film that abounds in intertextual narrative devices. While the movie alludes to scenes in earlier (American and European) zombie films and parodies certain aspects of the genre, its originality lies in its new codification of zombies through the Cuban experience during and after the Special Period. Film critic Carla Grossman makes a similar claim in her article "Zombies utópicos." She writes that Brugués' film not only satirizes the zombie genre, but does so from a code rooted in revolutionary discourse.[22]

Anne Marie Stock points out that many of the satiric precepts in *Juan of the Dead* can be linked to the Cuban cinema previously produced by the ICAIC. For example, she mentions the use of the horror genre and comedy in Juan Padrón's *Vampires in Havana* series,[23] Juan Carlos Tabío's postmodern satiric comedies about Cuban society (such as *Plaff* and *The Elephant and the Bicycle*) and Fernando Pérez's ruminations about the city such as *Madagascar* and *Suite Habana*.[24] Stock even points out specific images that parody canonical Cuban cinema, for example when Juan looks towards the street from his building with a telescope in a direct reference to Gutiérrez Alea's *Memories of Underdevelopment*, which is considered the greatest Cuban film of all time.[25]

Brugués' exploration of the apocalyptic zombie genre presents some of the visual staples of Cuban cinema in a new light. In addition, both Grossman and Stock have pointed out how the Cubanness of the film is redeployed through the exciting new manner in which the city of Havana is portrayed. More specifically, what could be perceived as a voyeuristic cliché in Cuban films is presented here in a fresh new manner through the use of traditional nationalistic monuments in new setups that are part of the comedy. Stock mentions specifically the CGI destruction of the FOCSA Soviet slum, the collapse of which provides a better view of dusk, and the portrayal of the parking of the Habana Libre Hotel as a zombie heaven among others.[26]

Where does the film belong within the zombie film genre tradition? *Juan of the Dead* returns the zombie concept to the Caribbean, but the colonial setting from *White* Zombie and *I Walked with a Zombie* is gone, or at least it has been transformed. The film's zombies are closer to Romero's version of the monsters, because they are not created by the hegemonic social structures, and the film focuses mostly on how the survivors and the Cuban revolutionary government react to the chaos brought about by the monsters.[27] In addition, Brugués uses the family melodrama structure of previous anti-hegemonic zombie films but applies its ideals to the Cuban family and its specific ideological and gender issues and controversies.

One could argue that the British zombie film *Shaun of the Dead* is the narrative most similar in tone to *Juan of the Dead*. Besides the obvious influences like the similarity of titles, which both emphasize the name of the protagonist, or like specific scene allusions such as the impaling of zombies on pipes sticking out of the ground, the two films are part picaresque comedies that place their antiheroes in apocalyptic settings rather than upbeat science fiction/horror adventures. Shaun and Juan are male characters that do not fit the national concepts of masculinity, but eventually begin to fit in when the traditional social structure collapses.

As I explained earlier, the family melodrama has often been used in zombie films to depict the changes in society. Film scholar Thomas Schatz has written that one of the most popular melodramatic themes is the clash between generations in an aristocratic family.[28] While it is obvious that *Shaun of the Dead* is influential in the creation of *Juan of the Dead*, it is important to point out the difference in how masculinity is represented in the two films, and how that affects the construction of melodrama in the two. Besides the two characters' obvious existential issues about manhood, in *Shaun of the Dead*, Shaun is a proper middle-class worker inside a European capitalist country (Great Britain), while in *Juan of the Dead*, Juan is a fisherman/con artist/criminal in a poor revolutionary leftist society (Cuba).

In their book *Melodrama*, film scholars John Mercer and Martin Shingler write that the basic model for melodrama concerns the conflicts and tensions of a middle class.[29] According to this model, Shaun would be a more traditional subject on par with the other zombie films in which the fall of the family structure symbolizes the fall of some traditional hegemonic structure. For example, Shaun is constantly compared to other British men such as his successful roommate, his new stepfather, and the judgmental best male friend of Shaun's girlfriend. Still, he remains a likable character to most audiences around the world because Shaun and his pals fit in our comfortable ideas about civilization. In fact, at the end of the film, after the British army kills most of the zombies, Shaun has matured a little due to his experience with zombies, but he and his surviving friends go back to their status quo (playing videogames). On the other hand, Juan is a different character because

6. The Idealogical Evolution of the Caribbean Zombie

he does not have Shaun's middle-class trappings; he is a divorced scoundrel, and does not have respectable affiliations. He is annoyed by people who work for the Cuban government (the closest thing to representing "morality"), and his pals from the hood include his violent best friend Lázaro and his huckster son Vladi Califonia, alongside crooks AfroCuban Primo and transvestite/transgender China. These social affiliations make the characters outsiders to both the ideals of the Cuban revolution and "civilized bourgeois modernity" in general.

When studying horror films, it is important to have a grasp of what is defined as the nation's other in order to understand the terrifying traits that defy masculine hegemony. That is why I began my discussion of *Juan of the Dead* by explaining how the zombie other shifted from its original Caribbean colonial settings in which AfroCaribbean culture was the threat to the capitalist modernity of post–George Romero era where the zombies were a metaphor for the civil rights movement's uprisings. According to horror cinema scholar Robin Wood, there are several types of "other" that are typically emphasized in the genre such as women, other cultures, the proletariat, ethnic groups, alternative ideologies, children, and homosexuality and bisexuality.[30] All of these designations appear one way or the other as characters in *Juan of the Dead*, and the director uses them to mock the decaying revolutionary Cuban society that, although well intentioned, cannot help itself from its incompetent state.

As the film plot develops, we are introduced to Juan's outcast survivor group who were his de facto family before the zombie uprising. This group is very different to their counterparts in other zombie films, because, with the exception of Juan's daughter Camila, all of the members are criminals and are not connected to the Cuban state or government. They lack "revolutionary morality" and fight between themselves over money and profits, but they are certainly all on the same page when they see the zombie apocalypse as an opportunity to acquire goods to survive. This "sleaziness" may seem outrageous to audiences who live in countries with stable economies, but after the famines suffered during the Special Period, Cuban audiences would completely understand the gang's attitudes about life and therefore not perceive them as villains, but antiheroes. When Juan's emigrant daughter (who is temporarily visiting the island) confronts him about his lack of altruism and reproaches him for charging other regular Cubans for protection from the zombies, he answers that in Cuba when things go wrong economically, that is what you are supposed to do to survive. This is a specific wink to the Cuban audience that other international viewers may not be able to understand if they do not have a grasp of the suffering experienced on the island. It is one of those moments where the meaning is intertextually affected by the local collective experience.[31]

Just like many American zombie films tend to mock local authorities, throughout the entire film *Juan of the Dead*, the Cuban revolutionary government is portrayed as intrusive and incompetent. Juan and his criminal buddies have to watch out for the CDR cronies that spy for the government and who harass his group into going to neighborhood meetings. It is precisely at this social event, after being bored with singing Cuba's national anthem, and being chastised by a party member, that they first encounter a zombie. The Cuban government TV newsroom dismisses the attack as a political subversion organized by dissidents, and Juan finds that explanation ironic because he knows the perpetrator personally, and he is well aware of the fact that the "dissident" zombie is actually a staunch party supporter, or, as he exclaims: "En mi vida nunca había visto un gordo más chivato y más maricón que ése" (I've never seen a bigger fat pussy squealer in my life).

During the entire film, the Cuban government keeps informing the public that everything is fine, and continuously blames Cuban ideological dissidents for all the chaos. This newscast narrative device was used in Romero's films as well to convey how the American authorities did not have a grasp on what to do with the zombie outbreak. Here, the main deformation of the narrative lies in how the Cuban revolutionary government is unable to save its people while vehemently denying any danger. The government's last stand to save society is presented in the scene (similar to the plots in *28 Days Later* and *Planet Terror*) where the army kidnap Juan's gang to establish a local community. After disrobing them and chaining them to other survivors, the soldier yells at them, "Con la comunidad todo, sin la comunidad nada," an obvious pun on Castro's slogan "Con la revolución todo, sin la revolución nada." This is a direct intertextual joke that is hilarious to viewers familiar with Cuban

6. The Idealogical Evolution of the Caribbean Zombie

popular culture, specifically Fidel Castro's speech "To the Intellectuals," which gave complete power to the ICAIC, as discussed in Chapter 2 of this book. The Cuban soldiers' plan to set up a new society and redeem Juan's gang fails miserably, and signals the end of Juan's group because the character of China gets bitten in the process and begins the final path of destruction for the group.

While Juan's crew is portrayed in very sympathetic terms because of their resourcefulness and constant defiance of social rules (and the Cuban government), some American reviewers have criticized the characters' tendency to use homophobic slurs. For example, the horror critic of the very influential fan website aintitcoolnews.com chose *Juan of the Dead* as one of the best films of the year, despite his painful struggle with what he perceived to be a very homophobic theme throughout the film:

> I think part of the reason why my experience watching *Juan of the Dead* was less than jaw dropping was the overall theme of homophobia throughout the entire movie. As much as the film is filled with amazingly comedic takes on age old zombie lore and cinematic tradition, there is an uncomfortable amount of off color humor about homosexuals. Ranging from Juan's friend calling those he dislikes derogatory terms for homosexuals to Juan's own distaste towards his openly gay partners in crime, this film is rife with homophobia from beginning to end. On the one hand, this is a Cuban film, made in Cuba, by Cubans, and while I want to respect that Cuba may not be as culturally accepting toward homosexuals, it doesn't make me any more comfortable sitting through a film which occasionally treats gays almost as bad as the zombies that are raging through the streets. There's nothing overtly violent towards homosexuals in this film, but the disdain put upon them by using the term in a derogatory fashion as well as the way the homosexual characters are looked at by the title character is enough to make any open minded individual uncomfortable.[32]

The reviewer is noticeably taken aback by the abundance of the word *maricón* in the film. Many in the Caribbean would dismiss this as nothing but American political correctness, however, even though slurs may be used innocently or as a habit in Cuba (and in the film), they are no less offensive when applied against people whose sexual orientation or queer identity have made them outcasts in their respective societies. When I saw the film, I thought the use of the slur was problematic because I had become aware of pertinent social issues while living in the United States. At the same time, I realized that the use of the word *maricón* is customary for characters of Juan's social environment, despite potential audiences' discomfort with the term. This is thus one of those contradictory moments where one does not agree with the use of the slur yet has to acknowledge its employment in the film as a marker of realistic Cuban dialogue. There are two reasons why I think *Juan of the Dead* might deserve a more lenient critique. First, the characters never use the word directly against China, *the* queer character of the film. Secondly, China is one of the most interesting and beloved characters because her/his defiance of authorities is a fantastic display of how nobody in Cuba knows how to handle his/her queer identity and challenge of heteronormativity. The fact that China is portrayed as a rebellious and interesting character demonstrates that queerness is not scorned in the film but, on the contrary, is represented as a path of resistance to authority.

As discussed in Chapter 2, a lot of academic criticism has focused on the development of gay culture in Cuba, especially in the analysis of the landmark Special Period film *Strawberry and Chocolate* that introduced Cuba's first homosexual protagonist, whose sympathetic defiance of the Cuban revolutionary society has made him an important character in Cuban cinema. However, while the character of Diego is very rebellious in terms of ideology, he is a very tame gay character when defying gender conventions, and specifically when compared to previous queer characters in other Hispanic national cinemas such as La Manuela in Arturo Ripstein's *Un lugar sin límites* (*A Place Without Limits*, 1978) and Miguel in Pedro Almodóvar's *¿Qué he hecho para merecer esto?* (*What Have I Done to Deserve This?*, 1984). *Strawberry and Chocolate* was released in the 1990s, by which time international queer cinema was at an advanced stage, even in formerly traditionalist countries such as Mexico and Spain. This is why sometimes the film and the character are more interesting to a foreign audience in terms of the "ideological" other than necessarily being an exposé of the intricacies of Cuban queer culture.

The character of China is a crossdresser with male genitalia (as the character mentions while being chained by the army) that seems more like a character from a film by the Spanish master Pedro Almodóvar. In

6. The Idealogical Evolution of the Caribbean Zombie

the Spanish director's films, the queer/crossdressing characters belong more to the decadent corners of Spanish sexuality that defy the remnants of the conservative fascist Spanish society, and are not necessarily portrayed as refined intellectuals like the character of Diego in *Strawberry and Chocolate*. Almodóvar is very influential on the international market, and it would not be an overstatement to say that his films almost single-handedly made queer characters acceptable in the international Hispanic mainstream, and thus a model that some young Hispanic filmmakers would follow in their contemporary projects. Scholar Abel Sierra Madero, who wrote a comprehensive book about the history of Cuban gender perceptions, states that, for example, Almodóvar's *Tacones lejanos* (*High Heels*) was a very influential film for Cuban transvestites, who have used it since the 1990s as a learning tool.

Alexandro Brugués had previously used the actor Jazz Villá in *Personal Belongings* to play another gay character, the best friend of the female protagonist, a device typical of Hollywood romantic comedies. In this film, Villá's role is small but is used to mock the character of a rich Spanish woman who wants to marry a Cuban man because she got pregnant as a result of her promiscuous lifestyle in Cuba. The film presents as a joke the fact that the Spaniard is seduced by the gay character played by Villá, and she decides to marry him because the sex they had was unforgettable. This is one of those narrative devices where the gender ambivalence of the character does not allow the viewer to determine if, by presenting this romance, the filmmaker is mocking Cuban sexuality or Spanish decadence. Maybe he is doing a little of both, because he is putting a gay man in the sexualized role of a Cuban gigolo, and the character is more successful at it than heterosexual Cuban men.

In an interview published by HavanaTimes.org, actor Jazz Villá mentions that, even though he began and developed his career with the Cuban acting group Teatro El Público, currently he is in Spain where he focuses mostly on dancing performances. After he saw Brugués at the premiere of *Personal Belongings* at the Malaga International Film Festival, he read the *Juan* script and told the filmmaker that he wanted to participate in such a historic production. Brugués sent him a new revised script with the character of China specifically written for Villá, and the actor was honored to accept. His performance is very sympathetic and charming because China represents a pure id of desire that neither the government nor even Juan can contain.

In Brugués' *Juan of the Dead*, China and her partner Primo serve as good counterparts to Juan's more traditional worker macho sexuality. While Juan and his best friend Lázaro are typical Cuban workers who are useless to society but thrive at nebulous business endeavors, including the black market, they are presented as leading unfulfilling lives. They are oversexed men, heterosexual, and they have accomplished the idea of family by having a daughter and a son respectively. However, the film presents them as "losers" because they are not satisfied by the sex, and do not have good relationships with their offspring. Juan has an uncommitted affair with a more affluent married woman while struggling to fix his relationship with his daughter. On the other hand, Lázaro masturbates by spying on couples from the rooftop of their apartment, including his lesbian neighbors. He also laments that his son is beginning to follow him in his criminal ways, and that he is using his handsome features to seduce tourists.

Their rivals and partners are China and Primo, two AfroCubans[33] that are also thieves and friends, although it is unclear whether they are also lovers. China is a crossdresser with male genitalia, and constantly hits on men which positions him/her as a queer character. This aspect of the character amplifies her/his otherness, and Cuban audiences would likely perceive him/her as a racial and gender other. The construction of China and Primo resembles that of the exaggerated Chinese and AfroCuban minstrel characters in Juan Padrón's *More Vampires in Havana*. However, China and Primo are very sympathetic characters, and they are arguably the characters that challenge Cuba's traditional society. Primo, as a tough AfroCuban male, is the more docile of the pair, but China's campy behavior is very interesting in terms of gender performance because he/she displays both masculine and feminine traits, something that is important for subversive queer representations as developed by Judith Butler in her theories about gender performance. In her book, *Bodies That Matter*, Butler specifically discusses the normative constructions of gender binaries by society and the importance of the abject which rejects social reason and does not fit ideas based on biological sex.[34]

6. The Idealogical Evolution of the Caribbean Zombie

When China has to haggle with Juan as a criminal she is able to defy his masculinity and not be afraid of him, thanks to having Primo as a sidekick. However, she can also be as violent as the other males, and becomes an integral part of the group when they are slaying zombies. China is "one of the boys" whenever she needs to be. However, the reason China is actually one of the most important heroes/heroines of the film, is because her sexuality sets up in motion the climax of the film. When he/she is captured by the soldiers, while everyone (including Juan) is completely submissive to the soldiers, China is the only one that defies the authoritarian military figure who is forcing them to get naked and rebuild Cuban society. One of the funnier scenes in the film is when China tries to seduce the soldier and hits on him while being arrested. This particular scene is very funny from a Cuban point of view, because it may be interpreted as a parody of when Cuban forces were sending gay and "undesirable" citizens to be reeducated. The dour behavior of the Cuban soldiers, while having this anarchic figure sexualizing her/himself in front of them, gives the audience a subversive pleasure. China is so relentless in her/his defiance to any authority, that she/he is the only one who defies Juan's leadership in the group. This is why when Juan sees that the zombified China has followed them all the way to the Plaza de la Revolución, he is so nasty with his/her body. He cannot stand her relentless opposition to his leadership.

It is very disappointing in the film that China and Primo are the only ones from the group who die and do not survive the story. While the other heterosexual and "white" criminals may be tolerated, China's particular demise can be interpreted by American critics to be anti-queer, especially with the constant demeaning use of the word *maricón* and the brutal and sadistic manner in which Juan slays China. When Juan slays the zombified China, he takes such pleasure in hurting him/her that watching her death at the hands of Juan can be uncomfortable for more politically correct audiences. Some could justify that the violence against China is only because he/she was an annoying character (which is what Juan says), but others could interpret the act as the slaying of queer identity. This trend is confirmed by the fact that two other lesbian characters are also previously killed in the film. Thus, the film is problematic because it is not clear if it aims to promote queer identity through the character of China and the lesbian couple or if by killing them it is returning in the end to a Cuban heteronormativity. Even the character of Juan suffers this queer ambivalence when he agrees to allow Lázaro to perform oral sex on him because Lázaro believes he is going to die, but suddenly the movie backs away and says it was all only a joke. Brugués knows how to push buttons but does not dare to completely cross into what could be extremely controversial, the visualization of gay sex in Cuban cinema.

In contrast, the two characters that represent the future of Cuban society are Juan's daughter Camila, and Lázaro's son Vladi California, both young, handsome, and heterosexual. Yet, they do not represent the typical Cuban couple either and may be a form of ideological other. Vladi's con jobs and womanizing behavior may be perceived as a Cuban stereotype, but he is also a pothead, which makes him unfocused. In addition, he is an anti-revolutionary character, a feature portrayed in the scene in which he says he would move to the first place where people have never heard of Cuba or Fidel Castro. Camila is an emigrant who left with her mother when the latter divorced Juan, and, because she was raised in Spain, she speaks and behaves like a Spaniard. Her allegiance to Cuba is questionable, as she constantly criticizes Juan and the island of Cuba, and even compares the two when she says to him at some point: "Tú eres como esta isla; nunca cambias" (You are like this island; you never change). At the end of the film both Camila and Vladi leave the island, representing the Cuban youth that has had to leave the island to improve their lifestyles. Thus queer characters do not survive, but the modern heterosexual traditional couple cannot exist on the island either.

In the end, Juan is the only one that stays on the island, similarly to the character of Ruy in Zambrano's *Habana Blues*, because he loves living in Cuba, the island, which he sees as separate from its revolutionary government. He likes his neighborhood and his people, but he knows the hard lifestyle on the island is not for everyone, which is why he gladly helps his friends and his daughter escape. After a tearful goodbye, the film ends with a wonderful edited sequence, in which Juan confronts alone the rest of the zombies, but assures himself that he "will be fine."

6. The Idealogical Evolution of the Caribbean Zombie

Throughout the film, Juan keeps saying that he survived Angola, the Special Period, and "the thing that came after" (the 2000s). The zombie apocalypse is just another phase in Cuban history that he and the Cuban people will survive as long as they never give up. This is a wonderful metaphor about the resilience of the Cuban people that goes beyond the ideological branding of the revolution.

Throughout the film, Juan has been presented as a criminal, but also a nice neighbor who cares about the people in the neighborhood. This contradiction is crucial to Juan's redemption in the climax of the story. At the beginning of the film, a child taunts Juan by saying that his father, a police officer, could beat him up. Juan's response is that his father is a "sodomita" (sodomite). At the end of the film, before his crew is able to escape the island, Juan hears screams, and sees that same child fleeing his father who has become a zombie and wants to eat him. Juan is able to stop the infanticide: he kills the homicidal father by impaling him on a sharp pole while yelling at him: "sodomita."

This scene could be interpreted as an ambiguous taunt from the director is that Juan slays a police officer from the revolutionary government, and then proceeds to send his son to the United States with his outcast friends. By this time, the Cuban revolutionary government has been destroyed, their attempt to get rid of the zombies has failed miserably, and the government officials have also become a zombie threat that can only be fought by social outcasts to the revolution. Juan has become the ideal father of melodramas who looks after his daughter and Cuban youth, and, while flawed, has supplanted the stoic revolutionary father from the past. This scene has a certain ambivalent dark humor, in which Juan supplants the authority of the Cuban state but by killing him with what the Cuban audiences would perceive as a "gay" act.

Even though some viewers may find issues with how gender and sexuality are presented in the film, *Juan of the Dead* still represents a new manner of daring filmmaking in contemporary post–Special Period Cuban cinema. Its importance lies in the fact that it is still a revolutionary film that has manipulated the intertextual aspects of the zombie genre to create an entertaining product with international distribution, while reshaping our expectations of Cuban cinema. What is particularly interesting is that it also modifies the conventions of the genre because of its socialist Caribbean setting, but also in the context of the revolution, as the filmmakers defy conventions of didactic realism, Cuban nationalism, and audience expectations to deal with issues of gender and race. Hopefully this is the future of Cuban cinema.

Conclusion

The main question the reader may have at this point is "Where is Cuban cinema headed today?" The answer is not simple, but I will try to delineate a structured response through the brief analysis of Juan Carlos Cremata's *Viva Cuba* (2005) and Ian Padrón's *Habanastation* (2011), two recent children's films that have been critically acclaimed locally and abroad, sent to represent Cuba at the Academy Awards, and well received by Cuban audiences. My goal in this analysis is to review some of the main points I have covered in the book about Cuban cinema after the Cold War. I will address specifically the availability of new production companies and alternate sources of film funding besides the ICAIC, as well as the emergence of a more daring criticism of the Cuban government and of Cuban culture that provides alternative viewpoints. Despite these innovations, the ICAIC remains dominant in Cuba, but Cuban filmmakers are moving away from the established patterns while still being influenced by the studio.

Both *Viva Cuba* and *Habanastation* are children's narratives, an emerging genre in Cuban cinema, that deal with topics related to class, ideology, and how the lives of Cuban children are marked and separated by societal differences established by the adult world. *Viva Cuba* is a road movie, in which two young children, Jorgito and his friend Malú, travel across the island to find Malú's estranged father. The trip is an attempt on the part of Malú to stay on the island instead of going with her mother who is emigrating to be with her boyfriend abroad. In the film, the differences between the young protagonists Jorgito and Malú are ideological, because Jorgito's parents are revolutionaries, while Malú's mother does not like living in Cuba, has bourgeois pretensions, and is going to live abroad with a foreigner. In *Habanastation*, the contrast

Conclusion

between child protagonists Mayito and Carlos is mostly about class and living conditions, and the differences in ideology are more subtle than those in *Viva Cuba*. Mayito, the son of a famous rich musician who has access to foreign goods, e.g., the Playstation 3 referenced in the title, gets lost in a slum in western Havana, and has to rely on his poor high school friend to survive in the area until he is able to contact his parents.

The first aspect of the two films that has to be addressed is their funding and production. During the Special Period, as discussed in Chapter Four, most Cuban films were made under the umbrella of the ICAIC, with some funding from coproduction companies from abroad. Juan Carlos Cremata was the first Cuban filmmaker on the island to be able to produce a film completely outside of the ICAIC, as *Viva Cuba* was funded by foreign companies and produced by the ICRT, another Cuban institute.[1] The ICAIC, which still controls all film distribution within Cuba, rejected Cremata's funding proposal for a musical titled *Candela*, but agreed to distribute *Viva Cuba* locally after the film won the prestigious children's prize at the Cannes film festival.[2] Padrón's *Habanastation* in turn was a collaboration between the ICAIC and the ICRT, but it also included various funding sources from abroad. This shows that the ICAIC no longer holds a monolithic control over the island's cinematic production as it used to. Both films were successful locally and abroad, and rewarded with an Academy Awards submission, which shows that they are accepted as part of the national industry.

As part of the national industry, the two films can also be seen as representative of the larger debates of Cuban nationalism and identity. More specifically, *Viva Cuba* addresses issues surrounding the Elián González historical controversy, and *Habanastation* deals with the Cubans' increased awareness of class differences on the island. Elián's political situation raised debates about how Cuban adults from different ideologies wanted to decide his destiny without consulting him. Many criticized both the Miami exile community and the Cuban government for being interested exclusively in spouting ideology through his figure, a situation that created a lot of resentment around this topic. In the United States, this event was also traumatic, and it even

Conclusion

made it into science fiction shows such as *Star Trek: Voyager*.[3] Still, Cremata's *Viva Cuba* is the first film to address the debate from the children's point of view, while constructing the adults subscribing to different ideological strands (revolutionary and anti-revolutionary) as conceited and flawed. Unlike *Viva Cuba*, *Habanastation* is not historically linked to Elián, but its narrative structure is used instead to address issues of class difference within the revolution. At this point in time, due to the commercial and critical success of the children's film genre, it is very likely that these two films will be followed by others using the same mold.

In addition to addressing topical contemporary issues, the two children's films are also very compelling for their incorporation of criticism of the use of revolutionary discourse to conceal problems. This is specifically represented in the school scenes at the beginning of the two films, in which the directors ridicule the insertion of revolutionary and nationalist discourse in various children's activities, and through the teachers and their lessons. Another device (previously discussed in Chapter Two), the use of voices of dissent to redefine Cuban nationalism, is also evident in the children's films, in the presence of characters that do not buy into the school's discourse (Malú and Carlos respectively), which presents a more dialogical perspective of Cuban reality that does not fit the parameters of a monolithic revolutionary point of view.

The problem with these films is that, even though they are not completely produced by the ICAIC, they are still connected to the ICRT, a conservative government institution, which is probably why the interesting critique of the Cuban school system in the first parts of both films later devolves into sentimental narratives which forge artificial bonds between characters. In *Viva Cuba*, once the children escape from their homes, they embark on an epic road trip from Havana to the farthest point in the East of Cuba. Ann Marie Stock admires how the director used this narrative device to create a bond between the characters, and how he took the opportunity to film small, and more unknown locales around the island.[4] I personally found the road trip segment of the film very disappointing because it is an ICAIC narrative device that has already been used for similar purposes in Tomás Gutíerrez Alea and

Conclusion

Juan Carlos Tabío's *Guantanamera*, in Humberto Solás' *Honey for Oshún*, and to a certain extent in Juan Carlos Tabío's *The Waiting List*. In *Habanastation*, there is no road trip, but Mayito's experiences in the slum give him the opportunity to bond with his poor companion Carlitos. Both the road trip and day in the slum are narrative devices used to remove the characters from their comfort zone, specifically the characters of Jorgito and Mayito, who have families that have benefitted from the Cuban revolution, and may be in a position of power in relation to their friends. Still, the fact that the plots of both films rely on such unconventional events to be able to provide an escape to harsh reality, make the films as manipulative as those produced under any capitalist entertainment industry.

Viva Cuba is certainly a more utopian film than *Habanastation*. When the children protagonists travel alone from one side of the island to the other, they never encounter criminals or pedophiles, and Cremata treats both foreign and local audiences to a very folkloric view of the island, that includes peasants, guijes (African spirits), the beach, and other staples of "Cubanness." This is pointed out by scholar Georgia Seminet who sees the trip as a nostalgic view of the island designed to solidify the dissenting voices in Cuba.[5] On the other hand, *Habanastation* provides a more balanced view of the Cuban slum, as it shows its violent and criminal aspects (dog fights, gangs), but also the good people that inhabit these spaces. At the end, Mayito, whose father is a jazz musician with access to Spain, gives Carlitos, the slum kid, his Playstation 3 as a sign of his friendship. This ending is very emotional for the audience, but also very sentimentally old-fashioned and lacking any type of rationality. The gesture is beautiful, but materialistic, because, in the end, this expensive game console will not make life better for anyone in the slum. During the entire film, the director criticizes the disparate living conditions in Cuba, which involve lack of education, food, and deplorable living spaces for the slum dwellers; yet in the end everything is expected to become better because the rich child gives away his toy.

Another element in both films that is more consistent with earlier ICAIC representations of the government as incompetent but well-intentioned is the representation of the police force. In *Viva Cuba*, the police officers are handsome and affable. They are extremely helpful to both families when their children escape, and act as mediators between the feuding parents. At some point in the film, Malú's mother can be heard talking to her foreign husband. When asked why she does not bribe the army so that they look for her daughter, she replies that this institution cannot be bought like in other countries. In *Habanastation*, the police save the children from a violent youth gang, and they even serve as a sort of parental figure to Carlos. Even though both films are critical of the bad economy and the revolutionary discourse, the filmmakers are very careful to portray the agents of the Cuban revolution in a positive manner.

This is why I believe that the most critical of the government recent Cuban film is *Juan of the Dead*. In this film, the bonding between characters was already established before the zombie calamity, and the apocalypse does not make them love Cuba any more. At the end of the film, Juan decides to stay in Cuba, but mostly because he is comfortable on the island, and he understands the necessity for others to leave. The revolutionary government collapses, and perhaps the most daring moment of the film is when Juan has to slay one of the military/cop zombie officials to save the monster's young son. *Juan of the Dead* uses the zombie apocalypse structure to actually depict the fall of the government, which is the most groundbreaking aspect of Cuban cinema I have seen to this day. This is not because I would like the revolutionary government to fail, but rather because it is impressive that a Cuban film dares to depict the fall of the government, and to portray government officials as threatening to ordinary citizens. This, to me, shows a new level of maturation in the Cuban cinema industry, because it demonstrates that Cuban filmmakers are finally able to distinguish between escapist fantasies and political commitment. Thus, making fun of or criticizing the government in such an aggressive way as it appears in *Juan of the Dead* means neither that the film is anti-revolutionary nor that it does not show commitment to the Cuban people.

One element that I do appreciate about *Viva Cuba* and *Habanastation*, however, is the lack of explicit sexuality in the films due to the young age of their protagonists (and target audiences). After the Special Period, foreign financing has affected the portrayal of

Conclusion

Cuban sexuality on the screen, and now foreign producers constantly demand graphic sex scenes to be included in the films. This is perfectly parodied in Juan Carlos Tabío's *So Far Away* (*Aunque estés lejos*), in which a Spanish producer demands Cuban women to have sex on screen. The film ingeniously and ironically incorporates this artificial sexuality into its plot through a meta parody of Cuban-Spanish coproductions. Still, it is difficult to understand the exploitative aspects of the depiction of Cuban sexuality, unless one has seen the entire history of the Cuban film industry, and specifically the attempts of foreign producers to maintain the exotic allure of the island for foreign audiences. I sincerely hope that in the future, Cuban filmmakers will continue to display pride with their revolutionary values, but at the same time will be able to evolve from certain racial and sexual stereotypes demanded by foreign interests, but also promoted by Cuban nationalist discourse.

There are several historical events that give me hope about the island's cinema industry prospects. The transition of power from Fidel to Raúl Castro still shows a controversial nepotistic element, but Raúl has been more open to change, and to evolving the Cuban economy. Nowadays, the internet and other types of media are more available on the island, and Cuba is beginning to look more like China rather than the Soviet Union in terms of socio-political and economic development. Still, no matter how open the Cuban economy becomes, the island's cinema will still be controlled by the state, which is why the critical views expressed in Cuban films will be channeled through certain genres, and will be difficult to decode for anyone outside of local Cuban audiences or specialists familiar with the idiosyncrasies of Cuban cinema.

In 2013, ICAIC's long-tenured president Alfredo Guevara died at the age of 87, but he had already been substituted in 2000 by Omar González. In a recent interview, González discussed the latest controversies regarding the ICAIC, which included the fact that they no longer control the island's movie theaters, with the exception of five theaters in Havana. Other topics on which he touched were the lack of digital projectors and the integration of young Cuban filmmakers to the ICAIC structure.[6] In another online interview, he specifically addressed the issue of the new independent Cuban directors, by maintaining that the

Conclusion

ICAIC is always attempting to be at the vanguard of cinema, and if this means a new cinematic diversity, they will embrace it.[7]

Gónzalez expressed pride in the ICAIC animation studios (which made four animated long features simultaneously), and in the festivals sponsored by the Institute (such as Festival de Nuevo Cine Latinoamericano, Festival de Cine Pobre, Festival de Documentales and la Muestra de Cine Joven) which provide screening venues for young filmmakers from Cuba and from other poor nations from around the world. In addition, he was very pleased with the re-emergence of their film criticism label Ediciones ICAIC, which has published important books about Cuban cinema that I myself have used as a reference in this book. Most importantly, he praises the ICAIC's stability and how older employees that have worked for several decades at the Institute may serve as experienced mentors to the new Cuban filmmakers.

In 2013, González relinquished his position at the ICAIC, and his assistant Robert Smith was appointed president. Smith's presidency has already experienced a number of controversial debates as the ICAIC has been placed under the control of the Cuban Ministry of Culture (Ministerio de Cultura). This structural change has magnified the bureaucratic process of official Cuban filmmaking. Filmmaker Fernando Pérez has discussed in online interviews[8] how he is now able to make independent Cuban films. He points out, however, that the ICAIC has failed to interact with independent Cuban filmmakers and to take advantage of the opportunity to integrate them better, as the Muestra de Cine Joven festival (designed to showcase new talent) has not been well promoted on the island. On the other hand, at a meeting of ICAIC animators, filmmaker Alexander Rodríguez said that the problem is not necessarily the ICAIC but the outdated financing system that hampers creativity.[9]

As an independent Cuban filmmaker, Alejandro Brugués (director of *Juan of the Dead*) specifically points out how his production was independent from the ICAIC, but still relied on the Institute's support to produce the film:

> You can do a painting independently, but not a movie. A film needs the support of many people. If ICAIC hadn't given its support it would have likely been someone else, the National Video Movement, for example. ICAIC helped with permits and gave institutional support. We shot in

Conclusion

Cubanacán Studios. We have always had a good relationship with ICAIC. They have the expertise and resources. They have their own way of doing things and we have ours. This creates a combination, a middle point where you use the best of each party and that gives the best results.[10]

In the end, it is very important that an institution like the ICAIC keeps itself relevant because it has been the most stable and important cinema studio in the Caribbean. Its continuous support of intellectual filmmakers, and their commitment to the Cuban revolution and its workers is worthy of admiration. The list of Cuban classics produced under its guidance is magnificent, and it is commendable that the institution survived the end of the Cold War. However, it is important that they start supporting constant independent work outside of their umbrella. The ICAIC still casts a shadow esthetically and culturally over independent filmmakers, but things are certainly looking promising for a Cuban national cinema respected around the world for its revolutionary esthetics, while remaining one of the most fun sources of Hispanic/Latin/AfroCaribbean/Marxist cinema today.

Chapter Notes

Introduction

1. At the time, selling private property was illegal in Cuba. The only legal way to acquire a new residence was to barter with other homeowners. This process is known on the island as "permutar" (literally: to exchange or swap). In November 2011, the selling of private property was finally legalized by President Raúl Castro, and Cuban citizens were able to sell their houses legally for the first time since the 1959 revolution.
2. ICAIC (Instituto Cubano de Artes Industriales y Cinematográficas) is the Cuban Film Institute. The name translates literally as Cuban Institute of Industrial and Cinematographic Arts.
3. Díaz and del Río, 12.
4. "En todos estos títulos se imitaba el folklorismo, adaptado en Cuba, de la comedia ranchera o el melodrama de origen mexicano, ambos pasados por la riquísima tradición musical nacionalista y por la tipología del teatro popular, o se imitaba abiertamente el folletín radial" (Díaz and del Río, 13).
5. Paranagua, 7.
6. Piñera, 40.
7. "Después de intentar infructuosamente incorporarse al cine del ICAIC en 1959, Peón regresó definitivamente a México, donde declaró con amargura: Tres veces fui a mi patria para hacer el cine cubano y fui recibido con banda de música en el aereopuerto, y en las tres oportunidades tuve que irme por suscripción popular" (Díaz and del Río, 14).
8. Walfredo Piñera, 65–66.
9. Castillo, 25.
10. Ibid., 27.
11. Ibid., 25 and Piñera, 70.
12. Piñera, 63.
13. Castillo, 29.
14. Fornet, 80.
15. Movie theaters had been nationalized, and content was provided only through government-approved sources.
16. Sandra del Valle, 65.
17. Pérez, 54.
18. Fornet, 82.
19. Díaz and del Río, 37.
20. For more details about the disastrous release of *Cecilia*, please refer to Michael Chanan's book *Cuban Cinema*. Another article that discusses the film in detail is Cuban researcher Sandra del Valle's "Definirse en la polémica: *PM, Cecilia* y *Alicia*."
21. The 2000s have not been officially named to this point, which is why one of the main jokes of the Cuban film *Juan de los muertos* (*Juan of the Dead*, 2010) is when the protagonist says: "I survived Angola, Mariel, the Special Period, and this thing that came after."
22. Hernández Reguant, 4.
23. Ibid., 7.
24. Venegas, "Filmmaking with Foreigners," 40.
25. Ibid., 39.
26. Ibid., 48.
27. Michael Chanan explains the role of *Cine Cubano* in his book *Cuban Cinema*:
    Julianne Burton has suggested that ICAIC was always leery of professional critics and therefore decided early on to assume the critic's task itself by creating the journal *Cine Cubano*. If it is true that many Cuban filmmakers believed the exercise of criticism to be a

Notes—Chapter 1

responsibility of the filmmaker, not to be left to journalists and literati, the journal was also an expression of the same imperative that guided the creation of film magazines throughout Latin America whenever a nucleus of film-makers committed to the new cinema movement took root: a magazine was a declaration of existence, a claim for attention, an instrument in the construction of an identity. Publications of this kind tend to share with the films of the movement they belong to many of the same artisanal qualities, and are devoted more to championing a cause and disseminating positions than traditional forms of critical reflection. *Cine Cubano* set new standards in the service of propagation and the education of its readership, and showed its spirit in its own distinctive modern typography and design. Abroad, the magazine became a primary source of information about Cuban and the new Latin American cinema in general. At home, the readership included the expanding circle of critics at a time when their numbers were growing with more space to fill in a press transformed by the revolution [424].

Chapter 1

1. Lewis Carroll's *Alice in Wonderland* and Astrid Lindgren's *The Adventures of Pippi Longstocking*.
2. Henceforth referred to as *Alicia*.
3. Redruello, 87.
4. Ibid., 88.
5. "In a summary of the Berlin Film Festival published by the magazine *D+C* (March, 1991) one reads: there Alicia found a society of strange characters trapped in an asylum for the mentally insane ran by a director with a large beard" (A.G. 1992, 18).
6. *Quiéreme y Verás* (1994), *Kleines Tropikana* (1997), *Hacerse el Sueco* (2000), *Lisanka* (2009), and *La película de Ana* (2012).
7. See, for example, Michael Chanan's chapter "Wonderland" in his *Cuban Cinema*.

8. This is how Michael Chanan describes the controversy surrounding *Alice in Wondertown*:
The crisis was compounded by the announcement around the same time of a scheme to merge ICAIC with Cuban television and the film unit of the Armed Forces, as part of a general plan of rationalization of human and material resources by the state, in the face of the greater economic crisis that had befallen Cuba with the collapse of Communism in Eastern Europe. At ICAIC, following unprecedented protests by the film directors, the situation was resolved by the end of the summer. The institute survived, but the film remained banned, and the head of the Institute, Julio García Espinosa, was replaced by the return of its founder, Alfredo Guevara [*Cuban Cinema*, 457].

9. Soles, 85.
10. The Charles Chaplin Theater is the main cinema venue in Havana.
11. Sandra del Valle, 89.
12. The Monty Python troupe has been involved in its own cultural controversies, especially after the satire *Life of Brian* was banned in a number of Christian countries.
13. Alice is waiting for her bus in a Cuban diner close to the bus station, and sees a glass of dirty water similar to the one the mayor was offering her earlier in the film.
14. Porbén, 10.
15. In the cartoon shown in the film, a little bird is buried in a big pile of excrement. The bird does not like the smell but grows accustomed to it, as it is a safe environment. When it finally decides to fly away, however, it is captured by a cat and eaten.
16. In the introduction to his interview with the director for the American journal *Cineaste*, Dennis West (1993) compares the controversy created in Cuba by Diaz Torres' *Alicia* to that created in the U.S. by *Birth of a Nation* (D.W. Griffith, 1915). He adds:
Alice opened in Havana in 1991 to endless lines of ticket buyers, but the

Notes—Chapter 1

government suspended exhibition after only four days. The official newspaper *Granma* and other media attacked *Alice* for being counterrevolutionary, while clandestine video copies circulated widely throughout Cuba and even in Miami and other U.S. cities. *Alice* became *cause célèbre*, and the question of artistic freedom versus political exigency was debated at the highest levels of the revolutionary leadership [24].

17. Here is an example of one of the citations that appeared in *Cine Cubano* (A.G., 21):
> From *Tribuna* (a Cuban newspaper):
> For attempting to go against our principles, the film is unacceptable. We cannot allow, in the historical phase in which our nation is living, a Cuban film to offend the dignity of those who fight to control their own destiny, tied to nobler causes and willing to improve our work with suitable ideas and with respect to the purest aspects of our historical heritage [Ada Oramas].

18. West, 24.
19. García Espinosa, "For an Imperfect Cinema," 81.
20. Martínez Alfaro, 270.
21. Chanan, *Cuban Cinema*, 457.
22. Millán Agudo, 146
23. Breton, 24.
24. Short, 11.
25. Millán Agudo, 21.
26. "The Baroque and the Marvelous Real," 103.
27. José Martí is one of Cuba's greatest nationalist heroes promoted by the Cuban Revolution.
28. Díaz Torres mentions that the word *bureaucrat* acquired a negative connotation after the film.
29. *The Man of Maisinicu* is a black and white film released in 1974 that follows the infiltration of a government agent into the ranks of the enemies of the Revolution. The film is allegedly based on real events, but esthetically it resembles a typical film noir about FBI agents infiltrating the Mafia.
30. "Self-consciousness as the dominant in the construction of a character's image requires the creation of an artistic atmosphere that would permit his discourse to reveal and illuminate itself. Not a single element in this atmosphere can be neutral: everything must touch the character to the quick, provoke him, interrogate him, even polemicize with him and taunt him; everything must be directed toward the hero himself, turned toward him, everything must make itself felt as discourse about someone actually present, as the word of a 'second' and not of a 'third' person." (Bakhtin, 64)

31. Desirée Díaz quotes former ICAIC president Alfredo Guevara about the film's double meanings and interpretations:
> Este problema de las múltiples lecturas, y de las dos principales, pudo ser para *Alicia en el pueblo de Maravillas* una prueba de calidad y valor excepcional pero ha sido, en cambio, la clave de su 'maldición.' Porque involuntariamente resulta para algunos obra maldita, y para otros maldita obra. [...] nadie se ha preguntado si no será acaso el verdadero problema, esa necesidad de explicación que el filme provoca; y a partir de esa eventual toma de conciencia si no convendría a cada receptor preguntarse (también explicarse) el porqué de sus propias reacciones [212].

> [The problem of multiple readings, and of the two main ones, could have been for *Alice in Wondertown* a test of quality and exceptional value, but it has become instead the key to its curse. Because involuntarily it becomes a damnable work for some and an ill-fated work for others. [...] Nobody has asked himself/herself if this isn't really the true probem, this necessity of explaining the meaning that the film provokes; from the consequent awakening of consciousness, if each receptor [reader or viewer] would ask (as well as explain to) himself/herself the reason behind his/her own reactions] [translated by the present author].

32. The Caracol award is given by "La Asociación de medios audiovisuales y radio de la Unión de Escritores y Artistas de Cuba (UNEAC)."
33. Hutcheon, *Theory of Parody*, 101.

Chapter 2

1. In the book by Carlos Galiano and Rufo Caballero, *Cien años sin soledad: Las mejores películas latinoamericanas de todos los tiempos* (La Habana: Letras Cubanas, 1999), a Latin American film canon was based on the votes of several prestigious film critics from Central and South America. *Memories of Underdevelopment* and *Lucía* were the first and third film with most votes respectively. The impact of the films in academia is important although it is debatable whether the films have been seen by the Latin American masses.

2. For more information about Solás' early life, see his interview conducted by Robin Ravelo del Valle included in the book *Tras las huellas de Solás*.

3. Gutíerrez Alea studied filmmaking in Italy, and Solás' life changed when he saw De Sicca's *Umberto D* (1952) (Flores González 11).

4. Film historian Michael Chanan quotes Alfredo Guevara, former head of the ICAIC, recognizing the disagreements about socialism among the revolutionaries:

> The situation according to Alfredo Guevara, was that the evolution of the Revolution toward socialism was for many people a great surprise, which created many anxieties. At the beginning, many people found it easy to be progressive. The condemnation of corruption, for example, was a matter of national pride: corruption wasn't Cuban, it was something created by the gringos. That a process had been set in motion, however, leading toward socialist solutions was something relatively few comprehended [*Cuban Cinema*, 123].

5. Cabrera Infante writes in his book *Mea Cuba*:

> I helped Sabá, my brother, with the completion of a documentary he was making with the cinematographer Orlando Jiménez Leal- at the time the youngest photographer in Cuba, capable of handling a CinemaScope camera when he was fifteen, quite a film feat. As its title suggests, *P.M.* would be a view of Havana after dark, the camera peeping into the small cafés and bars and dives patronized by the common Cuban having a last time before the political night closed in. I liked the idea. I gave them the money to edit the documentary, print two or three copies, and design the titles. All this was done outside the Film Institute-that is, officialdom, in our TV channel labs but quite openly. *Lunes* got the exclusive rights to show the picture on its program and we showed it. There was no censorship for us on television. As in my magazine, we were our own boss. After all, we were the offspring of *Revolución*, the newspaper of the Revolution, the voice of the people. We were omnipotent—sort of [484].

6. Cabrera Infante, 484.

7. Guevara, 372.

8. Guevara refers to the "New Man" in masculine terms, a locution that has been criticized in Cuban culture.

9. Guevara, 372–375.

10. Ibid., 371.

11. "To sum up, the fault of many of our artists and intellectuals lies in their original sin: they are not true revolutionaries. We can try to graft the elm tree so that it will bear pears, but at the same time we must plant pear trees. New generations will come that will be free of original sin. The probability that great artists will appear will be greater to the degree that the field of culture and the possibilities for expression are broadened" (Ché Guevara, 224).

12. Astrid Santana Fernández de Castro points out three things that had affected the perception of intellectuals after the Cuban Revolution: (1) Fidel's speech: "Las palabras a los intelectuales" (1961); (2) the first congress for writers and artists in 1961; and (3) the perception that the foreign cinema screened in Cuba was decadent and bourgeois (15).

13. These melodramas emphasized the pleasures of wealth and its attainment by the poor through Christian Catholic faith.

14. Film scholar Adrian Danks writes: "From a contemporary perspective, the most remarkable aspect of *Lucía* is its ability to move dynamically between vari-

Notes—Chapter 2

ous modes of cinema and eye-popping tableaux of equal beauty and horror" (504).

15. In her article "De Sergio a Diego: La Diáspora en el cine de Tomás Gutíerrez Alea," Desirée Diaz writes that Sergio did not leave with the Cuban bourgeoisie to escape this particular social class, but remained on the island without joining the revolution. This ambiguous position leaves him in a limbo:

"Para el personaje, el hecho de quedarse en la isla supone también un intento de escape, de refugio, en este caso, una huída de la clase social a la que pertenece, la burguesía, y con la cual no comparte determinados valores. Sergio no se queda 'con' la revolución, sino que se queda para no 'quedarse' con la burguesía y esta posición ambigua lo deja físicamente en la isla, pero psicológicamente en un limbo, en una especie de no—lugar que es también el espacio creado y habitado por la diáspora" [83].

16. Stam writes: "The Desnoes novel clearly derives, then, from the line instituted by Dostoevsky in *Notes from Underground*, i.e. the tradition of the irritable, spiteful, inconsistent, unreliable first-person narrator, who is undeserving of our confidence or our respect" (*Literature Through Film*, 210).

17. Schroeder, 140.

18. The *Sight and Sound* reviewer, Don Allen, was surprised by the film's dialogism; the review begins with the following lines: "It seems as improbable that Tomás Gutíerrez Alea's *Memories of Underdevelopment* should have been approved for export by the Cuban authorities as that Buñuel should have made *Viridiana* under Franco's nose. Both films in their different ways undermine, or significantly question, the cultural values of the country which sanctioned them" (222). Gutíerrez Alea has always denied assessments that define him as counterrevolutionary.

19. Burton, "*Memories*," 234.

20. In his interview with Julianne Burton, Gutíerrez Alea explains the attraction of Sergio:

In my view, the Sergio character is very complex. On one hand, he incarnates all the bourgeois ideology which has marked our people right up until the triumph of the Revolution and still has carry-overs, an ideology which even permeates the proletarian strata. In one sense Sergio represents the ideal of what every man with that particular kind of mentality would like to have been: rich, good-looking, intelligent, with access to the upper social strata and to beautiful women who are very willing to go to bed with him. That is to say, he has a set of virtues and advantages which permit spectators to identify to a certain degree with him as a character [Burton, "Individual Fulfillment" 189].

21. Gutíerrez Alea makes the following comments on Godard's achievements:

In the heat of the post-war period in France, a "new wave" of young directors appeared who threw themselves impetuously into revolutionizing filmmaking without going beyond the limits of the petty bourgeois world. Among them, Godard stands out as the great destroyer of bourgeois cinema. Taking Brecht as his point of departure—and the New Left as his point of arrival—he tried to make revolution on the screen. His genius, inventiveness, imagination, and clumsy aggressiveness gave him a privileged place among the "damned" filmmakers. He managed to make anti-bourgeois cinema but he could not make people's cinema. Noteworthy epigones like Jean-Marie Straub, admirable for his almost religious asceticism, have already institutionalized that position and some think they are making a revolution in the superstructure without needing to shake up the base [Gutíerrez Alea, "The Viewer's Dialectic," 114].

22. Shaw, 17.

23. Gutíerrez Alea, 129.

24. One of the first examples was the movie *Lejanía* (dir. Jesús Diaz, 1985) that attempted to portray Cuban exiles in a more nuanced manner.

25. These debates about how exiles or emigrants were perceived on the island were very important after the Special Pe-

riod. When asked in an interview what aspects of *Memories of Underdevelopment* have aged, actor Sergio Corrieri provided the following response:

Well, for example, everything in the film that refers to the emigration problem in Cuba is no longer seen in the same way today. The emigration problem has changed a lot—its reasons and causes are totally different. In the Sixties Cuban emigration was predominantly ideological. The first wave of emigrants were naturally those who were implicated by the Batista regime, the generals, the police, and the torturers. After them came those who were affected by the revolution, the land and property owners, those whom the revolution hurt in their pocketbooks. That was also partly an ideological emigration.

I think that Cuban emigration today is quite different. All right, naturally there is a quota of ideological emigration, but there is an even larger quota of economic emigration. There is even a wave of what we could call "cognitive" emigration, in the sense that many people leave Cuba not because they want the revolution to disappear, but simply because they want to see the world, to see other realities, other societies. That is entirely something else. In the Sixties those that left were gusanos, traitors. But that's not so today. At least not in every case [Miller 22].

26. Tomás Gutiérrez Alea was a cancer patient at the time, and needed the help of Juan Carlos Tabío to complete the film.

27. Chanan, *Cuban Cinema*, 474.

28. Chanan writes the following about the role of feminism in Cuban homophobia: "[The repression of gays] seems to me [...] the result of the advancement of women within the Revolution [...] Especially in a society as intensely machista as Cuba, the advancement of women represents a threat to men, or to a certain kind of man, and men whose own sexuality is thus threatened are all to liable to start taking it out on other men" (*The Cuban Image*, 6).

29. Smith, 254.

30. In Smith's words:

Another critic who makes quite explicit his identification with the "socialist ideas" of Cuba is Briton Michael Chanan, author of an exhaustively documented history of Cuban cinema. Chanan's *The Cuban Image* opens with an attack on *Improper Conduct*, then recently released (he was also prominent in attacking Almendros when he presented the film at the London Film Festival). In Chanan, as in Rich, but more explicitly, the critique of representation fuses with an overt political commitment that leads its author into sophistries based once more in a rhetoric of reversal [...] Chanan attacks the film for its "relentless disregard" for dialectical argument, [lack of] exploration of the contradictions [the interviews] posed, or respect for the viewer's powers of discrimination" [5].... In the end one has to doubt whether all these stories can be true [253].

31. Wilkinson, 287.

32. Ibid., 289.

33. "The revolutionaries adopted extreme postures in many arenas, not just the military and economic matters, but also in terms of behavior and even sexuality. In order to protect the country from everything 'corrupted,' one had to be ever more nationalistic, and to become more nationalistic it was necessary to revive some of the county's best and worst traditions, including homophobia [...] It is only fair to insist that the homophobic construction of Cuban nationalism is an indisputable reality, and that not all of the homophobic excesses of the revolution can be attributed to the personal prejudices of its leaders. It should therefore be said that what was truly extraordinary about the situation at that time was not the homophobic positions themselves, but their convergence, extremism, and institutionalization" (Bejel, *Gay Cuban Nation*, 95–96).

34. D'Lugo, 171.

35. Film scholar Emilio Bejel explains the film's popularity with the following lines:

The most extraordinary aspect of

Notes—Chapter 2

Strawberry and Chocolate was neither its cinematographic quality nor its theme of homosexuality per se, but rather that it was produced and released in Socialist Cuba and dealt with rights of homosexuals in that society. Of course, had it been a poorly made film, the theme and country of origin by themselves would not have given rise to such success. *Strawberry and Chocolate* was well made, however, the acting was excellent (with Mirta Ibarra truly exceptional in the role of Nancy), and above all, the human warmth of certain scenes (especially those where David and Diego communicate through an understanding that is progressive and complex) served to capture the attention and sensibilities of many audiences ["*Strawberry and Chocolate*: Coming Out of the Cuban Closet?" 66].

36. Evora, 56.
37. Ibid., 55.
38. Scholar Emilio Bejel finds the lack of gay sex in the film problematic because that made it safe for a traditional Cuban audience, and it does not dare to be more radical in comparison to other texts such as *The Kiss of the Spider Woman* (Bejel, *Gay Cuban Nation*, 161).
39. Mercer and Shingler's book *Melodrama: Genre, Style, and Sensibility* explores melodrama and its evolution from a generic film industry definition to an academic concept related to depiction of family dynamics. Among the scholars they quote as being relevant in the modern redefinition of the concept are Thomas Elsaesser and his writings on directors such as Douglas Sirk in articles such as "Tales of Sound and Fury: Observations on the Family Melodrama" and Thomas Schatz's chapter on family melodrama that appeared in his book *Hollywood Genres*.
40. Oroz, 51.
41. Gutiérrez Alea says: "No tengo fijación ni limitaciones en ese sentido: puedo poner el acento lo mismo en una que en la otra, en lo intelectual o en lo emocional, porque es un juego permanente que me permite cortar la emoción con la razón e impulsar la razón con la emoción, potenciándola" [Evora, 112].

["I don't have an obsession or limitations in this sense: I can place the emphasis on one or the other, on the intellectual or on the emotional, because this is a permanent game that allows me to cut down the emotion with reason and to enthuse reason with emotion, thus making it more powerful"] [translated by the present author].
42. Bejel, 67.
43. Smith writes:
Moreover, by replaying the clichéd equation of homosexuality and bourgeois decadence in the person of the fastidious, tea-sipping Diego, *Fresa y chocolate* precludes any specific political discourse by masking it in the gaudy show of sexual dissidence: Diego's flamboyance hides the fact that, even within the terms of the film's overt narrative, it is not homosexuality but the slightest sign of resistance to officialdom that is intolerable to the regime [93].
44. The one that I personally prefer is *El siglo de las luces* because there the melodramatic excesses are contained by the magnificent plot, complex politics and character development of Alejo Carpentier's original novel.
45. In the summer of 2000, at the time *Honey for Oshún* was being shot, Elián was the main topic of conversation, due to the exaggerated efforts of the government to politicize events related to the child's fate. I was present at the massive rally that the main character watches in his hotel at the beginning of the film, a self-reflexive cinematic strategy that most Cuban audiences would immediately recognize. In some of the first sequences of the film, the main character's flashbacks establish how he was violently taken (or nearly kidnapped) from the island. The fact that he is watching the political rally that inspired his fictional story sets up the symbolism in a clear way for the audience, now intrigued by how this fictional Elian will reencounter both his physical and his metaphorical mother.
46. It is an amusing fact that, because of this fame, Perugorría was able to play the

role of one of the greatest bourgeois literary figures in Latin America: *Doña Babara*'s Santos Lucardo. That a coproduction among several Latin American countries cast this Cuban actor suggests how successful Gutíerrez Alea and Solás were in encouraging a performance that would make audiences around the world believe that a Cuban could convincingly mimic an upper-class member of Venezuelan society, even though the story was framed in Communist narratives.

47. Ramsdell, 123.

Chapter 3

1. I explore this experimental proletarian cinema in my discussion of *Suite Habana*, which, with some modifications, mimics this type of filmmaking.

2. In his "The Work of Art in the Age of Mechanical Reproduction."

3. "Some of the players whom we meet in Russian films are not actors in our sense but people who portray *themselves*- and primarily in their own work process. In Western Europe, the capitalist exploitation of the film denies consideration to modern man's legitimate claim to being reproduced. Under these circumstances the film industry is trying hard to spur the interest of the masses through illusion-promoting spectacles and dubious speculations" (Benjamin, 1178).

4. *Bicycle Thieves* has a social message but it is a family melodrama that manipulates the emotions of the audience.

5. Arthur Miller gave a very positive review to the film that was published by *The New York Times* in January 8, 1950. André Bazin discussed the film in his article "Neorealism and Pure Cinema: The Bicycle Thief."

6. In one of his early pre-revolutionary essays, García Espinosa praises Italian neorealism, seeing it as a good model for the Cuban national cinema as opposed to the work imported from Mexican studios (*Algo de mí*, 172).

7. García Espinosa, "Recuerdos de Zavattini," 60.

8. "Cuban directors who supported the 1959 revolution also identified with post–World War II Italian films, linking the social changes in post-fascist Italian culture to those brought about by the revolution of 1959. Since both countries were depleted of resources after their respective historical turmoil, progressive directors saw the neorealist style as a way of counterbalancing Hollywood hegemony and the previously conservative nature of their respective national cinemas, such as the fascist films promoted under Mussolini in the case of Italy, and the conservative Hispanic melodramas screened in Cuba before the Revolution" (Chanan, *Cuban Cinema*, 147).

9. Zavattini's screenplay for *El joven rebelde* (*The Young Rebel*, 1961) was produced by ICAIC, an important moment for the young Cuban film industry in that it provided a recognized European professional who could possibly help in the distribution of ICAIC productions in film festivals outside the island.

10. Évora, 23.

11. One of the posters of *Histories of Revolution* promotes the film by stating that revolutionary soldiers play themselves in the scenes that reproduce the battles of Sierra Maestra.

12. Évora, 23.

13. Ibid., 24.

14. García Espinosa is adamant about the dangers of intellectual directors seeking European approval: "When we look toward Europe, we wring our hands. We see that the old culture is totally incapable of providing answers to the problems of art. The fact is that Europe can no longer respond in a traditional manner but at the same time finds it equally difficult to respond in a manner that is radically new. Europe is no longer capable of giving the world a new 'ism'; neither is it in a position to put an end to 'isms' once and for all. So we think that our moment has come, that at last the underdeveloped can deck themselves out as 'men of culture'" (78).

15. "Muchas veces se dice que 'Por un cine imperfecto' no es un ensayo, ni la espina dorsal teórica de un movimiento cin-

Notes—Chapter 3

ematográfico, sino simplemente un llamado de alerta política ante los caminos que producto del éxito se les ofrecían a los cineastas" (Herrera, 31).

["It has been said many times that "For an Imperfect Cinema" is not an essay, nor the theoretical backbone of a film movement, but simply a call for political awakening against the opportunities opened before the filmmakers as a result of their success"] [translated by the present author].

16. Venegas writes: "Como teoría estética hablaba de una energía creativa y de una visión que insistía en que los artistas buscaran sus caminos desde sus propias realidades y no a partir de otros modelos industriales… Apartándose de las jerarquías de producción y desafiando los patrones de calidad regidos por empresas con intereses propios, la producción de arte pudiera crear comunidades expresivas que cultivaran procesos en lugar de formas de producción destinadas a satisfacer un común denominador en el mercado masivo" (55).

["As an aesthetic theory, he spoke of a creative energy and a vision that stipulated that the artists must search for [an artistic] path from within their own reality and not borrowed from other industrial models… By distancing itself from the hierarchies of production and defying quality control imposed by business entities with their own agenda, art production could create artistic communities that would nurture artistic processes instead of forms of production aimed only at satisfying a common denominator on the mass-production market"] [translated by the present author].

17. García Espinosa, "For an Imperfect Cinema," 79.

18. In his book *Algo de mí*, García Espinosa himself recognizes the influence of Brecht in his imperfect cinema manifesto. He also quotes the German playwright in his postmodern film musical *Son o no son*.

19. Taylor, n. pag.

20. Douglas, 292.

21. Blasini writes: "*Plaff*'s ostensible 'carelessness' in terms of style, performance, and technique is explained as a consequence of rushing the film's production simply to meet a deadline—the day that commemorates the role of filmmakers in society. This 'carelessness' also serves as a way of emphasizing that the production of Cuban films should respond to relevant contemporary issues such as the everyday struggles of a country with minimal material resources rather than vainglorious ones like the narcissistic exaltation of artists" (200).

22. Baron writes: "Whereas in the 1960s, self-reflexive filmmaking carried with it the sense that the filmmakers were educating the audience as to the whys and wherefores of how a film was made and what it represented, in this film the audience is already informed and "in on the act," thus questioning the supposed 'authority' of the filmmakers themselves. So, with *Plaff!*'s repeated references to the film institute and humorous nods and winks to some of the financial challenges of making films in Cuba, the film develops a 'knowing' self-reflexivity" (55).

23. According to Woods, "Postmodernism is a knowing modernity, a self-reflexive modernism, a modernism that does not agonise about itself […] instead of lamenting the loss of the past, the fragmentation of existence and the collapse of selfhood" (9).

24. Baron, 56.

25. Ibid., 58.

26. Ibid., 59.

27. Ibid.

28. Chanon, 475.

29. With regard to shooting "reality," Gutíerrez Alea writes, "Thus we find it no longer sufficient just to take the cameras and capture fragments of that reality. This can still be a legitimate type of filmmaking, but only when, and if, the filmmaker knows how to select those aspects which, in close interrelation offer a meaningful image or reality, which serves the film as a point of both departure and arrival" ("The Viewer's Dialectic," 109).

30. Gutíerrez Alea, "The Viewer's Dialectic," 123.

31. This is an homage to Glauber Rocha's *Antonio Das Mortes* (1969).

32. Adell, 74–75.

33. Elliot Young on *Suite Habana*'s box office:

The reaction to the film by Havana audiences when it was screened in the

Notes—Chapter 3

summer of 2003 was phenomenal. Originally the film was scheduled for a short run at the Charlie Chaplin cinema, a venue that caters to art and European films, but the packed theater, night after night, with audiences openly crying and spontaneously erupting in standing ovations, created a public pressure that forced an extension of the screening for several months. The film was eventually screened at more popular movie houses like the cine *Yara*, and a as a result it reached a fairly wide audience, at least in Havana [36].

34. The cover for the bootleg version of *Suite Habana* contains the following tagline: "La película que censuró el gobierno cubano. *Suite Habana* está prohibida" [The film censored by the Cuban government. *Suite Habana* is banned]. Many eBay sellers are based in Miami, and similar announcements enhance sales. The myth that *Suite Habana* was banned in Cuba circulated widely, causing some scholars to be interested in the film's release, perhaps a consequence of those looking toward the production of another *Alice in Wondertown*.

35. Caballero, 300.

36. Juan Antonio García Borrero notes that this film represents a period when ICAIC was making straightforward films with clear narratives that would be accessible to the public (78). I myself consider this to be a bland propaganda film about the revolution.

37. Stock, "Imagining the Future in Revolutionary Cuba: An Interview with Fernando Pérez," 72.

38. The citizens play themselves, but their day is set up and manipulated for narrative purposes. Dara Goldman describes the film as "a documentary filmed in the style of cinéma verité: using no professional actors nor formal script, the camera seemingly observes the featured individuals going about their daily activities during a 24-hour period" (869).

39. Stock, "Imagining the Future in Revolutionary Cuba: An Interview with Fernando Pérez," 73.

40. Fernando Pérez was also a film critic, and in 1974 he wrote an article explaining the greatness of Eisenstein's montage in *Battleship Potemkin* and *October* (Pérez, "Un tratado cinematográfico").

41. This editing style was developed by Soviet directors, foremost among them Sergei Eisenstein, who defined in his publications four types of montage: metric, rhythmic, tonal, and overtonal. Metric montage is related to specific timed cuts which give the audience a stable temporal frame for the switching of images (72). Rhythmic montage changes the editing pace from image to image, and its construction is based on the manipulations of rhythm (73). Tonal montage arranges the images in order to visually seek an emotional response from the audience (75). Overtonal montage combines these mentioned above to provide a more complex narration (78). Eisenstein explains this in detail in his essay "Methods of Montage."

42. Elliot Young notes that Pérez "reinvents cine imperfecto by calling attention to the medium without turning his film into a mouthpiece for a didactic political message" (36).

43. Thompkins offers an elaborate explanation of Fernando Pérez's use of Eisenstein's montage techniques in her "Montage in Fernando Pérez Valdés' *Suite Habana*."

44. Thompkins writes: "Pérez subverts these generic conventions by eliminating dialogue. As a result, the characters of *Suite Habana* appear to become more introspective, and to engage almost mechanically in their daily activities; therefore, they seem to be looking inward, so their features appear motionless" (37).

45. It is unclear how the two are related. When watching the movie, I am inclined to think Raquel is Ivan's mother. However, other researchers have interpreted it as a wife-husband or brother-sister relationship.

46. Goldman, 877.

47. Young, 39.

48. Ibid., 46.

49. Caballero, 300.

50. Ibid., 298.

51. In contrast, Nestor Almendros and Oscar Jimenez Leal's documentary *Improper Conduct* (that I discussed in Chapter

2) was shocking by having people expressing themselves directly to the camera.

Chapter 4

1. When I taught my *Hispanic Musicals* class, I noticed that many of my students' perception of the musical genre is limited to Disney and Broadway musical adaptations. Latin American musicals, however, are mostly romantic dramas or comedies that feature a famous performer, and whose numbers may or may not be linked to the plot.

John Mueller has outlined how musicals in general use performances in different manners. Some have numbers that advance the plot, while others contain musical performances that do not advance the plot but enrich it, e.g. by means of duets that serve to display the emotions of the characters. Sometimes, Latin American musicals feature plenty of music, but the numbers are not related to the plot. They are instead included because the audience wants to see a particular singer perform.

2. Castilla, 20. Castilla claims that these characters were so embedded in Cuban narratives, that even the World War II thriller *Fantasmas del Caribe* (*Caribbean Ghosts*), with dialogues by famous Cuban writer Alejo Carpentier, had to include the three comedic archetypes in its plot.

3. The word "mulatto" is a social concept that is very relevant to countries that have had slavery and migration patterns from African regions as a consequence of Western imperialism. This word is usually used to describe individuals with a biracial heritage that includes black ancestry. This term can be very problematic because during the Caribbean colonial and slavery periods, being a mulatto provided a limited social status with advantages over other black members of society. These mulattos had more access to white hegemony, but their rights were still limited by the racist imperialist establishments.

4. Mendieta Costa, 40.
5. Ibid., 41.
6. Ibid., 43.
7. Bhaba writes:

Colonial mimicry is the desire for a reformed, recognizable Other, as a subject of a difference that is almost the same, but not quite. Which is to say, that the discourse of mimicry is constructed around an ambivalence in order to be effective, mimicry must continually produce its slippage, its excess, its difference. The authority of that mode of colonial discourse that I call mimicry is therefore stricken by an indeterminacy: mimicry emerges as the representation of a difference that is itself a process of disavowal. Mimicry is thus the sign of a double articulation; a complex strategy of reform, regulation and discipline, which "appropriates" as it visualizes power. Mimicry is also the sign of the inappropriate, however a difference or recalcitrance which coheres the dominant strategic function of colonial power, intensifies surveillance, and poses an immanent threat to both "normalized" knowledges and disciplinary powers [86].

8. This self-mocking mimicry is evident in Cuba's two most important 19th-century anti-slavery and nationalist novels: Gertrudis Gómez de Avellaneda's *Sab* and Cirilo Villaverde's *Cecilia Valdés o La Loma del Ángel*. In *Sab*, a mulatto named Sab falls in love with Carlotta, his employers' daughter. The family prefers to marry her to a dull rich foreigner whose only advantage over Sab is his aristocratic name. His nobility title is valuable to Carlotta's family because they are almost bankrupt at the time. The day of the wedding, Sab dies without achieving his romantic goals, but saves the family with money he won playing the lottery.

In *Cecilia Valdés*, a young mulatta named Cecilia tries to ascend into the Cuban aristocracy by seducing Leonardo de Gamboa, a pompous young man from an upper-class Cuban family. The irony is that she should be part of the family because she is the bastard child of Leonardo's aristocratic father. Her racial status has excluded her from these riches, and at the end of the novel she is committed to a mental asylum along with her mother who also

Notes—Chapter 4

was a victim of the Gamboa family's plotting.

Both novels were very important to the nationalist movement in Cuba because they showed that, even though the mulattos interacted within the Eurocentric culture, their African heritage made sure that they would never have complete access to power and economic gain in the Spanish colonial system. Marriage, sex, and miscegenation were the key to both Sab and Cecilia's economic success in their respective narratives, and this is why it was very important that their rejection at the hands of the colonial establishment led to both mulattos' destruction. In their times, these novels were considered the perfect allegories of the failure of Spanish colonialism in Cuba.

9. *El negro que tenía alma blanca* (*The Black Man Who Had a White Soul*) is a novel about a Cuban dancer who lived in Spain and France. The novel was adapted three times for the screen in Spain.

10. The Soviets were more interested in antagonizing the Americans rather than the Spanish because the project was intended as a response to the nuclear missile crisis in 1962.

11. Michael Chanan writes: "According to the director himself: 'I wanted to make the ugliest film in the world, that is to say, to eliminate customary expectations like suspense, the primacy of the image, virtuosic mise-en-scène, beautiful photography, etc., and for the film to be sustained only through its dramaturgy'" (397).

12. Chanan, 396.

13. Ibid., 396–97.

14. Many film scholars could have issues with these statements. *Son o no son* sees musicals made in capitalist countries as incapable of disseminating political statements, but it ignores Hollywood political musicals such as Norman Jewinson's *Fiddler on the Roof* and Milos Forman's *Hair*.

15. Film historian Michael Chanan writes in regards to the film's satire: "It is as if the film takes its own premises too seriously, afraid to carry them beyond a certain limited level of permitted double entendre; and in this respect it is marked by the political caution of the moment" (*Cuban Cinema* 398).

16. Hernández-Reguant, 87.

17. As I mentioned earlier in the chapter, many of the vaudeville performances in the Alhambra were very influential in early Cuban cinema.

18. On page 50 of the novel, she specifically explains that she sometimes faked torticollis in order to avoid playing the mulatta role.

19. Cuban film scholar Cristina Venegas wrote a very detailed article titled "Filmmaking with Foreigners," in which she analyzes many of the aspects involved in coproduction Cuban filmmaking during the Special Period.

20. Chanan, *Cuban Cinema*, 480.

21. The Tropicana cabaret is very influential in Cuban culture because of his musical shows. It has been featured in pre-revolutionary films such as *Tropicana* (1957), ICAIC films such as *Son o no son* (1978), *Adorables Mentiras* (1992), and others.

22. Hernández-Reguant, 82.

23. At the beginning of the film, the AfroCuban Armando does not believe she could dance so well because he perceives her as a white woman; however, when she gives birth to a black baby, he admits: "Pudiera ser, aquí el que no tiene de Congo lo tiene de Carabalí" [It could be, here, whoever isn't a descendant of a Congo tribe, must be from a Caravalí tribe].

24. These songs are "oldies" that continue to be played on certain specialty radio stations and are also available on CD.

25. Ry Cooder adds modern electric guitar sounds that are clearly out of place within the traditional music of the Cuban performers. He may argue this is fusion, but it certainly does not sound right in terms of musicality.

26. Tanya Hernández, 63.

27. Films such as *Buena Vista Social Club* do not threaten the regime or Cuban culture; the songs included in this documentary are less transgressive for contemporary audiences than when they were originally released in the 1950s and 1960s.

28. Fernandes, 118–119.

29. Baker, *Buena Vista in the Club*, 36.

Notes—Chapter 5

30. Baker, "*Cuba Rebelión*: Underground Music in Havana," 3.

31. See, for example, the films I discussed in Chapter 2.

32. In her article about the mainstream Cuban Hip Hop group *Orishas*, scholar Lea Ramsdell explains that their music is perceived as alternative in Europe but their lyrics emphasize the Cuban stereotypes about rum, cigars, hustling etc. (Ramsdell, 107). Ruy and Tito are this type of alternative characters as they hustle and are sexualized but never do anything extravagant related to drugs or crime.

33. A number of coproductions between Spain and Latin America replicate themes and filmic devices used by the renowned Spanish director. The Argentinean film *La niña santa* (*The Holy Girl*), for example, features a large female cast in a play revolving around organ donors.

Chapter 5

1. In her article, "Les dessins animés cubains," Cuban scholar Azucena Plasencia writes that this is the only Latin American animation studio open since the 1960s that has produced at least 80 minutes of animation every year, and that has won the acclaim of audiences and critics in four continents ["Fundados en 1960, son únicos en el panorama latinoamericano al mantener una producción estable de 80 minutos anuales en la pantalla, sin dejar de hacer películas a lo largo de 43 años. La calidad profesional y artística de sus obras está avalada por la exitosa recepción tanto del público como de crítica, en cuatro continentes"] (139).

2. Wells, 10.

3. Bazin writes:

Originality in photography as distinct from originality in painting lies in the essentially objective character of photography. For the first time an image of the world is formed automatically, without the creative intervention of man. The personality of the photographer enters into the proceedings only in the selection of the object to be photographed and by way of the purpose he has in mind. Although the final result may reflect something of his personality, this does not play the same role as is played by that of the painter. All the arts are based on the presence of man, only in photography derives an advantage from his absence. Photography affects us like a phenomenon in nature, like a flower or a snowflake whose vegetable or earthly origin are an inseparable part of their beauty [13].

4. Bazin writes:

Only the impassive lens, stripping its object of all those ways of seeing it, those piled-up preconceptions, that spiritual dust and grime with which my eyes have covered it, is able to present it in all its virginal purity to my attention and consequently to my love. By the power of photography, the natural image of a world that we neither know nor can see, nature at last does more than imitate art: she imitates the artist [15].

5. "This is why people enjoy looking at images, because through contemplating them it comes about that they understand and infer what each element means, for instance that 'this person is so-and-so.' For, if one happens not to have seen the subject before, the image will not give pleasure qua mimesis but because of its execution or colour, or for some other such reason" (Aristotle, 39).

6. McCloud, 30.

7. Ibid., 36.

8. According to György Lukács "[w]hen followed through logically, Expressionism repudiated any connection with reality and declared a subjectivist war on reality and all its works" (1043).

9. See, for example, Kracauer.

10. Lukács adds: "Great realism, therefore, does not portray an immediately obvious aspect of reality but one which is permanent and objectively more significant, namely man in the whole range of his relations to the real world, above all that outlast mere fashion" (1049).

11. In Eisenstein's words,

I'm sometimes frightened when I watch his films. Frightened because of some absolute perfection in what he does. This man seems to know not only the magic of all technical means, but also all the most secret strands of human thought, images, ideas, and feelings. Such was probably the effect of Saint Francis of Assisi's sermons. Fra Angelico's paintings bewitch in this way. He creates somewhere in the realm of the very purest and most primal depths. There, where we all are children of nature. He creates on the conceptual level of man not yet shackled by logic, reason, or experience [2].

12. Eisenstein writes,

Disney is a marvelous lullaby for the suffering and unfortunate, the oppressed and deprived. For those who are shackled by hours of work and regulated moments of rest, by a mathematical precision of time, whose lives are graphed by the cent and dollar. Whose lives are divided up into little squares, like a chess board, with the sole difference that whether you're a knight or a rook, a queen or a bishop-on this board, you can only lose. And also because its black squares don't alternate with white ones, but are all of protective grey color, day after day. Grey, grey, grey. From birth to death. Grey squares of city blocks. Grey prison cells of city streets. Grey faces of endless street crowds. The grey, empty eyes of those who are forever at the mercy of a pitiless procession of laws, not of their own making, laws that divide up the soul, feelings, thoughts, just as the carcasses of pigs are dismembered by the conveyor belts of Chicago slaughter houses, and the separate pieces of cars are assembled into mechanical organisms by Ford's conveyor belts. That's why Disney's films blaze with colour. Like the patterns in the clothes of people who have been deprived of the colours in nature. That's why the imagination in them is limitless, for Disney's films are a revolt against partitioning and legislating, against spiritual stagnation and greyness. But the revolt is lyrical. The revolt is a daydream. Fruitless and lacking consequences. These aren't those daydreams which, accumulating, give birth to action and realize the dream. They are the "golden dreams" you escape to, like other worlds where everything is different, where you're free from all fetters, where you can clown around just as nature itself seemed to have done in the joyful ages of its coming into being, when she herself invented curiosities worthy of Disney: the ridiculous ostrich next to the logical hen, the absurd giraffe next to the loyal cat, the kangaroo mocking the future madonna! [4].

13. "Donald Duck in the cartoons and the unfortunate in real life get their trashing so that the audience can learn to take their own punishment" (Leslie, 120).

14. Leslie, 121.

15. Adorno and Horkheimer, 1235.

16. The commercial failure of *Fantasia* is documented in the featurette "The Making of *Fantasia*" that was included in the original DVD release of the film.

17. "Instead of flying with his mother to an unknown paradise, Dumbo ends up as a highly paid star for the same circus director who beat his mother" (Kracauer, qtd. in Leslie, 200).

18. Leslie, 200.

19. For an example of this type of criticism, see Claudia Card on Pinocchio in the reader *From Mouse to Mermaid: The Politics of Film, Gender, and Culture*.

20. Cobas, 153.

21. Ibid., 153.

22. Plasencia, 139.

23. Ibid., 143.

24. Padrón says:

Porque en ese momento- te hablo cuando yo llegué- la animación era muy intelectual, películas experimentales ... Yo tenía dieciséis años, lo que quería hacer eran historias de aventuras. Pero se estilaban esas cosas, ya te digo, medio experimentales, que nadie entendía un carajo, quizás era porque todavía no se dominaba mucho el lenguaje. En el ICRT tenía más libertad, incluso comienzo a trabajar para la prensa. Fue una época muy linda de mi vida [Sotto Díaz, 153].

[Because at that moment—I mean

Notes—Chapter 5

when I arrived—animation was very intellectual, experimental films... I was sixteen, what I wanted to do were adventure stories. But what was in fashion at the moment, I am telling you, were those semi-experimental narratives that nobody understood. Maybe it was because they hadn't mastered the language yet. At the ICRT I had more freedom, I even began working for the press. It was a great moment in my life] [translated by the present author].

25. Roberto Cobas, 154.

26. For example, the character of the genie in *Aladdin* emulates the live-action speech pattern and acting of Jack Nicholson.

27. "Letter to Elián," 24.

28. The video was posted on You Tube.com as "Elpidio Valdés habla de su visita en Miami."

29. Mario Masvidal claims in his article that *Vampires in Havana* is the most popular Cuban animated film (93).

30. Sotto Díaz, 158.

31. Ibid., 159.

32. Vampire mythology can be traced to early Balkan folktales that dealt with the undead. These stories were Bram Stoker's inspiration for his novel *Dracula*, in which he pitted Anglophone characters against a Romanian historical figure/vampire who represented the other from the Balkans, a European region that had been conquered by the Ottoman Empire.

This narrative can be considered orientalist because it exemplifies the British Eurocentric hegemony's perception of the Balkans as a monstrous other, whose bloodletting nationalism against their Ottoman conqueror had turned them into a dangerous entity. Dracula and his vampires are sexualized in comparison to their Anglophone antagonists, and they represent lust and violence in opposition to Christianity and the British "civilization." However, as the vampire genre has evolved and now mostly produced by Hollywood, vampire characters have become more attractive to the audiences because of their eroticism, and are now often situated geographically in the Americas. Some examples of good, attractive vampires in their new American setting are Edward in Stephenie Meyers' *Twilight* saga, and Angel in Joss Whedon's *Buffy the Vampire Slayer* series.

33. This is confirmed by Mario Masvidal, who writes that animation has enjoyed a freedom of expression in Cuba that live action and documentary features never had. He sees animation as a type of id where the Cubans can see themselves in a more introspective and symbolic manner:

El animado en Cuba goza de mayor libertad de expresión, tanto formal como de contenido, que el propio cine de ficción y el cine documental, que no han tenido muchas posibilidades de explorar el divertimiento en el sentido más corriente del término, pues a menudo se han erigido como espacios de debate ideológico, como instrumentos de crítica y de reflexión social, o como vía de introspección psicológica del (o para el) nuevo sujeto. Enfocado desde la perspectiva del psicoanálisis –y pecando de intruismo profesional, pero auxiliándome de dicha corriente-, podría argumentar que el animado es un espacio más propenso para la manifestación del id-del inconsciente [101].

34. There is a reference to *Vampires in Havana* in the live-action Cuban movie *Vertical Love*. Two of the strangest characters in the latter film are a pair of Siamese twin sisters who represent the split political views of the Cuban people. One is pro–American, not unlike Cuban expatriates in Miami, while the other is patriotic and wants to stay on the island. As a result, in one scene, their brother points out that one likes Disney and the other likes Padrón's *Vampires in Havana*, as a symbol of their opposing worldviews. This statement splits Disney and Padrón's *oeuvre* according to the creators' ideological messages and national origins: nonetheless, the two share many filmmaking principles that this scene does not acknowledge. Both disguise ideology in fantasies that are acceptable to children through narrative metaphors that make sense through the language of animation.

35. Sotto Díaz, 161.

Chapter 6

1. See my discussion of the film in Chapter 1.

2. It is a shame that this ideologically biased representation has been so influential around the world because it is a negative portrayal of serious spiritual rituals that were important in reaffirming certain aspects of black identity in the Americas and in resisting slavery.

3. When I use the term "melodrama," I am referring to the theoretical idea developed by film scholars, such as Thomas Elssaeser, about how certain filmmakers use the societal concepts of family to visualize and contextualize the issues of the time. A number of film scholars such as John Mercer and Martin Shingler, have studied this phenomenon, and consider these themes the essential narrative frame of what is known in Film Studies as melodrama. As a result, various studies have been undertaken of the oeuvre of directors such as Douglas Sirk, Reiner Maria Fassbinder, Pedro Almodóvar, and other filmmakers who are known for focusing on the dysfunctional idea of the traditional family and its reflection on their respective national cultures. However, zombie genre filmmakers have also used melodramatic devices to convey the fall of the hegemonic families as a symbol of the decay of the status quo, which is why I believe this to be one of the most compelling horror genres to mainstream audiences in general.

4. Scholar Gyllian Phillips writes:

Seabrook implicitly recognizes the benefits of postcolonial culture, as it moves a little farther away from the polarizations of white supremacy. He also shows the attempts of Americans to reduce the threat to their own racial sovereignty, mainly by importing a kind of Jim Crownism, posed by a "mere existence of a 'black republic'" [31].

5. "On a larger ideological scale, I argue, the fear of European style colonialism found in the spectre of creolization, the threat of mixing and contagion, is relieved by this shift of ownership. Further, Legendre, as a character, is represented, albeit ambiguously, as a figure of creolization, and serves as implicit foil to American imperialism, which is exclusively white, rational, and therefore better than the inevitably syncretic models from Europe" (Phillips, 33).

6. Foster writes:

While aspects of *I Walked with a Zombie* are certainly condescending about Voudu as a cultural practice, these sections tend to be undercut by the construction of whites, as deceitful, diabolical and ultimately mad, primitive and associated with death and deception. In the world of *I Walked with a Zombie*, all that is supposed to be "civilized" is in a state of decay and collapse, and only the native culture is seen as living and vibrant [157].

7. "The family structure is seen to be much more stable and honest among the servants that Betsy encounters, than among the 'moral' whites" (Young, 112).

8. Young writes:

Ultimately, it is not the film's intention to tell us whether zombies really exist. The film is an examination of the different, but equally valid, belief systems and perceptions of the world. The zombie may or may not exist: what is important to remember is that the whole colonial system, which has such a legacy on the island of Saint Sebastian, has turned everyone into a kind of zombie [116].

9. Hervey, 42.

10. Fay, 82.

11. In the documentary *Birth of the Living Dead*, George Romero says that his main inspiration was Richard Matheson's classic *I Am Legend*. In this book, a surviving human is fighting vampires until he realizes that society has changed to the point that he is now the monster, and not the vampires. Romero says that the book is about revolt, and how the masses rise up.

12. This is an update to what Romero did in the sixties, and certainly has a more modern political content that younger audiences are more likely to grasp.

13. Foucault, "Chapter 3: Domain," n. pag.

14. Eslinda Nuñez played the second

Lucía character in Humberto Solás' *Lucía* (1968).

15. Stock, "Resisting Disconnectedness," 62.

16. It is important to note that even though Herrera's company La 5ta Avenida is not affiliated with the ICAIC, it is recognized by the state, and registered in Bolivia.

17. Padrón, 389.

18. In the first segment of *Aunque estés lejos*, a female Cuban who lives in the United Sates returns to Cuba and falls in love with a local. At the end she decides to stay in Cuba because she has found true love. As the segment ends in a kiss, the fiction is interrupted by a Spanish producer who tells the Cuban filmmakers that nobody would believe this plot.

19. Stock, 61.

20. Stock writes: "The ICAIC is acknowledged in the credits, as is Cuba's Ministry of Culture and a number of other state agencies, Brugués and Herrera (who also cameos as a zombie) wisely elected to compete in the global marketplace by aligning themselves with rather than distancing themselves from Cuba's national culture" (62).

21. Stock, 62.

22. Grossman, 96.

23. I discussed this filmmaker in Chapter 5.

24. Both filmmakers were discussed in Chapter 4.

25. Stock, 61.

26. Ibid., 59.

27. By not blaming the authorities for the zombie outbreak, *Juan of the Dead* diverges from the post–9/11 films *28 Days Later* and *Planet Terror*.

28. Schatz, 237.

29. Martin and Shingler write:

First and foremost, the basic model chiefly concerns the conflicts and tensions of a middle-class family. More often than not, this conflict is between the generations. In general, the drama is set within an affluent or upwardly mobile situation and, whilst social and economic concerns are often present, the emphasis tend to be on personal emotional traumas [12].

30. Wood, 10–11.

31. Juan's daughter Camila, who has been raised in Spain, is the only one from the survivor group that displays a moralistic behavior, with which Juan complies, because he wants to gain her respect in the hope that she will no longer see him as a loser and a criminal, an opinion apparently also shared by Juan's alienated ex-wife and mother-in-law. Throughout most of the film, Juan is unsuccessful at playing the ideal masculine hero, and more often than not, his group ends up accidentally killing the victims that they are trying to help.

32. Ambush Bug, n. pag.

33. Although it is always problematic to define the race of a person, China would likely be perceived as mulatto/a by the Cuban audiences.

34. Judith Butler writes:

The forming of a subject requires an identification with the normative phantasm of "sex," and this identification takes place through a repudiation which produces a domain of abjection, a repudiation without which the subject cannot emerge. This is a repudiation which creates the valence of "abjection" and its status for the subject as a threatening spectre. Further, the materialization of a given sex will centrally concern *the regulation of identificatory practices* such that the identification with the abjection of sex will be persistently disavowed. And yet, this disavowed abjection will threaten to expose the self-grounding presumptions of the sexed subject, grounded as that subject is in a repudiation whose consequences it cannot fully control. The task will be to consider this threat and disruption not as a permanent contestation of social norms condemned to the pathos of perpetual failure, but rather as a critical resource in the struggle to rearticulate the very terms of symbolic legitimacy and intelligibility [n. pag.].

Conclusion

1. ICRT stands for "Instituto Cubano de Radio y Televisión," or Cuban Institute of Radio and Television.

2. Stock, "Chapter 4: Opening New Roads: Juan Carlos Cremata Malberti Redefines Revolutionary Filmmaking," n. pag.

3. See episode "Child's Play" (season 6, episode 19), a metaphor for the Elián González debate.

4. Stock, "Chapter 4: Opening New Roads: Juan Carlos Cremata Malberti Redefines Revolutionary Filmmaking," n. pag.

5. Seminet writes: "The film nevertheless suggests that the nation will find its strength in its collective memories of the past grounded in common myths and the natural beauty of the Cuban countryside as well as the vibrancy of its youth" (200).

6. García García, n. pag.

7. Pedregal, and Pedregal Casanova, n. pag.

8. Rivero, n. pag.

9. Hernández, n. pag.

10. Maristany Castro, n. pag.

Bibliography

A. G. "Alicia a través de los espejos" ["Alicia Through the Looking Glass"]. *Cine Cubano* 135 (1992): 16-25. Print.

Adell, Elena. "*Pon tu pensamiento en mí* y *El elefante y la bicicleta*: El protagonismo del cine dentro de la filmografía cubana." *Torre de papel* 12.1-2 (March 2002): 63-81. Print.

Adorno, Theodor, and Max Horkheimer. "Dialectic of Enlightenment." *The Norton Anthology of Theory and Criticism*. Trans. Harry Zohn. Eds. Vincent Leich, William E. Cain, and Laurie Fink. New York: Norton, 2001. 1223-1239. Print.

Allen, Don. "*Memories of Underdevelopment* Review." *Memories of Underdevelopment and Inconsolable Memories*. Eds. Tomás Gutiérrez Alea, Edmundo Desnoes, and Michael Chanon. New Brunswick: Rutgers University Press, 1990. 222-223. Reprinted from *Sight and Sound* 38.4 (Autumn 1969): 212-213. Print.

Amaya, Hector. *Screening Cuba: Film Criticism and Political Performance During the Cold War*. Urbana: University of Illinois Press, 2010. Print.

Ambush Bug. "*Juan of the Dead*." ainitcoolnews.com aintitcoolnews, 19 Aug. 2012. Web. 20 Aug. 2012. http://www.aintitcool.com/node/57683#6.

Arenas, Reinaldo. *Antes que anochezca* [*Before Night Falls*]. Barcelona: Tusquets, 1992. Print.

Aristotle. *Poetics*. Loeb Classical Library no. 199. Cambridge: Harvard University Press, 1995. Print.

Baker, Geoffrey. *Buena Vista in the Club: Rap, Reggaetón, and Revolution in Havana*. Durham: Duke University Press, 2011. Print.

———. "*Cuba Rebelión*: Underground Music in Havana." *Latin American Music Review* 32.1 (2011): 1-38. Project MUSE. Web. 12 February 2014. http://muse.jhu.edu/.

Barnet, Miguel. *Canción de Rachel*. 1969. Barcelona: Libros del Asteroide, 2011. Print.

Baron, Guy. "Not Afraid for a Critical Space: Discovering the Post Modern in Cuban Cinema: The Case of *Plaff o demasiado miedo a la vida*." *Romance Studies* 29.1 (2011): 54-65. Print.

Bazin, André. "The Ontology of the Photographic Image." *What is Cinema?* Vol.1. Trans. Hugh Gray. Berkeley: University of California Press, 1967. 9-16. Print.

Bejel, Emilio. *Gay Cuban Nation*. Chicago: University of Chicago Press, 2001. Print.

———. "*Strawberry and Chocolate*: Coming Out of the Cuban Closet?" *South Atlantic Quarterly* 96.1 (Winter 1997): 65-82. Print.

Benjamin, Walter. "The Work of Art in the Age of Mechanical Reproduction." *The Norton Anthology of Theory and Criticism*. Trans. Harry Zohn. Eds. Vincent Leich, William E. Cain, and Laurie Fink. New York: Norton, 2001. 1166-1186. Print.

Bhaba, Homi. "Representation and the Colonial Text: A Critical Exploration of Some Forms of Mimeticism." Ed. Frank Gloversmith. *The Theory of Reading*. Sussex: Harvester Press; Totowa, N.J.: Barnes & Noble, 1984. 93-122. Print.

Bibliography

Blasini, Gilberto Moisés. "The World According to Plaff." *Visible Nations: Latin American Cinema and Video*. Minneapolis: University of Minnesota Press, 2000. 193-218. Print.

Breton, André. *Manifeste du surréalisme*. Paris: Gallimard, 1924. Print.

Burton, Julianne. "Individual Fulfillment and Collective Achievement: An Interview with Tomás Gutíerrez Alea." 187-198. Gutíerrez Alea, Tomás, Desnoes, Edmundo, and Michael Chanan. *Memories of Underdevelopment and Inconsolable Memories*. New Brunswick: Rutgers University Press, 1990. Reprinted from *Cineaste* 8.1 (Summer 1977): 8-15. Print.

———. "*Memories of Underdevelopment* in the Land of Overdevelopment." *Memories of Underdevelopment and Inconsolable Memories*. Eds. Tomás Gutíerrez Alea, Edmundo Desnoes, and Michael Chanan. New Brunswick: Rutgers UP, 1990. 232-247. Print.

Butler, Judith. *Bodies That Matter*. New York: Routledge, 2011. Kindle.

Caballero, Rufo. *Lagrimas en la lluvia. Crítica de cine, 1987-2007*. La Habana: Ediciones ICAIC, 2008. Print.

Cabrera Infante, Guillermo. "Mea Cuba." *The Cuba Reader: History, Culture, Politics*. Eds. Aviva Chomsky, Barry Carr, and Pamela María Smorkaloff. Durham: Duke University Press, 2003. 481-487. Print.

Card, Claudia. "Pinocchio." *From Mouse to Mermaid: The Politics of Film, Gender, and Culture*. Eds. Elizabeth Bell and Lynda Haas. Bloomington: Indiana University Press, 1995. 62-71. Print.

Carpentier, Alejo. "The Baroque and the Marvelous Real." *Magical Realism: Theory, History, Community*. Eds. Lois Parkinson Zamora, and Wendy B. Faris. Durham: Duke University Press, 1995: 89-108. Print.

———. "On the Marvelous Real in America." *Magical Realism: Theory, History, Community*. Eds. Lois Parkinson Zamora, and Wendy B. Faris. Durham: Duke University Press, 1995. 75-88. Print.

Carroll, Lewis. *The Annotated Alice in Wonderland and Through the Looking Glass*. New York: Norton, 2000. Print.

Castillo, Luciano. "Rápida mirada al cine de los soñadores." *Conquistando la utopia: El ICAIC y la Revolución 50 años después*. Ed. Tupac Pinilla. La Habana: Ediciones ICAIC, 2010. 11-42. Print.

Chanan, Michael. *Cuban Cinema*. Cultural Studies in the Americas. Vol. 14. Minneapolis: University of Minnesota Press, 2004. Print.

———. *The Cuban Image: Cinema and Cultural Politics in Cuba*. London: BFI; Bloomington: Indiana University Press, 1985. Print.

Cobas, Roberto. "Juan Padrón et l'animation." *Le cinéma cubain*. Paris: Éditions du Centre Pompidou, 1990. 153-158. Print.

Cornejo Polar, Antonio. "*Mestizaje* and Hybridity: The Risks of Metaphors." *The Latin American Cultural Studies Reader*. Eds. Ana Sarto, Alicia Ríos, and Abril Trigo. Durham: Duke University Press, 2004. 760-764. Print.

Danks, Adrian. "*Lucía*." *1001 Movies You Must See Before You Die*. Ed. Steven Jay Schnieder. London: Barron's, 2005. 504. Print.

de la Campa, Román. "Globalización y nostalgia: *Buena Vista Social Club*." *Sargasso: A Journal of Caribbean Language, Literature, and Culture* (2003-2004): 39-56. Print.

del Río, Joel. "Insurgencia, dinámica y potestad del cine joven en Cuba." *Conquistando la utopia: El ICAIC y la Revolución 50 años después*. La Habana: Ediciones ICAIC, 2010: 167-183. Print.

del Valle, Robin Ravelo. "Interview." *Tras las huellas de Solás*. La Habana: ICAIC, 2000. 15-36. Print.

del Valle, Sandra. "Definirse en la polemica: *PM, Cecilia y Alicia*." *Conquistando la utopia: El ICAIC y la Revolución 50 años después*. La Habana: Ediciones ICAIC, 2010. 63-91. Print.

Desnoes, Edmundo. *Inconsolable Memories*. Translated by the author. New York: New American Library, 1967. Print.

Díaz, Desirée. "*Alicia en el pueblo de Maravillas*: Otra pelea cinematográfica contra los demonios de la censura." *Cuba: Cinéma et révolution.* Eds. Julie Amiot-Guillouet and Nancy Berthier. Lyon: Grimh, 2006. 205–212. Print.

———. "De Sergio a Diego: La Diáspora en el cine de Tomás Gutíerrez Alea." *Voir et lire Tomás Gutíeerez Alea: La Mort d'un bureaucrate.*, Ed. Emmanuel Larraz. Dijom: Centre d'Etudes et de Recherches Hispaniques du XXe siècle; Université de Bourgogne, 2002. 77–92. Print.

———. "Un clásico se recicla/Un Classique se recycle." *Cinémas d'Amérique latine* 9 (January 2001): 38–40. Print.

Díaz, Marta, y Joel del Río. *Los cien caminos del cine cubano.* La Habana: Ediciones ICAIC, 2010. Print.

Díaz Torres, Daniel. "Los olvidados." *Cine Cubano* 78–80 (1973): 134–135. Print.

———. "Sobre el diablo y las liebres" ["About the Devil and the Rabbits"]. *Cine Cubano* 156 (2004): no pag. Print.

D'Lugo, Marvin. "From Exile to Ethnicity: Nestor Almendros and Orlando Jímenez-Leal's *Improper Conduct* (1984)." *The Ethnic Eye: Latino Media Arts.* Eds. Ana López, and Chon Noriega. Minneapolis: University of Minnesota Press, 1996. 171–182. Print.

Dorfman, Ariel, and Armand Mattelart. *Para leer el pato Donald: Comunicación de masa y colonialismo* [*How to Read Donald Duck*]. Buenos Aires: Siglo Veintiuno Editores, 1975. Print.

Douglas, María Eulalia. *La tienda* negra: *El cine en Cuba* [1897–1990]. Cinemateca de Cuba: La Habana, 1997. Print.

Eisenstein, Sergei. *Eisenstein on Disney.* Trans. Alan Upchurch. Ed. Jay Leydad. London: Methuen, 1988. Print.

———. "Methods of Montage." *Film Form: Essay in Film Theory.* Trans. Jay Leyda. New York: Harvest, 1973. 72–83. Print.

Elsaesser, Thomas. "Tales of Sound and Fury: Observations on the Family Melodrama." *Imitations of Life: A Reader on Film & Television Melodrama.* Ed. Marcia Landy. Detroit: Wayne State University Press, 1991. Print.

Évora, José Antonio. *Tomás Gutíerrez Alea.* Madrid: Cátedra, 1996. Print.

Fay, Jennifer. "Dead Subjectivity: White Zombie, Black Baghdad." *CR: The New Centennial Review* 8:1 (Spring 2008): 81–101. Print.

Fernandes, Sujatha. *Cuba Represent: Cuban Arts, State Power, and the Making of New Revolutionary Cultures.* Durham: Duke University Press, 2006. Print.

Fernández de Castro, Astrid Santana. *Literatura y Cine: Lecturas cruzadas de Memorias del subdesarrollo.* La Habana: ICAIC, 2010. Print.

Flores González, Luis Ernesto. *Tras las huellas de Solás.* La Habana: ICAIC, 2000. Print.

Fornet, Ambrosio. "Trente ans de cinéma dans la Révolution." *Le cinéma cubain.* Paris: Éditions du Centre Pompidou, 1990. 63–78. Print.

Foster, Gwendolyn. "The Corruption of the Family and the Disease of Whiteness in *I Walked with a Zombie*." *A Family Affair: Cinema Calls Home.* London: Wallflower Press, 2008. 149–159. Print.

Foucault, Michel. *History of Sexuality.* New York: Vintage, 1990. Kindle file.

Galiano, Carlos, and Rufo Caballero. *Cien anos sin soledad: Las mejores películas latinoamericanas de todos los tiempos* [*A Hundred Years Without Solitude: The Best Latin American Films of All Time*]. La Habana: Letras Cubanas, 1999. Print.

García Borrero, Juan Antonio. *Guía crítica del cine cubano de ficción.* La Habana: Arte y Literatura, 2001. Print.

García Espinosa, Julio. *Algo de mí.* La Habana: Ediciones ICAIC, 2009. Print.

———. "For an Imperfect Cinema." 1969. *New Latin American Cinema Vol. 1: Theory, Practices, and Transcontinental Articulations.* Ed. Michael T. Martin. Detroit: Wayne State University Press, 1997. 71–82. Print.

———. "Recuerdos de Zavattini." *Cine Cubano* 155 (2004): 60–65. Print.

García, Enrique. "Miscegenation and Family Apocalypse in Robert Rodríguez' *Planet Terror*." Forthcoming in *Robert Rodriguez and the Cinema of Possibilities.* Ed. Frederick Aldama. Austin: University of Texas Press, 2015. 142–156. Print.

Bibliography

García García, Yeneily. "ICAIC: más allá de la luneta de una sala oscura." *Cubahora.* 24 March 2014. Web. 30 October 2014.

Goldman, Dara. "Urban Desires: Melancholia and Fernando Pérez's Portrayal of Havana." *Bulletin of Hispanic Studies* 85.6 (2008): 867–881. Print.

Gómez de Avellaneda, Gertrudis. *Sab*, 5th ed. Madrid: Cátedra, 2004. Print.

Grossman, Carla. "Zombies utópicos." *Cinémas d'Amérique latine* 21 (January 2013): 95–109. Print.

Guevara, Ernesto. "Man and Socialism." *The Cuba Reader: History, Culture, Politics*. Eds. Aviva Chomsky, Barry Carr, and Pamela Maria Smorkaloff. Durham: Duke University Press, 2003: 370–374. Print.

Gutíerrez Alea, Tomás. "The Viewer's Dialectic." *New Latin American Cinema. Vol 1: Theory, Practices, and Transcontinental Articulations*. Ed Michael T. Martin. Detroit: Wayne State University Press, 1997. 108–134. Print.

Hernández, Helson. "Actor Jazz Vila & Cuba's First Horror Flick." *Havana-Times.org* Havana Times, 9 December 2010. Web. 15 January 2014.

Hernández, Normando. "Expone el ICAIC detalles de su proceso de reestructuración." *Normando Hdez blogia.* 15 May 2013. Web. 30 October 2014.

Hernández, Tanya. "*The Buena Vista Social Club*: The Racial Politics of Nostalgia." *Latino/a Popular Culture*. Eds. Michelle Habell-Pallán, and Mary Romero New York: New York University Press, 2002: 61–72. Print.

Hernández-Reguant, Ariana. "Multicubanidad." *Cuba in the Special Period: Culture and Ideology in the 1990's*. Ed. Ariana Hernández-Reguant. New York: Palgrave, 2009. 69–88. Print.

Herrera, Manuel. "De lo perfecto a lo imperfecto y viceversa." *A cuarenta años de por un cine imperfecto*. La Habana: Ediciones ICAIC, 2009. 31–36. Print.

Hervey, Ben. *Night of the Living Dead*. Basingstoke: Palgrave Macmillan, 2008. Print.

Insúa, Alberto. *El negro que tenía el alma blanca*. Madrid: Castalia, 1998. Print.

Kracauer, Siegfried. *From Caligari to Hitler*. 1947. Princeton: Princeton University Press, 2004. Print.

Kristeva, Julia. "The Bounded Text." *Desire in Language: A Semiotic Approach to Literature and Art*. Ed.s Leon S. Roudiez et al. New York: Columbia University Press, 1980. 36–63. Print.

———. "World, Dialogue and Novel." *Desire in Language: A Semiotic Approach to Literature and Art*. Ed. Leon S. Roudiez et al. New York: Columbia University Press, 1980. 64–91. Print.

Leslie, Esther. *Hollywood Flatlands: Animation, Critical Theory, and the Avant-Garde*. London: Verso, 2004. Print.

"Letter to Elián by Elpidio Valdés." *Cine Cubano* 147. 24. Print.

Lindgren, Astrid. *The Adventures of Pippi Longstocking*. Trans. Florence Lamborn. Ilus. Michael Chesworth. New York: Viking, 1997. Print.

Lukács, György. "Realism in the Balance." *The Norton Anthology of Theory and Criticism*. Ed. Vincent Leitch. New York: Norton, 2001. 1030–1057. Print.

Maristany Castro, Carlos Eduardo. "*Juan of the Dead*: The Making of a Cult Film Hit, Part One." *Cuban Art News*. 08 March 2012. Web. 28 January 2013.

Martínez Alfaro, María Jesús. "Intertextuality: Origins and Development of the Concept." *Atlantis: Revista de la Asociación Española de Estudios Ingleses y Norteamericanos* 18.1-2 (1996): 268–285. Print.

Masvidal, Mario. "Mirar los muñe: un acercamiento crítico a los animados producidos por el ICAIC." *Conquistando la utopia: EL ICAIC y la revolución 50 años después*. La Habana: ICAIC, 2010. 93–106. Print.

Matheson, Richard. *I Am Legend*. New York: Rosetta Books, 2011. Kindle.

McCloud, Scott. *Understanding Comics: The Invisible Art*. New York: Harper, 1994. Print.

Mendieta Costa, Raquel. "Exotic Exports: The Myths of the Mulatta." *Corpus Delecti: Performance Art of the Americas*. Ed. Coco Fusco. London: Routledge, 2000. Print.

Mercer, John, and Martin Shingler. *Melo-*

drama: Genre, Style, and Sensibility. London: Wallflower, 2004. Print.

Meyer, Stephenie. Twilight (series). Boston: Little, Brown, 2005–2008. Print.

Millán Agudo, Francisco J. *Las huellas de Buñuel: Influencias en el cine latinoamericano* [*Buñuel's Footprints: Influences in Latin American Cinema*]. Teruel, Spain: Instituto de Estudios Turolenses, 2004. Print.

Miller, Paul. "*Memories of Underdevelopment*, Thirty Years Later: An Interview with Sergio Corrieri." *Cineaste* 25.1 (December 1999): 20–23. Print.

_____. *A cuarenta años de Memorias del subdesarrollo*. La Habana: Ediciones ICAIC, 2008. Print.

Naito López, Mario. *Cuarenta años de Lucía*. La Habana: Ediciones ICAIC, 2008. Print.

Oroz, Silvia. *Melodrama: El cine de lágrimas en América Latina*. Ciudad de México: Universidad Nacional Autónoma de México, 1996. Print.

Paranagua, Paulo Antonio. "Trajectoire du cinéma cubain: du-sous développement a l'autonomie." *Le cinéma cubain*. Paris: Éditions du Centre Pompidou, 1990. 7–12. Print.

Paz, Senel. "El lobo, el bosque y el hombre nuevo" ["The Wolf, the Forest, and the New Man"] [1990]. Garrandés, Alberto, ed. *Aire de luz: Cuentos cubanos del siglo XX*. Havana: Editorial Letras Cubanas, 1999: 442–464. Print.

Pedregal, Alejandro, and Ramón Pedregal Casanova. "Omar González, presidente del ICAIC: 'El socialismo no se hace para que todo el mundo sea igual. Se hace para que todo el mundo sea diferente.'" *Cubainformacion*. 2 January 2013. Web. 30 October 2014.

Pérez, Fernando. "Un tratado cinematográfico" ["A Cinematographic Treatise"]. *Cine Cubano* 89–90 (1974). Reprinted in *La vida es un silbo*. La Habana: Ediciones ICAIC, 2004. 123–138. Print.

Pérez, Manuel. "El ICAIC y su contexto entre 1959 y 1963: Nacimiento, primeros pasos, primeros contratiempos …" *Conquistando la utopia: El ICAIC y la Revolución 50 años después*. La Habana: Ediciones ICAIC, 2010. 43–61. Print.

Phillips, Gyllian. "*White Zombie* and the Creole: William Seabrook's *The Magic Island* and American Imperialism in Haiti." *Generation Zombie: Essays on the Living Dead in Modern Culture*. 2011. Jefferson, NC: MacFarland, 2011. 27–40. Print.

Pierre, Jose. "Buñuel gótico, prerrafaelista y surrealista" ["The Gothic, Pre-Raphaelite, and Surrealist Buñuel"]. Residencia de Estudiantes. *Luis Buñuel: El ojo de la libertad: (catálogo de exposicíon)* [*Luis Buñuel: The Eye of Liberty: (An Exhibition Catalog)*]. Febrero-Mayo 2000. Madrid: Publicaciones de la Residencia de Estudiantes, 2000. Print.

Piñera, Walfredo. "Le cinéma pré-révolutionnaire." *Le cinéma cubain*. Paris: Éditions du Centre Pompidou, 1990. 63–78. Print.

Plasencia, Azucena. "Los 'muñequitos' cubanos/Les dessins animés cubains" *Cinémas d'Amérique latine* 11 (January 2003): 139–147. Print.

Porbén, Pedro. "El panóptico insular en *Alicia en el pueblo de Maravillas*." *Argus-a* 2.9 (July 2013): n. pag. PDF.

Ramsdell, Lea. "The Mythical Return to the Mother(land): Cinematic Representations of the Garífuna and the Cuban Diasporas." *Hispanic Journal* 29.2 (September 2008): 115–126. Print.

Redruello, Laura. "Algunas reflexiones en torno a la película *Alicia en el pueblo de maravillas*." *Cuban Studies* 38 (2007): 82–99. Print.

Reyes, Dean Luis. "El etnocentrismo blando: mambises y vampiros como guerrilla anticolonial en el cine de Juan Padrón." *Portal del cine y el audiovisual latinoamericano y caribeño* [formerly *Miradas*]. Fundación del Nuevo Cine Latinoamericano, n.d. Web. 16 December 2013.

Rivero, Mónica. "Fernando Pérez: Nosotros queremos una ley de cine." *Progreso Semanal*. 2 May 2014. Web. 30 October 2014.

Schatz, Thomas. *Hollywood Genres: Formulas, Filmmaking, and the Studio System*. Philadelphia: Temple UP, 1981. Print.

Schroeder, Paul A. *Tomás Gutiérrez Alea:*

Bibliography

The Dialectics of a Filmmaker. New York: Routledge, 2002. Print.

Seabrook, William. *The Magic Island*. New York: Literary Guild of America, 1929. Print.

Seminet, Georgia. "A Post-Revolutionary Childhood: Nostalgia and Collective Memory in *Viva Cuba*." *Studies in Hispanic Cinemas* 8.2 (2011): 189–202. Print.

Shaw, Deborah. "Tomás Gutíerrez Alea's Changing Images of the Revolution From *Memories of Underdevelopment* to *Strawberry and Chocolate*." *Contemporary Cinema of Latin America*. New York: Continuum, 2003. 9–35. Print.

Short, Robert. *The Age of Gold: Surrealist Cinema*. Persistence of Vision. Vol. 3. London: Creation Books, 2003. Print.

Sierra Madero, Abel. *Del otro lado del espejo: La sexualidad en la construcción de la nación cubana*. Casa de las Américas, 2006. Kindle.

Smith, Paul Julian. "Cuban Homosexualities: On the Beach with Néstor Almendros and Reinaldo Arenas." Ed. Sylvia Molloy. *Hispanisms and Homosexualities*. Durham: Duke University Press, 1998. Print.

———. *Vision Machines: Cinema, Literature, and Sexuality in Spain and Cuba, 1983-93*. London: New York: Verso, 1996. Print.

Soles, Diane. "Administración de la crítica: tácticas de censores y cineastas cubanos en los noventa." *Cultura y letras cubanas en el siglo XXI*. Ed. Araceli Tinajero. Madrid: Frankfurt: Iberoamericana-Vervuert, 2010. 77–94. Print.

Sotto Díaz, Arturo. "Un vampiro mambí o vice versa" ["A Mambí Vampire or Vice Versa"]. *Conversaciones al lado de Cinecittá*. Ed. Arturo Sotto Díaz. La Habana: Ediciones ICAIC, 2009. 149–163. Print.

Stam, Robert. *Literature Through Film: Realism, Magic, and the Art of Adaptation*. Malden: Blackwell, 2005. Print.

Stock, Ann Marie. "Imagining the Future in Revolutionary Cuba: An Interview with Fernando Pérez." *Film Quaterly* 60.3 (Spring 2007): 68. Print.

———. *On Location in Cuba: Street Filmmaking During Times of Transition*. Chapel Hill: University of North Carolina Press, 2009. Print.

———. "Resisting Disconnectedness in *Larga Distancia* and *Juan de los muertos*: Cuban Filmmakers Create and Compete in a Globalized World." *Revista Canadiense de Estudios Hispánicos* 37.1 (Fall 2012). Web. 20 February 2013.

Stoker, Bram. *Dracula*. 1898. New York: Norton, 1997. Print.

Taylor, Anna Marie. "Imperfect Cinema, Brecht, and *The Adventures of Juan Quin Quin*." *Jump Cut: A Review of Contemporary Media* 20 (1979). Web. 20 February 2013.

Thompkins, Cynthia. "Montage in Fernando Pérez Valdés' *Suite Habana*." *Confluencia: Revista Hispánica de Cultura y Literatura* 26.2 (2011): 31–45. Web. 15 December 2013.

Venegas, Cristina. *A cuarenta años de por un cine imperfecto*. La Habana: Ediciones ICAIC, 2009. 55–57. Print.

———. "Filmmaking with Foreigners." *Cuba in the Special Period: Culture and Ideology in the 1990's*. Ed. Araina Hernández-Reguant. New York: Palgrave, 2009. 37–50. Print.

Villaverde, Cirilo. *Cecilia Valdés o La Loma del Ángel*. Madrid: Cátedra, 1992. Print.

Wallace, Inez. "I Walked with a Zombie." *Zombie: Stories of the Walking Dead*. Ed. Peter Hainin. London: Seven House, 1985. 95–102. Print.

Wells, Paul. *Understanding Animation*. London: Routledge, 1998. Print.

West, Dennis. "Alice in a Cuban Wonderland: An Interview with Daniel Díaz Torres." *Cineaste* 20.1 (1993): 24–27. Print.

Wilkinson, Stephen. "Behind the Screen and into the Closet: Reading Homosexuality in the Cuban Revolution through *Conducta impropia*, *Antes que anochezca*, and *Fresa y chocolate*." *Identity and discursive Practices: Spain and Latin America*. Ed. Francisco Domínguez. Bern: Peter Lang, 2000. 283–305. Print.

Wood, Robin. "An Introduction to the American Horror Film, Part 1: Repression, the Other, the Monster." *American Nightmare: Essays on the Horror Film*.

Bibliography

Toronto: Festival of Festivals, 1979. 7–11. Print.

Woods, Tim. *Beginning Postmodernism*. Manchester: Manchester University Press, 2010. Print.

Young, Elliot. "Between the Market and a Hard Place: Fernando Pérez's *Suite Habana* in a Post-Utopian Cuba." *Cuban Studies* 38 (2007): 26–49. Print.

Young, Gwenda. "The Cinema of Difference: Jacques Tourneur, Race and *I Walked with a Zombie* (1943)." *Irish Journal of American Studies* 7.1 (1998): 101–119.

Filmography

Allers, Rogers, and Rob Minkoff, dirs. *The Lion King*. USA. Walt Disney Studios, 1994. Blu-ray. Walt Disney Studios Home Entertainment, 2011. 88 min.

Almendros, Néstor, and Orlando Jiménez Leal. *Mauvaise conduit* [*Improper Conduct*]. France. Antenne-2, 1984. 112 min.

Almodóvar, Pedro. *¿Qué he hecho para merecer esto?* (*What Have I Done to Deserve This?*) Spain, 1984. 101 min. DVD. Fox Lorber, 2003. 101 min.

———. *Tacones lejanos* (*High Heels*). Spain, 1991. DVD. Lionsgate, 2012. 112 min.

Alonso, Manolo. *Casta de roble*. Cuba, 1953. 81 min.

———. *Siete muertes a plazo fijo*. Cuba. 1950. 86 min.

Ball, Lucille, and Desi Arnaz, perfs. *I Love Lucy: The Complete Series*. Desilu Productions, 1951–1957. DVD. Paramount, 2007. 5,394 min.

Barba, Carlos, dir. *La mujer que espera* [*The Woman Who Waits*]. Cuba, ICAIC, 2005. 63 min.

Bayón Herrera, Luis, dir. *A la Habana me voy* [*I Am going to Havana.*]. Argentina and Cuba, 1950. 104 min.

Boyle, Danny, dir. *28 Days Later*. USA, 2002. DVD. 20th Century–Fox, 2003.

Brugués, Alejandro, dir. *Personal Belongings*. Cuba, 2006. DVD. Maya Entertainment, 2009. 95 min.

———. *Juan de los muertos*. [*Juan of the Dead*]. Spain-Cuba. La Zanfonia Producciones, ICAIC, and Producciones de la quinta avenida, 2011. DVD. Focus Features, 2012. 96 min.

Buñuel, Luis, dir. *L'âge d'or* [*The Golden Age*]. France, 1930. DVD. Kino, 2004. 63 min.

———. *Los olvidados*. Mexico, 1950. DVD. Ciné-Club, 2001. 80 min.

———. *Un chien andalou* [*An Andalusian Dog*]. France, 1929. DVD. Transflux Films, 2004. 16 min.

Cabrera Infante, Sabá, and Orlando Jiménez Leal, dirs. *P.M.* Cuba, 1961. 15 min.

Caparrós, Ernesto. dir. *Fantasmas del Caribe* [*Caribbean Ghosts*]. Cuba, 1943. 76 min.

Cazals, Felipe, dir. *Canoa*. Mexico, 1974. DVD. Desert Mountain, 2006. 115 min.

Chen, Kaige, dir. *Farewell My Concubine*. China. Miramax, 1993. DVD. Miramax, 1999. 172 min.

Chijona, Gerardo, dir. *Adorables mentiras* [*Adorable Lies*]. Cuba. ICAIC, 1989. VHS. ICAIC, 1999. 108 min.

———. *Un paraíso bajo las estrellas* [*Paradise Under the Stars*]. Cuba and Spain. ICAIC and Wandavisión, 1999. DVD. Vanguard, 2001. 90 min.

Craven, Wes, dir. *The Serpent and the Rainbow*. USA, 1988. Universal, 1988. iTunes. 98 min.

Cremata, Juan Carlos, dir. *Viva Cuba*. Cuba, 2005. DVD. Film Movement, 2007. 80 min.

De Sica, Vittorio, dir. *Ladri di biciclette* [*Bicycle Thieves*]. Italy, 1948. DVD. Criterion, 2007. 89 min.

———. *Umberto D*. Italy, 1952. DVD. Criterion, 2003. 89 min.

Díaz Torres, Daniel, dir. *Alicia en el pueblo de Maravillas* [*Alice in Wondertown*]. Cuba. ICAIC, 1988. DVD. First Run Features, 2009. 90 min.

———. *Hacerse el sueco* [*Becoming Swede*]. Cuba-Germany. ICAIC, 2001. VHS. ICAIC, 2002. 95 min.